Tough Cookies Don't Crumble

Turn Set-Backs into Success

Susan O'Malley, MD

INDIE BOOKS
INTERN

D1303309

No part of this publication may be reproduced or distributed in any forms or any means, without the prior permission of the publisher. Requests for permission should be directed to permissions@indiebooksintl.com, or mailed to Permissions, Indie Books International, 2424 Vista Way, Suite 316, Oceanside, CA 92054.

Neither the publisher nor the author is engaged in rendering legal or other professional services through this book. If expert assistance is required, the services of an appropriate professional should be sought. The publisher and the author shall have neither liability nor responsibility to any person or entity with respect to any loss or damage caused directly or indirectly by the information in this publication.

ISBN: 1941870139
ISBN 13: 978-1-941870-13-6
Library of Congress Control Number: 2015931315

Author photograph by Brigham & Co. Photography
Cover design by Victoria Vinton
Interior page design by Joni McPherson, mcphersongraphics.com

INDIE BOOKS INTERNATIONAL, LLC
2424 VISTA WAY, SUITE 316
OCEANSIDE, CA 92054
www.indiebooksintl.com

To my courageous mother whose perseverance
gave me my first smile
and
my beautiful husband whose love makes me
smile every day.

Do not pray for easy lives. Pray to be stronger men. Do not pray for tasks equal to your powers. Pray for powers equal to your tasks. Then the doing of your work shall be no miracle, but you shall be the miracle.

— Phillips Brooks

Table of Contents

Preface   xi

Chapter 1: What Do You Want?   1

Chapter 2: Find Your Reason   13

Chapter 3: Row Your Own Boat, Baby   27

Chapter 4: Flip Your Switch   41

Chapter 5: Don't Marry Your Destiny   53

Chapter 6: Put On a Helmet   69

Chapter 7: Embrace Embarrassment   83

Chapter 8: Ask for Help   95

Chapter 9: Figure Out the Rules   107

Chapter 10: Make a Friend of Fear   125

Chapter 11: Be Willing to Make Mistakes   139

Chapter 12: Be Your Own Champion   151

Chapter 13: Never Surrender   163

Epilogue   177

Acknowledgements   179

How to Get in Touch   185

Preface

We keep secrets. We all do. Things about ourselves we don't tell everyone. Things we only tell a privileged few, or maybe no one at all. And we're entitled—after all everyone does not need to know everything about you. Except if you're writing a book outlining how you got from there to here. Then, I don't think it's fair to keep secrets.

It was important to me to lay it all out for you—all the ugliness, the failures, the embarrassment, the mistakes. It was important because, having read books and attended seminars by successful women, I have been on the receiving end of confusion more than once in my life. All it does is make you feel bad about yourself and maybe make you feel like a failure. *Why can't I do it? She did it.* And then you realize, *I don't have the whole story.*

If you were having an intimate conversation with your best friend, you would tell the whole story. Here is mine. Here are the steps I used to take control of my life and make my wildest dreams come true. Here are the challenges from my own journey, as well as others I met along the way. Here are the lessons I learned.

I could have left many stories out of this book—stories showing how scared I was, how vulnerable I felt, how I wanted to give up. But then, big chunks would be missing and you wouldn't have the whole story.

Achieving success, however you define it, is hard. But it can be a lot of fun—especially when you laugh at yourself. It turns out you have to walk a rocky road to get to easy street. Here's to your journey.

Dr. Susan O'Malley
January 2015

CHAPTER 1
What Do You Want?

Pour yourself a drink, put on some lipstick, and pull yourself together.

— Elizabeth Taylor

What do you want? It took me many years to decide what I wanted. You must want something because you're about to start reading a book that outlines strategies to help you get the most out of your life. Maybe you were intrigued by the title, maybe you stumbled across this book in the self-improvement section of the store, or maybe someone gave it to you as a gift. However you came to hold this book in your hands, you know you're not settling into a hot steamy novel. So you must want something. We all do.

Do you want to start a business? Would you like to take your business to the next level? Perhaps you would like to attract more clients or add more programs? Are you looking for a better job or a promotion? Would you like to be a better leader in your organization? Are you struggling with work/life balance challenges? Trying to pass a licensing exam? How about just hoping for a better relationship with your family and friends? Would you like to take control of your life? I can tell you this—if you can define what you want, you have a better chance of getting it.

I couldn't define what I wanted until I was thirty years old. Even then, the definition kept changing. After years of floundering, I finally got my act together and decided I wanted to be a doctor. Years later, my dream expanded and I set my sights on being an entrepreneur, a public speaker, and an author. After many failed relationships, I decided that I deserved the best relationship I could have with a true soul mate or no relationship at all. Today I have all that and more. It didn't come easy and it didn't come cheap—but it came.

My Uphill Years

Let me take you back to the early eighties. I was a college dropout and had been working as a secretary in New York City for more than ten years when, at age thirty, I decided to be a doctor. Can you imagine the rolled eyes and elbow jabs when I made that announcement? The good thing about rolled eyes and elbow jabs is that they usually occur behind your back. Which is much less intimidating than to your face.

The journey was never easy. I returned to college, graduated, and then went through the medical school application process. Twice. The first time around, I was rejected from every medical school in the country—at the time, forty-two. The following year I was accepted to the Mount Sinai School of Medicine (renamed in 2012, the Icahn School of Medicine at Mount Sinai) in New York City three weeks before school started.

I was thirty-five years old and six months pregnant without a husband. My life was in such turmoil that I needed welfare assistance to afford to birth my baby. Not exactly the walking-talking example of the traditional medical student. Everything I wanted most in my life came about at the same time. I didn't know how I was going to do it, but I wasn't willing to give anything up. I delivered my beautiful son Ryan two days before the start of Christmas vacation and stepped back in line with my classmates at the beginning of January 1987. And the race really began.

I chose a career as an emergency room doctor so I could juggle the demands of medicine and single motherhood. There was something about having my emergency room schedule secured to the refrigerator door with brightly colored alphabet magnets that kept me grounded. I trained in New York, on Long Island and in the Bronx, and worked in two emergency rooms in Connecticut after my training.

At age fifty, I left mainstream medicine with a dream and not much else and opened a medical spa dedicated to helping women navigate the aging process without surgery. I spent seventy-five dollars to place a newspaper ad and sat at the reception desk waiting for the phone to ring. Initially, my interest in aging was to keep myself out of the plastic surgeon's office but over the years I have come to realize this is my calling in a way the emergency room could never have been.

And now at age sixty-three, I have refocused my life to include author and public speaker, proving it's never too late to have a dream and to make that dream come true.

The Back Story

Before we go any further, you should know a little more about me. I was born in Brooklyn, New York, to young parents who were totally unprepared for the experience. When my mother went into labor, they took the bus at midnight in a snowstorm to get to the hospital. It was February 1952. The day I arrived on the scene, my father's weekly paycheck was thirty-three dollars and my mother was unemployed. I'm told we took a taxi home. Let's just say, childbirth is a totally different experience today.

Over the years, our family grew to five children and we settled in Queens, New York. If you've ever been to Queens you know the houses are small and very close to each other. Seven of us lived in a twelve hundred square-foot house and crowded around a dinner table every night that was built for six.

This was a time when children shared bedrooms, everyone used the same bathroom, the phone was attached to the kitchen wall, and you had to negotiate with six other people to watch *your show* on the living room television. Not exactly lifestyles of the rich and famous.

My father was a maintenance worker for the New York Racing Association. He didn't have a college education, but he could fix things. He was meticulous in his work. He knew how to paint and how to plant flowers. He wore a green laborer's uniform with his name embroidered over the left breast and was part of the behind-the-scenes team that kept Belmont Race Track looking beautiful.

I learned a lot from my father. I learned the correct way to open a can of paint and how to store the brushes so they could be used again. I learned how to hold a hammer and the correct way to hang pictures on a wall. In the last year of his life without saying a word he taught me the greatest lessons— the true meanings of courage and optimism. Sadly, my father did not live to see me open my own business or write this book, but to this day I feel his presence.

My mother was at home with us during the day and supplemented our family income by working as a cocktail waitress at a bowling alley in the evenings. She, like most women of her generation, did not have a college education either. My mother was very creative and had dreams of being a fashion designer or an actress when she was a young woman. She was very talented and was able to teach herself how to do almost anything.

Over the years, my mother was the family hairdresser, the family decorator, and fashion coordinator. She made all of her own clothes and many outfits for my sisters and me. Her craftsmanship far surpassed what was found on the racks. After I was grown, my mother went to college and got a degree in drama. She finally was able to enjoy acting in some local plays and was an extra in many feature films. Although her scenes eventually wound up on the cutting room floor, her speaking part in *Baby It's You* earned her a Screen Actors Guild card.

I learned two important lessons from my mother that I carry to this day. The first is determination. The other is how to stretch a dollar. My husband appreciates this one.

Twenty Seconds That Changed My Life

When I was a toddler, I took a tumble down a flight of hallway stairs in a walker and smashed my face on a steel radiator. The impact sliced my two front baby teeth in half, with half landing on the dirty hallway floor and the other half jammed into my gums. The fall, which only took seconds, changed the course of my life.

We were living in an apartment on the second floor of a two-story house. When the front door opened downstairs, a gush of air would travel up the stairs and push our apartment door open. One Saturday morning, my mother came home with bags of groceries and forgot to dead lock the apartment door. The rest is history.

As a mother myself, I can't imagine the chaos and terror of that moment as my twenty-two-year-old mother dropped groceries all over the kitchen floor and came flying down the stairs to pull her bruised, bloodied and screaming baby girl out of a mangled walker.

My battered and bloodied face eventually healed and in due course the remnants of my baby teeth made their way through my gums. But everyone held their breath to see how my permanent teeth would develop.

My adult two front teeth grew in prematurely when I was five years old. One was at a ninety-degree angle and the other at a forty-five-degree angle. They were brown, jagged and pock marked and resembled driftwood on the beach. It was a horrifying sight even for those who knew what had happened. My jumbled teeth were uncomfortable and cut up the inside of my mouth. I felt like a monster.

They affected the way I ate and the way I talked. They affected my self-esteem and my self-worth. I stopped smiling. We spent my entire childhood traveling from one dentist to another and they all had the same advice: "Pull them out and give her false teeth." Can you imagine? There was no such thing as cosmetic dentistry in 1958.

It is a testament to my mother's perseverance that I can smile today. She refused to accept that answer and didn't stop until she found the dentist who could give us what we wanted and needed: a smile people could smile back at. Today I tap into that trauma whenever a woman seeks me out, believing she can't be beautiful. It's part of what has made me a trusted cosmetic doctor and a confidant to thousands of women.

Growing Up Without a Goal

I was the only one of my neighborhood friends who went to college, but it didn't last long. At eighteen years old, without any goal, direction, drive, or ambition, I dropped out of college after one year and became a secretary. Although that was my job for eleven years, my goal was to find a man to marry me. At the time, hitching my star to someone else's wagon seemed like my best option. At age twenty-nine, after another failed relationship, it was finally time to take stock of my life.

I never excelled at anything. I didn't sing, I didn't dance, and I didn't play sports. I just showed up. In 2009, I attended my fortieth high school reunion at The Mary Louis Academy (a Catholic college-preparatory school for young women). It was clear from that evening's conversations with classmates that there had been three tracks of study at the school. This came as a surprise to me since I had blocked out most of my high school experience. The first track was for overachievers, the second for good students with potential and the third— well, you know.

From the classes I recalled taking, it was clear I was in the lowest track. At the reunion, I was remembered as being pretty and funny, but no one offered up recollections of me as being smart. I was a "C" student in the lowest track—good grief!

Making Choices

As you read this, ask yourself: "Am I living the life I chose, or did my life choose me?" When you wait for things to happen, life chooses you. I know this firsthand. For years I showed up physically and waited for life to get better. All through my twenties, I would look at friends who had a great life and think they were just lucky. I had a job and an apartment and occasionally a steady boyfriend, but I didn't have a great life.

It took me more years than I would like to admit to figure out why. I'm here to share my secrets, but before I do, I ask you to think about your own life. Do you have the life of your dreams? Do you have a great life? What's holding you back from having your best life, a fulfilling career or satisfying relationships? What stalled your dreams? What killed them? Put another way, what is the enemy of great?

The answer might surprise you. It has nothing to do with not having opportunities or lack of education or not enough money. The enemy of *great* is *good*. I'd love to tell you I came up with this on my own, but I didn't. Jim Collins, business consultant and author of five books, among them *The New York Times* best seller, *Good to Great,* said it and inspirational speakers have been repeating it for years. I'm referencing Jim Collins because I finally got it, and I'm hoping you will too.

Do you have a good job? You know—the one that pays well but is so boring that you dread getting up every morning? Or even worse—the one that pays so well you can't leave because you'll never find another job to pay you as much as you're earning now? And, at this point, you have developed some pretty bad habits like paying the mortgage and buying food for the family.

If you can relate, you're not alone. A 2011 Gallup Poll reported that 71 percent of American workers are emotionally disconnected from their workplaces and are less likely to be productive. That means only one-third of Americans are enthusiastic about their work and making positive contributions.

I faced this dilemma when I walked away from my emergency room position. I was paid very well but after years of fulfillment, I just wasn't enjoying the work anymore. I was forty-nine years old, working around the clock and raising my son by telephone. It was exhausting and I found myself not wanting to show up for my shifts, especially overnight shifts.

Trust me, if you ever find yourself in the emergency room you want a doctor who would rather be working there than any other place on the planet. I knew it was time for me to go and I started exploring other options. I spent a year in an occupational health clinic treating work-related injuries. It was not fulfilling but at least I was not working around the clock.

After much soul-searching and conversations with family and friends, I decided to open a medical spa dedicated to helping women navigate the aging process without surgery. Can you imagine the looks of horror when I announced, at age fifty, I was leaving a steady six-figure income position in mainstream medicine to open a business I knew nothing about? And sit at the reception desk myself?

I've learned so many lessons over the years. Adversity can be a great teacher. It can teach you perseverance and courage; it can teach you to trust your instincts and push past your perceived limitations; but most of all, it can teach you how to forgive yourself and keep on going. So as you might have guessed, this is a book about lessons learned and the strategies used to make big dreams real—not only my dreams, but your dreams too.

As I reflect upon my humble start, I realized there were key strategies that helped me achieve my goals. To be clear, I didn't realize they were strategies at the time. I was just slogging through the mud of my life. I was just putting one foot in front of the other. But there was more than that. There was falling down and getting back up. There was figuring out what worked and what didn't. There was laughing and crying. There was fear and reward. There were mistakes and regrets.

You can call them lessons. You can call them strategies. You can call them whatever you like. They were a roadmap to get me to this place. If you need a roadmap, maybe they will help you too. Or maybe, you will recognize yourself and they will help you avoid slogging as hard or as far as I did.

I've accomplished a great deal and you can too. I've made a ton of mistakes and have overcome many obstacles. Many times, I was my own obstacle. I can be my own obstacle to this day. I recognize it much quicker now, and if I don't, the supportive people in my circle remind me. These are the strategies that helped me climb out of many holes and stand on firm ground. I hope they help you too.

So here is my story, inspirational I'm told. I never considered myself an inspiration, just a hard worker. If it inspires you, that would make me happy. If it makes you work harder, that would make me happier. If it helps you recognize yourself and push past your perceived limitations to the greatness that is your story, that would be the most rewarding of all.

CHAPTER 2
Find Your Reason

*We all live under the same sky, but we don't all
have the same horizon.*

— Konrad Adenauer

You can be anything you want to be when you grow up.
Did you hear that too? Did you ever say it to someone
else—maybe your own child or a niece or nephew? Growing
up in the 1950s, it was my mother's mantra. There were
two problems: first, it was so open-ended and didn't mean
anything to me, and secondly, I didn't believe it. They were
just words to me. I never believed it.

Now as an educated, enlightened adult I recognize the
true power of mindset. My young mother was doing her
best and trying to encourage me to be anything I wanted,
but unfortunately it would take years for her message to get
through.

Condoleezza Rice told the following story at the 2012
Republican National Convention. As a little girl she grew up
in Jim Crow Birmingham, a segregated city in the south where
her parents couldn't take her to a movie theater or a restaurant.
But they had her absolutely convinced that, even though she
couldn't eat a hamburger at a Woolworths' counter, she could

become president of the United States if she wanted. She became secretary of state. She believed. I didn't.

The Fallout

The aftermath of my accident became all-consuming. My first childhood memory was being in a dentist's chair with a bright light shining in my eyes. I didn't understand the severity of the situation, but I knew enough to be scared. And it kept happening. We visited dentists for years. I didn't understand why. I just wanted it to stop.

To compound the situation, my disfigured teeth affected my ability to speak correctly and so there were visits to the speech pathologist as well. *Will it ever end?* When my mother finally found a dentist with a plan, we transitioned from sporadic visits to many different dentists to one dentist and, finally, a schedule. The first part of his treatment plan was a year in full-mouth braces.

Braces were different in the 1950s. They were shiny and rough and macerated the inside of your mouth. Once a month, they were tightened one tooth at a time with a dental instrument that resembled a pair of sharp nose pliers and my head would feel like it was in a vise. It wasn't pleasant, but it was better than showing off my disfigured brown front teeth.

But the real terror came when my two front teeth were filed down with the drill and my mouth was fitted for a crown. To this day a trip to the dentist can send a chill down my spine.

What Do You Want to Be When You Grow Up?

When I was growing up I never thought I'd be anything. Kids grow up with dreams of being a doctor or nurse or astronaut or something. I didn't have hopes or dreams at all.

Sadly, at eight years old when well-meaning relatives asked me what I wanted to be when I grew up, I can remember thinking, *I want to be left alone.* I was so exhausted from the trauma of spending my childhood in the dentist's chair and the speech pathologist's office that I just wanted to be left alone.

At eight, I was smart enough to know I couldn't tell anybody that, so I would just shrug and say, "I don't know." I didn't realize the universe had already delivered the perfect profession to my doorstep.

Early on, I was tagged by some as lazy. Others, trying to be kind, labeled me as not living up to my potential. Looking back, I was probably depressed. My teeth were so horrifying that I sat in the classroom like a mute. The last thing I wanted to do was excel at anything and draw attention to myself. I never felt pretty or smart or exceptional in any way. In fact, I felt just the opposite. I felt ugly, stupid and dull.

At nine years old, my teeth were finally fixed. *Thank you Mom and Dr. Axelrod!* Now I looked like everyone else physically, but mentally the feelings of inadequacy didn't change. I left childhood without any dreams and entered my teenage years with low self-esteem that got carried way too far into adulthood.

As you examine your life, can you remember a time when you felt like you didn't fit in? Maybe you weren't pretty enough or smart enough? Sometimes feelings of inadequacy can motivate us to prove people wrong. *I'll show you. I am enough.* Other times we carry these feelings and let them take control of our lives. Wanting to hide in childhood set the stage for me to take a back seat for many years. I believed I wasn't smart. I felt lazy. I had no desire to reach whatever potential everyone was talking about.

Look to Your Pain

And yet today, the little girl who sat mute in the classroom not living up to her potential, and the teenager who perfected being part of the background noise of life, has grown up to become a doctor, an entrepreneur, and of all things, a public speaker. Little did I know my greatest wound in life would bring forth my greatest gift. Little did I know my pain would shape my calling and make it possible for me to help others.

Sometimes things happen when you're small and too young to understand the significance of the situation or what to do with it. That's what happened to me. When I went flying down the hallway steps as a toddler, a major shift occurred in my life. Unbelievably, it took me more than fifty years to recognize it.

I am called to run my medical spa and help women feel beautiful from the inside out, the same way I was called to write this book. It is a feeling that cannot be denied and sometimes cannot be explained. I floundered for many years without direction until I finally returned to college at age twenty-nine. When I set my sights on becoming a doctor, it was a dream. It might have been the first real dream I ever had but it came with so much work it never felt dreamy.

When I reached my goal, I worked in the emergency room for nearly ten years and I enjoyed every minute for a long time. I was good at my job and I enjoyed helping people and figuring out complex diagnoses. I treated thousands of people and saved hundreds lives over the years. It was truly important work but it never felt like a calling. It felt like a job at which I excelled.

I became an emergency room doctor because I was single with a child and needed to coordinate my life around being a mom and being a doctor. By age forty-nine, I was raising my son by telephone and working around the clock. I was exhausted.

I wanted to be a great parent and I wanted to be great at some type of service that wasn't going to kill me. I was no longer finding fulfillment in the emergency room and I didn't find it working a year in the occupational health clinic either, so I created my own.

When I opened the medical spa, I created a different way of contributing that brought it full circle. It turned out the trip down the staircase brought the gift. Shortly after opening, I recognized the irony that a little girl who didn't smile until she was nine years old grew up to help women smile every day.

It took a little while longer for me to realize that my wound was the gift. I know what it's like to be perceived as not being pretty, so I make ladies feel pretty every day. And that heals me as well.

It is only recently that I have been able to truly tap into the pain of my accident and its horrible aftermath. I understand what it feels like to not want to look at your own reflection in the mirror. I understand what it feels like to want to fade into the background so no one will notice you. That accident and its devastating consequences taught me the importance of beauty in a way no other experience could. Not only external beauty, but internal as well.

One of the reasons I initially decided on a career in the emergency room was for the ease of scheduling. Luckily for me, it was fulfilling but was never my purpose. I never really felt connected to my patients. The fulfillment came more from solving the problem and figuring out the solution, which in turn enabled me to do great things for my patients.

Finding Your Purpose

It was an entirely different experience when I opened my own business. The first time I did a treatment for someone in my spa and she looked in the mirror with tears in her eyes and said, "This is how I used to look!" I knew I was exactly where I was supposed to be. It was a seminal moment for me.

But I wrestled with it for a long time. Being an emergency room doctor was important work. Did I sell out for my own comfort? How could it feel so good to help women feel good about the way they look and yet be so conflicting internally for me with my education? When I realized I used to save lives and now I save self-esteem, the significance of my purpose became illuminating.

Who would have thought that a knock down the stairs would have given me a gift that's giving back to me and others in so many ways? Women trust me with their faces. It is, in my opinion, the highest honor.

As a toddler, the universe knocked me upside my little head and said *you're going to learn this lesson in a way that will be indelible to you.* I got my teeth knocked out—literally. Yet I spent years putting the accident out of my mind. It was something that happened a long time ago. I never understood its role in my life. I never understood it had a role in my life. I thought it was just an unfortunate accident. I never even spoke about it.

Is there something in your past that you haven't recognized yet as a gift? Bad things happen to good people all the time. Loved ones die, fortunes are lost, careers end. The list is endless. The choices are simpler. Are you a victim or victorious? The truth is, everything in your life had to happen exactly the way it did in order for you to be in the place you are today. What you do with where you are is another story.

Two Kisses for Maddy

Matthew Logelin, author of *Two Kisses for Maddy: A Memoir of Loss & Love,* was an ordinary guy living an ordinary life until tragedy struck in 2008. It took some time, but out of Matt's unspeakable horror came peace and comfort for millions. He had married his childhood sweetheart in 2005 and two years later they were delighted to learn that his wife Liz was pregnant.

After a difficult pregnancy which required home bed rest and finally hospitalization, their daughter Madeline was born on March 24, 2008. She was healthy although seven weeks premature. The following day Matt helped his wife out of bed for the first time in five weeks so he could wheel her to the neonatal intensive care unit to visit their daughter. Within seconds she collapsed in his arms and died of pulmonary embolism. She never even held her daughter.

Matt turned to blogging as an outlet for his grief and to document his journey as an unexpected single father. As news of his story spread, Matt found himself in the national spotlight being profiled in *People* magazine and *The Oprah Winfrey Show* to name a few. Initially, there was an outpouring of support that came to Matt in the form of dozens of packages a day. Total strangers were sending formula coupons, diapers, clothing, books, and much more to help ease his struggle. There was also an outpouring of advice and encouragement on his blog.

In 2009, Matt started to write his book and also founded The Liz Logelin Foundation, in honor of his wife. The foundation has given tens of thousands of dollars to widowed families. Through workshops and keynote presentations, Matt has worked extensively with people who have lost partners. His book, which rose to number twenty-four on *The New York Times* best-seller list and number eleven on the e-books list, has helped millions.

During an interview, Matt spoke about how, if his wife had lived, he would have never written a book or gone on to help so many in need. Little did he know his tragedy would bring this gift to millions.

Laura and Richard's Story

After failed marriages, including an alcoholic wife for him and an abusive husband for her, Laura and Richard not only found each other but true love and happiness as well. They were an unlikely pair. He was twenty-six years older and she was two inches taller.

Theirs was a fairy tale story. They both knew after the first date they would be together forever. It wasn't easy—he came with two teenage children and she with a two-year-old son. But it worked. Richard, a loving and generous person, quickly adopted her son and then they proceeded to add to their newly blended family.

He had a successful accounting business and she had a financial and insurance background. They grew their business out of a home office and spent quality time with each other and their children daily. Their big house was the destination for all the parties. It was where we all wanted to hang out.

In February 1992, Richard developed a pain in his back. Initially no one thought much of it. Alarm bells went off when it wouldn't respond to pain medication and wouldn't go away. In May, he was dead of pancreatic cancer. He left behind a thirty-eight-year-old wife, an unborn baby, four children under the age of ten and two young adult children from his previous marriage.

One of the saddest sights I ever saw was my childhood friend, with her seven-month pregnant belly, flanked by her four young children walking down a church aisle behind the casket of her dead husband. The best ten years of her life came to a screeching halt in three months.

Life went on for Laura. It always does. There were good days and bad days, happy days and sad days, days she wanted to remember and days she hoped to forget. Thankfully, good financial planning enabled her to raise her five children without having to work outside the home. She was a single mother for almost fifteen years, devoted to her faith and her children. When her youngest was finishing high school, Laura was feeling the desire to return to the workforce. She turned to what she knew best—financial planning.

She knew how to help people manage money but what she didn't know was how to get a business off the ground. She joined a mastermind group to learn the basics of building a business in the twenty-first century. The course covered everything from identifying your ideal client, to marketing, to the components of a successful website, and even how to write a newsletter. We had multiple extended conversations about business during that time and although she was applying all the basics, she just couldn't get traction.

One day she confided that she was feeling stuck because she couldn't get a business started and guilty because she was heavily invested financially in the mastermind program that wasn't producing results. She divulged, "I am really all too content right now in so many areas that it un-motivates me. I think I am convinced that commitment to work will steal the joy. I love lots and lots of things but not super passionately, except of course for my kids and family."

Laura had recently married a dear family friend who lost his wife and blended yet another family. Her children were grown and were having children of their own. She referred to this segment of her life as "Grandma Bliss."

"Did you always know you would love what you are doing?" she once asked me. The truth is I didn't. I, like most people, looked for my calling in my passion. When I couldn't find a passion, I assumed I didn't have a calling. I felt like the only person on the planet who didn't have a purpose. I liked a lot of things, but I never felt the passion I heard others express. I liked food, traveling, socializing with friends. I liked to paint a little and I could play a mean *Merrily We Roll Along* on the piano, but I could have never made a career out of any of that.

I had even tried that approach initially. When I originally decided on a career, I was going to be a nutritionist because I loved food. During the process, I found that I loved science, which led me on the road to being a doctor. I love solving a good mystery and when I combined it with a love of science, a career was born.

Don't get me wrong, I loved it for a long time. I loved working in the emergency room. I loved solving complex medical problems. I loved turning around a critically ill patient and watching him or her talking with family members an hour after my intervention. But it was never the kind of passion that burns deep inside. You don't know what that feels like until it happens to you.

Laura began to realize her best contribution to the world and to herself would be working with young widows. She knew what it was like to have five children expecting Santa to come when you still hadn't gotten yourself out of bed to go to the mall on Christmas Eve. She knew what was like to have to stretch a finite amount of money to accommodate the needs of five growing children as well as yourself. She knew what it was like to be so broken-hearted that you can't even get out of your pajamas and clean the kitchen or to make dinner, when what you really want to say to your children is, "You're hungry again?"

The day she decided to help young widows, everything fell into place. She signed up for bereavement courses and is completing end-of-life doula training. Doulas, who have long helped women through labor, are now assisting the dying and their families as they make this final transition. When Laura started giving workshops to young widows through the church, a business that eluded her for over two years was born.

Finding Your Story

Where is your story? Is your story rooted in your passion or your pain? Maybe you were one of the lucky ones who always knew. My brother, who served on the New York City police force for twenty years, knew from the time he was nine years old. At eight years old my younger sister told my mother she wanted to be a nurse when she grew up. "Why don't you be a doctor?" asked my mother. And that was it for her, doctor it was.

Or maybe you had a passion as a child but didn't believe it could ever be a catalyst for the goal of a lifetime. Maybe you were the little girl with the Easy-Bake Oven who never thought it could be possible to own the best bakery in town. Or you were the child who was always putting on plays in the backyard but never thought you could earn a living as an entertainer. Where you start doesn't have to be where you end, no matter how old you are. People change careers all the time—sometimes out of choice and sometimes because they are forced out of their comfort zone.

I am living proof that you can be passionate about different things at different times. At first glance it looks like my medical spa and my speaking and writing career are two different callings. It took me a while to realize they have the same root. I am called to empower women so they can realize how fabulous they are. I accomplish that by helping women stay beautiful externally through non-surgical cosmetic procedures and internally by helping them regain their self-esteem through my writings and speeches.

It took me years to find my calling. My story was under my nose my entire life and I never mentioned it to people. It was literally under my nose and in my mouth. Is your story hiding in plain sight too? What is your seminal moment? Maybe you were in your twenties or thirties when someone did or said something to you that left a mark. Maybe you were in your forties or fifties when devastation hit.

Early on in my medical spa journey, I knew in my heart I was destined to help women feel beautiful. The validation really came when I stumbled upon a quote from Jeffrey Van Dyk, chief executive officer of Big Vision Business: "Out of your deepest wound in life comes forth your greatest gift to share." Pay attention to your own life to see if there are any clues. Turn your wound into a gift.

Because, like Dorothy in the *Wizard of Oz*, it turns out you have the power. We all have the power. Dorothy always had the power to get home—she just had to be present to the power that was right under her nose. What's hiding in plain sight for you?

The Take-Away

We all have a calling but it can sometimes elude us. Traditional thinking advises us to find our calling in our passion. *If you do what you love, you'll never work a day in your life.* But what if you don't fit into that mold? Some of us will find our calling in our passion and it will be crystal clear right from the start. Others of us will find it in our pain. You might have been too hurt to embrace the lesson or too young to understand its significance. It's there for all of us but some of us have to dig deep to find it. If you can't find your calling in your passion, look to your pain. Trust me—we all have a purpose. Even you! Embrace your journey.

CHAPTER 3
Row Your Own Boat, Baby

It's not the size of the dog in the fight, it's the size of the fight in the dog.

— Anonymous

Row, row, row your boat *gently down the stream. Merrily, merrily, merrily, merrily, life is but a dream.* Do you remember this little song? Are you singing it to yourself right now? For me, it conjures up an image of two people lazily rowing a small boat aimlessly down a quiet stream. The sun is shining and the birds are singing.

Now don't get me wrong. I like a beautiful day as much as you do. I would love to be lazily coasting down a stream with someone I love. The problem is, in my opinion, people now think they can dream their way to success. You can't.

If you want to row your boat gently down the stream with no end point in mind, you can row all day long. Bring some wine and make it a party. But if you want to get to the other side of the stream, you need a plan. This is not to say you still can't have fun doing it, but you need a plan and it takes some work.

What's waiting on the other side of the stream for you? Is it a well-deserved promotion that keeps eluding you? Is it a new business with a logo you can't get out of your mind? Do you dream of seeing your name up in lights? Whatever it is, you have to want it badly enough that you're willing to get in your own boat and row. It's not enough to just row—you have to row with purpose and row with both oars, otherwise you'll just be going around in circles.

What Happened to Hard Work?

Have hard work, determination and willpower fallen out of favor? Beginning in childhood we give rewards so that people will feel good about themselves. The participation trophy is a prime example. There was a time when the exceptional player on a little league team got the trophy and the team that won the most games got the trophy. Now everyone gets the trophy just for showing up.

But it's worse than that. It's reached a point when the mediocre don't earn the reward, we take it away from the exceptional. St. Basil School, an elementary and junior high school in Calgary, Canada, did away with its honor roll. It seems the children who didn't make the cut had hurt feelings. So rather than push those children into excellence, the prize was taken away. What ever happened to, "If at first you don't succeed, try, try again?"

Teach Your Children to Row

It's hard enough to get in your own boat and row. It's even harder to give the oars to your children. As a parent, you want the best for your child. You want them to have an easy life. You don't want them to struggle. Unfortunately, it's not always realistic.

When my son graduated from college, he was having a difficult time finding a job. He was working as a waiter and had an unpaid internship for a men's health magazine. Because he was unable to fully support himself, my husband and I were his financial safety net.

The back-up plan if he couldn't make it work was for him to move in with us. I love my son, but I didn't want him back living with us. I knew it would not only disrupt our lives, but more importantly, would not move him forward. One day I was discussing this dilemma with a dear friend who gave me some great advice.

As the mother of seven children herself, she said I was handling the situation all wrong. Instead of funding him every month, I needed to give him a set amount of money and let him figure it out for himself. So, I told him I loved him, that the current situation wasn't working, and gave him a check to cover two months of living expenses.

With a heavy heart, I told him he could either figure it out, he could live in his car, or he could move in with his grandmother. He used the two-month advance wisely and when he couldn't make it work on his own, he moved to New York and lived with my mother. Within a year, he was able to turn a dead-end job in New York into a career in Washington, D.C. He got in his own boat and rowed to the other side.

When we give our children every comfort, we don't make self-reliant adults. We all want our children to have more opportunities and a better future than we had. The challenge is to strike a balance between good parenting and creating entitled children.

Advice from Steve Harvey

I once saw an Oprah's Lifeclass episode with Steve Harvey, author of *Act Like a Success, Think Like a Success*. A twenty-three year old girl and her mother Skyped in to get Steve's advice. She was living with her mother and was complaining that her mother didn't treat her like an adult. She had chores that she felt were "childish" and thought she was entitled to a weekly allowance. She went on to lament that she had a 2:00 a.m. curfew though she was still out having fun at that hour. She wanted to know how she and her mother could reach common ground and not battle over these issues.

She was back living at home because she had changed her major and transferred to a local college. A lot of her credits didn't transfer and it was like starting all over again. Her mother explained that she got up at 5:00 a.m. to go to work and, since the house was alarmed, when her daughter came in late her sleep was interrupted.

Steve Harvey told the girl she had to move. If she didn't want to live by her mother's rules, she had to move out of her mother's house. The young girl was astounded and the conversation went around and around. She admitted she wasn't expecting that answer and thought that Steve Harvey would show them how to find a compromise. "It's not easy moving and I don't want to move out and then struggle."

When did we teach our children that they shouldn't have to struggle? When did we teach our children that their needs and wants come before all others? I suppose this *things were different when I was a child* theory is a universal rite of passage of adults of a certain age. I must be at that age. Where are you? Are you at *that* age too? And where were you at twenty-three? Were you content to live at home?

When I was a child, I didn't get everything I wanted because we couldn't afford it. I saved up for things. I waited. My parents were never afraid they would hurt my feelings. Struggle is the foundation for strong will. Strong will is the foundation for a strong society. My fear is that, with the best of intentions, we are failing our children. In the end, we all lose. You have to get in the boat and row.

The New High School Experience

There's a new phenomenon happening in schools. I heard this from a front office employee of a local high school and at first thought she was joking. Unfortunately, she was not. It appears that so many kids were texting their parents to bring them "stuff" during the school day, the front office was overwhelmed. So tables were set up in the hallway as a drop-off point. Forgotten homework assignments, lattes and muffins from Starbucks, change of clothes, lunch from the local deli can all be delivered to the hallway drop-off point by doting parents so little Johnny can have all his needs met.

How convenient. If you forgot your homework, no need to get in trouble—just text Mom. Forgot your gym clothes?

No need to be embarrassed—Dad to the rescue. Who wouldn't love a latte in-between classes or a different lunch than what's being offered in the cafeteria?

How do you learn to solve a problem when someone is a text away to bail you out? How do you learn personal responsibility or delayed gratification when all your needs are instantly met? How do you ever learn about consequence and reward when you are shielded from consequence?

Our job as parents is not to shield our child from difficulty and adversity, but to foster motivated, disciplined adults who will one day contribute to society. When we shield our children from every problem, they grow up thinking that everyone else will solve their problems too. No one can row your boat but you.

A Story from Entertainment News

About five years ago, I saw a segment on an entertainment news program that stuck with me. I remember the segment like it was yesterday. The interviews were broken up between chief executive officers and workers. CEOs of different corporations were interviewed and all had the same impression. New graduates had difficulty working independently and also had a tough time dealing with criticism. The consensus was young people performed better in a group than solo.

I remember thinking of my son's elementary school experience and contrasting it to my own. In my classroom in the 1950s, the desks were one behind the other in organized rows. The only view you had was the back of the person's head in front of you and the teacher's face. In the early 1990s in my son's classroom, four desks were put together so that four students all faced each other. These large communal desks were scattered throughout the room with, what seemed to me, no particular order.

I remember his early teachers complaining to me he was always reaching over to one of the other desks if he needed a crayon. It was astounding to me that the school sat a five-year old boy in a communal space and then expected him to have boundaries and work independently.

But the best interview in the segment came last. Two young twenty-something men were interviewed about their work experience. One said that things were different now. It's not like when his father was employed and he stayed with the same company for fifty years. People of his generation didn't feel that kind of loyalty and were expected to change jobs frequently during their careers.

He went on to say if he didn't like the way he was being treated at his job, he would just go somewhere else where they would treat him better. But the piece-de-resistance came from the other one. "For years, my mother and my grandmother have been telling me I'm special. I believe them." Can you hear the double line forming for the participation trophy?

Equal Pay for Equal Work?

It's hard to preach a message of *hard work gets the rewards* when society glorifies athletes, actors, and the lucky. Is there seriously any person on the planet who is worth a $25 million salary because they can pretend to be someone else on film or throw a ball or run fast? Seriously?

When I finished my residency training, my first job as an emergency room doctor paid $150,000. I was literally working around the clock with some shifts that started at midnight and ended at 8:00 a.m. I cared for crying and terrified children, elderly people who couldn't communicate, and everything in between.

Some people had life-threatening illness or injury and others had the common cold. It didn't matter. I brought my "A" game to every patient, every day. If I was taking care of a critically ill patient when my shift ended, I didn't get to go home. I stayed until that person was stabilized. If the shift was non-stop and my charts had to be completed, I didn't go home. I stayed until every "T" was crossed and every "I" was dotted.

I held this job as the dot-com boom was taking place. Young people, some without college educations were part of start-up companies and were walking away with millions. I was despondent. It felt like these people had relied on an easy fix or had been in the right place at the right time and had reaped a great reward.

How could it be you could deliver mail for a start-up company and walk away with millions and I could save your life at 3:00 a.m. and bring home a little over $100,000 after taxes? Of course, the dot-com bubble burst and it turned out that most of the millions were in stock options that could now be used to wallpaper the bathroom. But it didn't matter to me at the time.

A Quick Fix is Not the Answer

You can have a dream and you can be successful, but you can't dream your way to success. You have to do the work. Sometimes we say we want something but we make choices that sabotage ourselves.

What do you want your legacy to be? In my twenties I wasn't willing to put in the work to move myself forward. I was bored and going through the motions, but deep down inside I was hoping someone else would do the work for me. You can't take a picture from the top of the mountain unless you climb up there yourself.

If you don't want to see the view from the top, that's fine too. But if you do, what are you willing to do to get there? How hard are you willing to work? When opportunity knocks, success is usually on the other side—disguised as hard work.

When I worked in the emergency room, it was surprising to me how many people were looking for a quick fix to good health. As part of most visits, vital signs and blood work were taken. Even though I didn't have a private relationship with my patients, the results made clear which patients were on a path leading to dependence on medication.

I viewed this as a bad path to be on and would try to counsel people. "Your blood pressure is up slightly and some of your blood tests indicate that there might be a problem down the road. You can still turn this around with diet and exercise." I can't tell you how many times someone asked me "Doc, don't you just have a pill I can take?" I don't get it. *Doesn't anyone want to row anymore?*

In the United States, the Declaration of Independence states: "All men are created equal." Opportunities and results, however, are not. Roadblocks are put in your life for a reason. They help mold your character and they help flex your willpower muscle. So if you haven't figured it out by now, this is not a book that will help you journal your way to joy. There's a reward waiting for you, but you have to roll up your sleeves and do some work.

Who is Dr. O'Malley?

By now you must be asking who is Dr. O'Malley and why should we listen to her? I'm not a celebrity. I don't have a television show. I'm not the chief operating officer of any major organization, and you've never seen me on a shopping network. I'm just a hard working girl with a story, probably boring by Hollywood standards.

I never had a drug or alcohol problem, was never homeless, and didn't suffer abuse at the hands of my parents. I went to school every day with a full stomach and clothes that fit me. But, like you, there were obstacles that could and did impede my success for a long time.

I suffered disappointments and setbacks that almost derailed me on more than one occasion. I know what it's like to be pulled in so many directions you think you will break apart. I wanted to give up many times but had reached a point where I was so heavily invested financially in my choice that there was no turning back. I wasn't trained to do anything else and I owed a lot of money. There were times I kept on going because I didn't know what else to do. I never had a Plan B.

Turning the "M" of Manifesting Upside Down into the "W" of Work

I've noticed people now spend great sums of money to study things like mindset and manifesting, believing their thoughts alone will create their reality. I didn't ask the universe to deliver me to medical school. I worked my butt off to get there and when I didn't get accepted, I worked my butt off some more.

When I was up all night with a crying newborn and found myself falling asleep in medical school lectures, I didn't cut pictures out of magazines and pin them on a vision board. I waited until the end of the day, got some sleep, and then got up the next day and did it all over again.

When I spent what felt like my entire internship year crying in the hospital bathroom because I was so physically, emotionally, and intellectually spent, and because the system is designed to make you feel like a stupid idiot who doesn't know anything, I didn't manifest a miracle. I dried my tears and then worked some more.

When I was growing up, my mother used to say, "The world doesn't owe you a living." I didn't fully understand what she was talking about until I started working towards a goal. Nothing comes for free.

It's important to have a positive mindset and it helps to have a dream, but it takes work to make your dream come true. Action and results don't come from magical thinking. Positive affirmations and manifesting miracles aren't going to get the job done. No amount of meditation and no dream board will ever take the place of work and willpower.

You have to want it so badly you're willing to wage
war to get it—you have to be willing to become a warrior
and a workhorse. You have to be willing to turn the M's of
manifesting, mindset and miracles upside down into the W's
of work, willpower and warrior.

Hard, But Not Impossible

One Monday morning in my freshman year of medical school,
a young classmate of mine came up to me with a quizzical look
on his face. He said he had been home to visit his parents over
the weekend. He told his mother about me, a classmate who
was a single mother with a newborn, and she told him, "That
was impossible." I smiled and said, "Here I am."

This is a story about what is possible, a story about
perseverance and empowerment—and about choices. And
about how, even when you make a series of not-so-good
choices, you can still have a good outcome if you work hard
enough.

In the end, we all want the same things. We want to feel
we have done the best job we could have done. We want
to feel validated, whether to ourselves or by someone else.
We want to be happy. And we want to feel those feelings in
relationships or business or on a personal level.

It took me many years to get to this point, and it took me
many years and many failures to figure out these strategies.
Taking your life to the next level always requires a change, be
it a change in attitude, approach, or circumstance. My greatest
hope is that my strategies will help you row your boat to the
destiny you deserve too.

The Take-Away

Success doesn't come from a quick fix, it comes from hard work. It's important to have a positive mindset and it helps to have a dream but it takes work to make your dream come true. Positive affirmations and manifesting miracles aren't going to get the job done. No amount of meditation and no dream board will ever take the place of work and willpower. If you are bound and determined to reach your goal, you have to roll up your sleeves and do whatever it takes.

CHAPTER 4
Flip Your Switch

*Courage is the commitment to begin without
any guarantee of success.*
— Johann Wolfgang von Goethe

I want to spend a moment talking about commitment. You know—when you tell someone you'll do something and you follow through. That's not usually the problem for most of us. Many of us, me included, will honor commitments made to others better than we will honor commitments we make to ourselves. Sometimes, we value others more than we value ourselves.

So before we even talk about a plan, you need to commit yourself to changing what you don't like about your life. In my family we have a saying: "Change is good. You go first."

I call it *flipping your switch*. We all have a different reason and a different time we find ourselves ready to commit to a change. Sometimes it's a rational reason and sometimes it's an emotional reason.

Maybe you're just ready, period, end of the story. You probably approach many decisions from a rational perspective and this is no different for you. Many women I talk to with this approach say the same thing. "I don't want to be here next year or ever again." And boom they are ready to make whatever changes are necessary. Cheryl's story is a prime example.

Cheryl and Larry's Story

She and Larry had a good life. They were in love and committed to each other with enough money to live in a nice home, raise three children, take an occasional family vacation, and socialize with life-long friends.

Twenty-two years and three children later, Cheryl found herself 100 pounds overweight. For years she would lose a little and gain it back. But now, nearing fifty, losing weight seemed to be an up-hill battle.

To compound the problem, Cheryl's body was no longer cooperating. The weight was taking a toll on her muscles and bones. She was in constant pain and becoming less mobile.

At one point she pulled a groin muscle resulting in excruciating hip pain. She needed months of medication and intense physical therapy. She was even taped up like a racehorse for stability but still needed a cane to walk any distance.

A few months later, intense foot pain brought her to her doctor again. This time she was diagnosed with a stress fracture of one of the bones in her foot necessitating eight weeks of a not so stylish boot. It seemed she was always seeking medical attention for some ache or pain. The wake-up call came when she fell twice in one month.

She didn't like where her life was headed and knew if she didn't commit to a change, she would wind up on a downward spiral. "I am willing to do the work rather than

pay the doctors or insurance company," she decided one
Saturday morning. "I have to get my body mechanics back
before I break something. I am willing to forgo hair, nails,
and anything else to engage a personal trainer." And she
ended with, "It's going to get ugly real soon."

It never really got ugly, which is not to say it was easy. It
was not easy, but over the last three and a half years, Cheryl
has lost sixty pounds. Her bones don't creak and she is mobile
again. She has energy and has been forced to buy new clothes.
Just for the record—her hair and nails survived the change.

When she would feel herself sliding backwards she
thought *not another penny more* to doctors and she kept on
going. She flipped her switch when she decided she was done
giving money to doctors.

My Experience with Smoking

When I was eighteen, I began smoking cigarettes. Smoking
was socially acceptable back then. Everybody smoked. People
smoked in restaurants, on airplanes, in the office, in the
doctor's office—anywhere and everywhere.

Ten years later and after one failed attempt at quitting, I
flipped my switch. I started noticing older women walking on
New York City streets hunched over with cigarettes dangling
out of their mouths and smoke lofting up into their faces. For
the sake of vanity, I decided this was not going to be me.

I was going to quit. Quitting was different in the
seventies. There was no pill or patch. There might have been
gum, but I don't remember it.

Since I made the decision it was just a matter of when, and now was as good a time as any. Because I had one failed attempt behind me, I decided to quit with an open pack of cigarettes in my purse. I knew if I threw them away in some magnanimous gesture that would not work for me.

If in a moment of weakness I bought another pack, I knew I would open it; and I knew if I bought them I would smoke one and that would be the end. Within twenty-four hours I felt like someone was pulling my lungs out through my nose.

That's when the anger took over. I had fooled myself into thinking if I really wanted to quit smoking, it wouldn't be a problem. Have you ever fooled yourself into thing something similar? *If I wanted to, I could stop eating desert, I could stop having a second glass of wine every night, I could quit smoking.*

I couldn't believe nicotine had done that to me and I had been a willing participant. Now it was the cigarettes or me. Every time I wanted to give in to the cravings, I opened my purse and looked at the open pack. It fueled my anger.

For me, I had made the decision and I knew it was the right decision so I wanted to honor it. Willpower and discipline were the tools I used to honor my commitment to myself. Oftentimes, we think of anger as a negative emotion. In this instance, I used the anger I was feeling at myself as a catalyst for positive change. Never underestimate the power of willpower and discipline, or even anger.

Some of us approach change from a more emotional perspective. Maybe you approach the decision with a little more emotion but with enough self-esteem to propel you forward on the fast track. "I deserve better than this." "You can't treat me that way." "I'm better than this." Does this sound like you? And it can be any decision—whether it's a relationship or a job or whatever it is. You just believe you deserve better than the situation is offering and you're ready to make a change.

As much as I wanted to be in either one of those categories, especially when it came to relationships or jobs, I just wasn't. I was the one with low self-esteem, the emotional wreck. I needed to have the tears streaming down my face and my chest heaving from crying before I was willing to move on and up. I usually found myself sobbing, "I can't take it anymore."

Rock bottom was a familiar place for me on more than one occasion. Rock bottom was the place I needed to be before I could gather up the strength to say, "We gotta get out of here." I know I'm not alone on that one. I don't know if you've ever been at rock bottom but my friend Rachael sure was.

Rachael's Story

Rachael was a pretty woman who didn't know her own value. She had a successful career in sales despite never having finished college. It was a sticking point for her but now at age thirty-one, she had resigned herself to it. She had been dating Tommy for almost two years. In my opinion, they had one thing in common. She liked him and he liked him.

Tommy's career was on the rise and Rachael, a people pleaser, was doing everything in her power to make his life easier. Tommy, who was five years younger, had recently been accepted to law school so they didn't see as much of each other.

Rachael convinced herself that he was just busy even though deep down she feared their relationship was changing. More often than not, she was finding herself with hurt feelings.

The turning point came one evening when she visited him at his dorm. He was now living in a dangerous section of New York City. She traveled almost an hour to see him, trekking on two New York City subways and walking three city blocks in the dark.

The evening was a disaster. He ignored her for the first hour because he was studying. He had nothing planned and talked about himself and his new life the entire time. She told me at one point she saw his mouth moving but didn't even hear words coming out. She could only hear her own voice in her head—*What am I doing here?*

Have you ever been in a relationship that you let continue long past the time you should have let it go? Maybe you were hoping he would change? Maybe you were so lonely that being with him was better than being alone? Maybe you were so heavily invested emotionally and embarrassed to admit to your friends and family that it wasn't right? Chances are they already knew.

When Rachael put her head on his pillow that evening she flipped her switch. Nothing was working the way she had planned. She knew he didn't value her the way she valued him. As he slept, she soaked the pillow with her own tears. *When my feet hit the floor in the morning, you will never hurt me again. I'm done.*

When the sun came up, they had a cup of coffee and she got back on the subway and rode away. She never saw him again. It broke her heart but she was in love with the fantasy of Tommy, not the real Tommy that showed up day after day. That experience helped her discover her worth. She had reached the point where she was able to say, *you can't treat me like this.*

Honoring Yourself

Sometimes you have to flip a switch to make a commitment to honor yourself. This sounds simple, but can be harder than you think. During my years of emergency medicine training, there were always colleagues who wanted to change shifts.

Someone would come up to me with some sob story of why they needed that day off and would I please switch shifts with them? I always felt obligated to give someone an immediate answer and many times would accommodate because I knew I probably didn't have any big plans for the day anyway.

Without fail, the day I showed up for the shift that was never assigned to me in the first place, it would be chaos from beginning to end. I would spend eight hours angry at myself for having agreed to it.

Then one day, I flipped my switch and realized I was under no obligation to give anyone an immediate answer. Even though I didn't have plans that didn't mean I had to accommodate them.

After I decided to commit to honoring myself, I changed my tactics. When someone would come to me and ask a favor, I would say, "Let me check my schedule and I'll get back to you."

I wasn't left staring at someone feeling obligated to answer. I wasn't left feeling guilty that I really didn't want to do it but if I didn't I wasn't being a team player. I was left with a feeling of empowerment. Even if I only took five minutes to make the decision, I got to decide what I wanted to do.

The Power of Your Words

Sometimes, what you say can help others flip their switch. As an emergency room physician, I found myself not only caring for the physical well being of my patients but for the emotional well being of family members as well.

A nurse came up to me on one particularly busy shift to let me know there was a family that wanted to speak to me. The family's daughter was being seen by my co-worker, the other doctor working that evening, but they wanted to speak with me. My mind started racing. Who are these people? Did I misdiagnose a family member of theirs? When someone at work says they want to speak to you, it usually isn't to tell you what a great job you're doing.

The mother and father came out of their daughter's room and met me in the busy hallway. "Do you remember us?" they asked. Now my mind was really racing. I didn't remember them and didn't know where this conversation was headed. "You took care of our daughter a year ago."

It came flooding back to me. Their twenty-something-year-old daughter had a long history of drug and emotional problems. They had been with her in the emergency room numerous times and were at their wit's end. That particular evening was a Saturday. I don't remember exactly what their daughter did to land her in the emergency room but I do remember that it wasn't life threatening and was clearly manipulative to the parents.

That night we also spoke in the hallway. "You have to walk away," I said. "It's eleven o'clock on a Saturday night and you two have been in this emergency room for hours while your daughter is sitting here comfortably laughing and having conversations with the staff. I'm sure there are ten other places you'd rather be. I'm getting paid to be here and there are ten other places I'd rather be myself."

It was my recommendation to admit her to a psychiatric facility to sort out her issues and let her start taking responsibility for her life and her behavior. My shift ended one hour later and that was the last I saw or heard from that family until I found myself standing in the hallway again.

"You gave us back our daughter and we wanted to say thank you." They went on to explain that shortly after I walked out that night, they walked out as well. They had tried for years to solve their daughter's problems and it had reached a point where they were being held emotionally hostage. "We cried all the way home," they said, "but we knew we had to do it."

A year later, she was drug free and her emotional issues were under control. That night they were in the emergency room only for a sprained wrist. What courage it took for those parents to flip their switch and commit to another way to solve the problem. For a long time, it felt to them that they had abandoned their daughter. Once they made the decision to change their approach, they honored the commitment they made to each other. In the end, everyone was a winner.

Find the Courage to Commit to Yourself

We all have a different reason. What is yours? Maybe you're in a relationship and know deep down you're not being honored. Maybe your company downsized and you find yourself laid off after many years of being a loyal employee.

Did someone else get your promotion? Do you really want to break free from your corporate cubicle and start your own business? Maybe the kids are finally out of the house and it's time for you. Are you realizing you have a limited work time left before retirement?

Maybe you're looking around and saying—*you know, I just don't want to do this anymore. I don't want to spend the next ten or fifteen years doing this.* I want to do what I really want to do or maybe what I've always wanted to do but for one reason or another never did.

Maybe you always promised yourself once you got to a certain level, you would—and you can fill in your own blank—play more tennis, take golf lessons, entertain, travel, and you find you're not doing that.

Many times it is harder to make the commitment to do something than to actually get your act together and do it. How many times have you spent months thinking about the task you need to accomplish? You know—you have to give a presentation or you want to write a book or you have a great idea for a business.

Then the self-doubt creeps in, followed immediately by procrastination. I formulated this book in my head for five years before I finally got myself together to write it. I told myself every story—it's been done before, this is not a new message, I don't have a brand name anyone will want to read, and, my personal favorite, this book sucks.

One day I flipped my switch and said *enough already*. Is it time to flip your switch? You have to make the decision that you're ready to change. Once you flip the switch, it is time to take action. And now you can create and talk about a plan to take you where you want to go. Whether it's as simple as, "I don't want to be here next year," or "You can't treat me like that," or "I can't take it anymore," this is your time and here is the plan.

In this book are the strategies that moved me from college dropout to emergency room doctor, entrepreneur, public speaker and author. Even though I have laid them out in a particular order, the order is not as important as the message. Many times you may find that you have to put on the helmet before you can figure out the rules. Or you may have to figure out the rules before you're ready to take a plunge. Or you may find yourself using more than one strategy at a time.

No matter, the point is, you have to be committed to doing whatever it takes to move you from here to there. The real obstacles to success are always internal. Unfortunately, there's no magic bullet. You have to do the work.

So unless you haven't figured it out by now, I'm not talking about, "I'll try." I'm talking about, "I will." Whether you want to start a business, change your career, find a soul mate— whatever it is for you, you have to be "all in." Are you in?

The Take-Away

The first step to making a positive change in your life is committing to honor your decision. Often we will honor commitments made to others better than we honor commitments made to ourselves. You need to commit to yourself that you will make whatever change you want to make and then honor it. Sometimes, it's harder to make the decision to change than it is to actually follow through with the plan. Once you honor your own commitment, it will make the follow through a little easier.

CHAPTER 5
Don't Marry Your Destiny

The pen that writes your life story must be held in your own hand.

—Irene C. Kassorla

At twenty years old I married my on-again, off-again teenage boyfriend. It seemed like a good idea at the time. Being *Mrs. Somebody* was going to give me credibility. If all else failed—and it already looked like it had—I was going to make a career out of being a wife and mother. As it turned out, two things failed: my self-esteem and my marriage.

We didn't see eye to eye on anything. I knew at the six-month mark that it wasn't going to work, but it lasted a year and a half. Years later, my girlfriend Mari Catherine summed it up the best: "At twenty years old you shouldn't be allowed to pick out a winter coat, let alone a husband. You just don't know what you're doing." She was right.

My College Experience

In 1969, at age seventeen, I had borrowed $3,000 from the Richmond Hill Savings Bank in Queens, NY, so I could go to college. Unbelievably, that's what tuition and room and board cost in the 1960s. I had just graduated from The Mary Louis

Academy in Jamaica Estates, New York. It was an all-girls catholic academy that trained young women to go to college.

All of those girls had big dreams and were not afraid to share them. I had no skills, no dreams and no direction. My low "C" average didn't give me a lot of options but—at the end of a college prep high school—if you didn't go to college you had just wasted four years of your life and your parents' money.

There was no federal aid package back then. If you needed money to go to college, you took it out of your own bank account or borrowed it from a bank. So, at seventeen years old, I signed the bank note and off I went.

My grades weren't good enough to get into a big name college or even City College in New York. But I did find a small liberal arts college in Tennessee that was willing to take my $3,000 and my grades.

To be clear, I didn't head off to Tennessee because I had any great love of the South. I was a New Yorker—I didn't know anything about the south. Tusculum College in Greeneville, Tennessee, was the only place I got accepted. It suddenly became more appealing.

I had a great year. I met some wonderful people and keep in touch with a handful to this day. I had a lot riding on that year but it ended the way it began—with me still waiting for something to happen.

When I left for college I had two goals: first, to get out of my crowded house and, second, to find some direction. Instead, I found thirty pounds and a $3,000 debt. Remember, I had borrowed that money and I had to pay it back. So my first big decision was whether to go back for another year or not.

I made some great friends but I still had no direction. Now at the end of that year, I was actually in worse shape than I was when I started. I still had no direction but now I owed $3,000. At eighteen years old, that sounded like the national debt.

College wasn't a safety net for me. It wasn't a place where I could take different courses and figure out what piqued my interest. It became apparent quickly I had no idea what to do with myself, and no money to spend on four years of education trying to figure it out.

I had a decision to make. *Do I invest $6,000 and hope for the best? Could 1970 be the year I figure it all out?* I didn't believe I could do it, so I didn't go back. Would it surprise you to find out that there would be many more instances over the years where I didn't believe I could do it and so I didn't try? As you look back on your life, have there been times when you didn't believe you could so you just walked away?

I was afraid to roll the dice. The thought of owing $6,000 and still having no direction was terrifying. So in 1970, at eighteen years old, I dropped out of college. My first big life decision made me feel like a failure and I returned to my parents' home to find a job. Looking back at my $3,000 bill and comparing it to today's college tuition, it's laughable. I wasn't laughing at eighteen.

Love Doesn't Always Conquer All

At twenty years old, my self-esteem was already destroyed. I grew up with disfigured teeth and always felt ugly as a child. Even after they were fixed, I didn't really feel pretty. A failed year of college and back in my crowded childhood home didn't do much to raise me up.

Now it was time to find a job. After four years of high school that prepared me to go to college, I wasn't trained to do anything. One typing class in my senior year provided the only marketable skill I had. And so, I became a secretary and started paying down my college debt.

To put this into context, in the 1970s, secretarial work was not highly regarded and you were referred to as, "just the secretary." Entering the workforce having failed at college, thirty pounds overweight and in a job that made me feel like a second-class citizen was demoralizing. The future was not looking bright.

At the tender age of twenty, again for the same reason— to get out of my crowded house—I married him. He was my on-again, off-again high school boyfriend. I thought it could work. He had a job and I thought he was as good a catch as any.

I needed to marry this man. He was the only way I was getting out of my house. He was my only hope for a career, for credibility and maybe even for happiness. I was going to marry my destiny. He became more important than I was and he knew it. It was a big mistake.

Have you ever been in a relationship hoping it would change your life? With someone who you knew, deep down in a quiet place within you, wasn't the best fit? Did you sacrifice yourself to make it work?

I was in a place where the relationship, and the possibilities it could bring, became more important than I was. There were red flags everywhere but I chose to ignore each and every one. I was so focused on what I didn't want that I never even gave thought to what I did want.

I didn't want to feel lost. I didn't want to live in my crowded house. I didn't want to be directionless. I didn't want to feel like a failure. I thought getting married would solve all those problems. It turns out you have to solve your own problems. No one can solve your problems but you.

By twenty-one years old, I was in my second of a series of secretarial jobs and fighting to save a failing marriage. Less than a year before, I had two hundred guests at my wedding. I walked down a long church aisle and stood in front of a priest and a packed house and said I was in it for the long haul.

When the union isn't right, the wedding becomes more important than the marriage. I focused on that wedding for a year. We paid for it ourselves by saving every penny and paying off the balance with money we received as gifts. Family members were still talking about what a great time they had at my wedding and my marriage was falling apart.

I was divorced by age twenty-two. To put this into context, in 1974 very few people got divorced. I was the first person in my very large extended family that walked away from a marriage. It wasn't commonplace and it hardly got discussed.

I remember my mother referring to my situation to inquisitive relatives by saying, "Susan is home" rather than, "Susan is divorced." I was despondent. I wasn't even twenty-three years old and I had already failed at college and marriage. *How did I wind up here?*

My Chaotic Twenties

The next ten years were filled with conflict. I set out on a quest to either find myself or find someone who would take care of me. Whichever showed up first was fine with me. The reality is that I looked harder for someone else than I did for myself.

In the 1970s women were marching in the street burning their bras. If I had joined them, my mother would have taken my bra and wrapped it around my neck. You would think that women fighting for equal rights would have empowered me, but they only made me feel more inadequate.

I knew they weren't marching for me. They were marching for educated women with promise. They were not marching for college dropouts who typed and filed and answered someone else's phone.

At that time, the world was changing. In the 1950s, women could be homemakers, even housewives. Now, in the 1970s, you were expected to *be something*. While it's true I was a secretary, a noble profession, it was never my passion. It never fulfilled me.

Even though I didn't have any goal or direction, I spent those secretarial years looking at every job in every company and asked myself the same questions. Would I want that job? Do I want to be president of that advertising agency? Do I want to be vice-president of that manufacturing company? Do I want to be a director of marketing, in charge of product development?

Each time, the answer was always "No." Now I was really lost, because not only was I not becoming something, I didn't even have a goal or a dream to work toward. I didn't even know what I would be if I had every opportunity at my disposal.

At age twenty-five, three years divorced, I realized I needed to get myself together. My plan—find another husband. After all, I was twenty-five, a quarter of a century, over the hill, too old for college. The day I turned twenty-five was one of the worst days of my life. All I could do was focus on what I didn't have. I didn't have a college diploma, didn't have a career, didn't have a husband, didn't have children, and didn't own a home. I really thought I didn't have a future.

Can you imagine thinking at twenty-five that you would be too old to do something? Feeling like you had no future? Although my parents had placed a value on education, I felt like I was the only person in the country without goals or dreams. I found myself asking on more than one occasion, "What is wrong with me?"

Finding Mr. Wrong, Again

Facing thirty, I was determined to get my life figured out. I decided I was not going to waste the next ten years as I had wasted the last. It took about a month, but I convinced myself that being married to my ex-husband hadn't been so bad.

After all, could anything be worse than where I was now—living in a studio apartment in New York City, with gates on the windows that kept out the burglars as well as the sunlight, in a secretarial job with no chance of advancement, with no college education, and staring at my thirtieth birthday alone and lonely?

We had some good times, I thought, and I could do worse. *I'll re-marry him. We'll have children.* I'll be set. I was so lost and lonely that I was willing to walk back into the fire. So, I tracked him down.

Finding my ex-husband was a quite a challenge. There were no cell phones and the Internet hadn't been invented. There was no Google or Facebook or LinkedIn. It took some serious detective work to find him.

He was living in Florida where he had moved years before. He had started his own business. He was witty and charming. He was cute. He had new friends and a new life and he didn't have a girlfriend. That was good enough for me.

Within a few months, I had totally re-arranged my life. I gave up my apartment in New York City. I quit my job, sold my furniture, packed up my belongings, and moved to Florida to start my new life. I wasn't going to turn thirty lonely and struggling. Who needed college? Who needed a career?

I had it all figured out. He was going to be my salvation. I was going to get my "Mrs." degree rather than a college degree. Women of my generation went to college to find a husband, so this seemed totally acceptable to me.

My girlfriends were appalled, but they didn't say much. Six months later, it was a disaster. He was staying out all night and I was crying. Not such a great plan after all. My hair was frizzy, my heart was broken, my dream was shattered, and I was more alone than ever. Thankfully, I never re-married him because it was time to come home.

I owe my college education to that man. If he had treated me just a little better, I would have stayed. I was so emotionally broken that a simple "I'm sorry" would have changed the course of my life. But he couldn't say it and I didn't stay.

So in 1979, I found myself in a unique position. Unique is the word I use now. Unique is not the word I used in 1979. After he drove me back to New York, I found myself with everything I owned in a U-Haul trailer in my parents' driveway and sleeping back in the bed I grew up in as a child. *How did I wind up here again?*

This was a devastating and depressing place to be and turned out to be the crossroads of my life. At twenty-nine years old, I had added yet another failure to my resume. But I learned an important lesson. You can't marry it – you gotta do it yourself.

I was willing to marry my destiny. I was willing to settle for less than I deserved and less than I could be. Because he ended the relationship, I went to college. If he was a little nicer to me, I would have stayed and I wouldn't be a doctor today. As I look back on that now, it is almost unbelievable to me.

That break-up brought the realization that no man was coming along to save me. I had to do the work. At age thirty I was willing to put on the same winter coat that didn't fit when I was twenty. Doing it a second time wouldn't make it the right decision.

Until you are clear about who you are and what you want, you can't find or be a great mate. I went back to my first husband because he was the devil I knew. I went back because I thought he would make a life for me. Because I didn't believe that I had the brains or the power to make a life for myself.

Did you ever find yourself giving up everything because you didn't believe in yourself? Because you thought someone else could make a better life for you than you could make for yourself? Because you thought that they were more qualified than you were? Maybe they had more money or a better job or more education than you?

Oops, I Did it Again

I thought I had learned that lesson but unbelievably, many years later with a different set of circumstances, I made the same mistake. I had finished medical school, internship, and residency, and was working in an emergency room in Connecticut. To the untrained eye, it looked like I had it all together. I had a highly respected career, was raising a beautiful and respectful son, and was surrounded by a circle of truly supportive family and friends. But inside, something was missing. I was lonely.

I started dating another physician that I met in my residency program and in less than a year's time, we were married. Although we only dated for a short period of time, I had trained with him for three years and felt that I knew him.

We were all so excited. David and I were both new emergency room doctors and had so much to talk about. We understood each other's work stress intimately. We both wanted children and he was initially excited to have a young son as part of the package.

Ryan was excited because he was finally going to get a father. I couldn't believe how lucky I was to have found a man who loved my son, wanted more children, and could afford to support a family.

I cut back on my hours at work and was home more for Ryan. One of our first official acts as a family was to buy a house. I remember sitting with the bank officer and going over our finances to determine the mortgage we could afford.

Because we had two physician salaries, on paper we qualified for a house that was $750,000. I absolutely refused to be house poor. My plan was to buy a house that could run on one income. Little did I know it would be mine.

After the newness wore off, David realized he made a mistake. He was considerably younger than I was and really had no interest being a father to someone else's son, or a husband to me. It was exciting to have me as a girlfriend but it became apparent that he felt trapped as a husband. He was miserable, and the more miserable he became, the harder I worked to keep it all together. My dream was going up in smoke right before my eyes.

I was now forty-five years old and I knew this was my last chance to have another baby. Ryan was nine years old and I wanted a second child desperately. Having grown up with four brothers and sisters, I couldn't imagine my son growing up alone.

There would never be time to start a new relationship and conceive another child. I wasn't even sure if I could conceive now, but this was clearly my best shot and I was going to take it. Ryan was becoming withdrawn and depressed. David was becoming withdrawn and depressed and I was doing everything I could to make everybody happy.

I was turning into the bridge builder and the fence mender. What a mess. Did you ever find yourself in between two people you loved and in a situation you knew was not destined for a happy ending?

I thought if I just worked hard enough, it would all work out. I thought I could do the work for David and for me. I was the woman who delivered a baby on Christmas break of medical school. I was the woman who raised a son by herself while juggling medical school, internship, and residency. Clearly, I could handle this.

One day, David announced he couldn't take it anymore and he was leaving. I remember being astounded. *Couldn't take what?* I thought to myself. *Couldn't take someone contorting herself to make you happy?* He moved out the next day. When I stared into a half empty closet, I sat on the floor and cried. And once again asked myself, *How did I wind up here again?*

Finding Myself in Therapy

The pain of that loss was so great it threw me into therapy. Once a week for a year I sat with my therapist and poured my heart out. I cried and cried long after I didn't think I had tears left to shed.

More than anything else, I mourned for what was supposed to be. I was supposed to have a husband, I was supposed to have someone to share the burdens, my son was supposed to have a father, I was supposed to have another child, I was supposed to live happily ever after.

The pain was so deep. Every week as I sat and cried my eyes out, my therapist offered me anti-depressant medication. And every week, I refused. I felt like someone had taken my clothes off, scrubbed my body with a wire brush and left me out in the wind. Every part of me hurt.

"I won't take any medication to mask this pain," I said. "I'm going to feel every bit of it for however long it takes because I'm never coming back here again." Now I realize that's not the best course of action for everyone, but that was what I needed to do for me to make it through. A year later, I walked out of her office with a new understanding of myself and with new optimism for life.

I married twice to make the life I wanted, hoping that someone would add something to my incomplete life. I knew in my heart both times that something was wrong. I ignored warning signs to get to my end point. The first time my end point was to make a career out of marriage. The second time it was to have another child and fill the void of loneliness.

Many years later, I married my now husband for all the right reasons. I didn't need anything from him and he didn't need anything from me. We both brought love, respect, and honor, to the other. We are better together than we would ever be apart.

Months before I met him I remember telling a girlfriend exactly how I felt. "I have a great life. I have a wonderful son, fabulous girlfriends, and a supportive family. I own my own home and have a solid, respectable career. If this is as good as it ever gets, I'm happy." I had finally stopped looking for someone else to add something to my life.

You can have a happy marriage and a career, or not, but it can't be your destiny because then someone else controls your destiny. No one can save you from yourself. Stop looking for someone to add something to your life. "You complete me" is a Hollywood fantasy. You're already complete. Don't give your power away. Don't give yourself away.

A Message from Iyanla Vanzant

Iyanla Vanzant is an inspirational speaker, spiritual teacher, and an author whose work has appeared on *The New York Times* best-seller list. I first found her on *The Oprah Winfrey Show* in the 1990s where, as a no-nonsense relationship expert, she dished out tough love and made people see their part in the mess they created. In case you haven't figured it out by now, I resonate with tough love. She now has her own television show on the *Oprah Winfrey Network* and during a recent show said this: "We need to understand, as women, we have that brokenness and we go looking to fill it. If you are broken, you're going to fill it with brokenness. If you are empty, you're going to fill it with emptiness, if you are wounded, you're going to fill it with woundedness. We all have to get healed. You have to do your work."

Blaze your own trail, whatever that is and where ever it takes you. Had I stopped short, I wouldn't have gotten to where I was meant to go. That huge disappointment at age twenty-nine propelled me forward, and, for the first time, forced me to become an active participant in my own life. That devastation set me on the road to becoming a doctor. It was the second disappointment that taught me who I really am and what I'm really made of. What are you made of?

The Take-Away

You are the only one who can make a life for you and that doesn't mean you need to have a college degree and a career. If you decide that being a wife and mother fulfills you—go for it. But you need to make that decision because you want it in your heart and not because there are no other options available. Until you know yourself and what you have to offer, you cannot find or be a great mate.

CHAPTER 6
Put On a Helmet

*You can't sit around and wait for the storm
to be over.*
You've got to learn how to dance in the rain.
— Anonymous

Remember the Nike ad campaign *Just Do It.?* A sneaker, a logo, and three words but you got the message loud and clear. Nike didn't say, "I know it's hard, but why don't you give it a try." They didn't say, "I know you're not really coordinated or athletically inclined but if you decide to do it, you might want to try our shoes." They said, *Just Do It.*

Then there is the lottery—*You gotta be in it to win it.* Nobody said, "Hey, if you're passing by a convenience store and you have a few extra dollars, why don't you buy a ticket and see what happens?"

I say: *Put on a Helmet and Get in the Game* because no one ever scored the winning touchdown sitting on the bench. I don't know much about football—my husband informed me that football players stand on the sideline and baseball players sit on the bench. But, sit, stand, whatever—my point is you have to play to win.

Decision Time

So at twenty-nine years old, I unpacked the contents of my life from the U-Haul trailer and moved back into my childhood bedroom with my new roommates, mom and dad. I had $1,000, a second-hand car, and a guaranteed place to live. It wasn't crowded anymore because everyone else had grown up and moved out.

And now it was time to make some decisions. After the devastation and depression wore off, for the first time in my life I felt like I had some breathing room and could take my time planning a career. I had heard someone say, "If you do what you love, you'll never work a day in your life." This sounded like good advice, but what do I love? This was the million-dollar question that always stopped me from finding a profession. I never really got excited about anything.

But then it came to me. Aha! I love food. It was obvious—I'll be a chef! I enjoyed cooking, mixing ingredients, coming up with new recipes and trying new combinations. I was finally passionate about something. I thought I had figured it all out.

Alas, I hadn't. I did a lot of research and found a culinary arts program at The New School in New York City. It would cost $1,000, every penny I had. Unfortunately, there was no financial aid so my choice would have wiped me out financially. Also, the school was in Manhattan and I couldn't drive into the city so I would be back and forth on the subway.

As the obstacles mounted my passion was dimming. When small obstacles can throw you completely off course, you know you're on the wrong road. So I did some serious thinking. It didn't take me long to realize what I really liked about food was eating it and having someone serve it to me. I really wasn't interested in cooking for strangers. This is a serious drawback for someone who is contemplating a career as a chef.

But I was on to something so I decided I would take my love of food, go back to college, and get a degree in nutrition. The answer was clear. I was going to stop looking for a man to marry me. I was going to have a career and make a life for myself, and I would make a career out of food, something I loved. I was going to stop layering failures on myself.

Up until that point I really was not in the game. I was sitting in the stands and sometimes standing on the sidelines hoping I was going to win the game, but doing nothing to participate. For the first time in my life, I started participating.

I went to college. I was twenty-nine years old and everyone else was nineteen. People always asked if it was hard for me to go back to college. It wasn't. This was a whole new experience and I loved it. I showed up to every class and spent hours studying. I had a goal, I had a plan, I had direction. This was the feeling I had been waiting for since I was eighteen. It couldn't get better than that.

Actually, it got worse. Within three months, I realized I didn't want to be a nutritionist. The classes were not stimulating to me, except for chemistry, which I found out I really enjoyed. Where did that come from? I was the "C" student on the lowest track in high school.

I knew if I did pursue a degree in nutrition, I would become a registered dietician working in a hospital. *Do what you love and you'll never work a day in your life* played in my head. If I became a dietician, I would not be doing what I loved and every day would be work.

Dieticians do important work, but it was not the career for me. Now I really felt lost. I thought, what now? How could this be? I'm in college and there still isn't a place for me. What am I going to do? Did you ever find yourself questioning your place in the world? Especially after you put time, effort, and brainpower, into getting yourself to that place? How could this not be the right place after I worked so hard to get here? That's what happened to me.

It was decision time again. I didn't know what the answer was, but I knew it wasn't nutrition. About this time, my sister, who is nine years younger than I am, had moved to Los Angeles and was pursuing her dream of becoming a doctor. We were both taking the same chemistry course, but her biology courses sounded much more interesting than my nutrition courses.

Planting Seeds

"Why don't you move to Los Angeles and we can go to school together?" she suggested. I remember thinking, *who just moves to Los Angeles? Just move…that was crazy.* "Why don't you become a doctor, too?" she added. *Become a doctor? I'm thirty years old. You don't just decide to become a doctor at thirty.*

You grow up with a doctor kit and your parents take those cute childhood pictures of you with your doll wrapped in ace bandages. You put bandages on the dog. You don't just declare at thirty years old, "I'm going to be a doctor." That was crazy talk.

What would people say? People would think I was
crazy. I don't know anything about California. I don't know
anything about being a doctor. But the seed was planted. For
the first time in my life, the seed of passion was planted. But
what was I going to do with it?

It didn't take long for the fantasy of living in Los Angeles
and being a physician to creep into my mind. I imagined
myself as a television character, perfectly coifed in a starched
white lab coat, enjoying lunch in the outdoor hospital
cafeteria having just delivered a beautiful pink baby to
beaming parents. I think music might have been playing.

I knew if I completed my nutrition degree that I would
eventually work in a hospital setting. Try as I may, I couldn't
conjure up the same nutritionist fantasy. (Just for the record,
the fantasy faded one month into my internship year when I
found myself, out of exhaustion and frustration, crying in the
hospital bathroom on what became a regular basis.)

So I set my sights higher and decided I was going to be a
doctor. And that's how I made the decision. I'd love to know
what went through everyone's mind when, at the age of thirty,
I announced after ten years of being a secretary and three
months of being a college student that I was going to become
a doctor.

But it didn't matter because as quickly as I talked myself
into it was as quickly as I was talking myself out of it. The
chatter and the negative talk started playing in my head.

What am I thinking? People start medical school when
they're twenty-two, not thirty. I don't even have a college
degree. I still have three years left in college. That meant I
wouldn't start medical school until I was thirty-three.

*What if I can't do the work? What if I'm not smart
enough? Just because I like chemistry what does that mean?
I like science, but that doesn't mean I can be a doctor. People
have life-long dreams of becoming a doctor, they don't decide
overnight. Who decides overnight?*

On the one hand, the new go-getter me knew if I was
working in a hospital and didn't know everything there was
to know, I would feel inadequate. I now understood the
childhood lesson everyone was trying to teach me about
reaching my potential.

Even though I had doubts about my ability to understand
medicine, I was willing to take a chance on my brainpower.
On the other hand, I would be thirty-three years old. I kept
coming back to thirty-three years old. It was a stumbling
block that I couldn't get around.

Who gave you the best advice you ever got? For me it
was my mother. She listened to this negative chatter patiently
for weeks and then put it in perspective in three sentences:
"Susan, one day you'll be fifty. You'll either be a doctor or you
won't, but you'll still be fifty. That's your choice."

In that instant all the clutter fell away and I knew I had to
go for it. I was scared to death for many reasons but I knew
I had to do it. You know the truth when you hear it. I started
school in Los Angeles the following semester. I put on my
helmet and I got in the game.

Look Ahead

You land where you look. Gymnasts have known that for
a long time. While training to dismount from the uneven

bars, gymnasts are trained to fix their gaze on a spot on the landing mat.

During a flip, they focus on a spot on the wall for as long as possible and are trained to find the spot immediately after the rotation is completed. Once they find their focal point, they know it's time to land.

I'm no gymnast, but I think this is a great metaphor for life—not the flipping part, the looking part. I didn't start looking ahead until I was thirty years old. That was really the first time in my life I had a goal. Before that I was looking down and I saw the road but I didn't see the path until I started looking ahead.

Where are you looking? The challenge is to look at where you want to be. Often, we say we want something but when you look at our actions it doesn't look like we want it at all. I remember when I was in my twenties, I said that I wanted a soul mate, a husband, but I then jokingly would add that the qualifications were he had to have a pulse and a job. Well, guess what I found?

I once saw a Dr. Phil show that illustrated this point. I don't remember all the particulars but he was interviewing a young woman who was lamenting the fact that she didn't have a boyfriend. He was asking many questions and it appeared that she had done very little to meet anyone new in a long time.

In typical Dr. Phil fashion he asked, "How do you plan on doing that, when he rolls over the hood of your car? You have to leave your house if you want to meet someone."

Nancy Juetten's Story

Sometimes you need to switch games to be successful. In 2001, Nancy Juetten owned a full service public relations firm. She was on top of her game, working with a lot of big name clients like Roger Staubach and Fran's Chocolates, chocolatier to the President of the United States. She was generating publicity items for her clients like the following:

> **Fine Dining Chef is a Sweet Addition to Fran's Chocolates** (*The Seattle Times*). "The queen of flavor and the king of savor, Fran Bigelow and Scott Carsberg, are preparing inventive treats for Valentine's and beyond together at the Fran's Chocolate factory on Capitol Hill, a family-run business also led by Fran's daughter Andrina Bigelow and son Dylan Bigelow. Carsberg, one of Seattle's most respected and formidable fine-dining chefs, joined on to help oversee the kitchen and develop new products at Fran's, one of the pioneers of fine chocolates in the U.S. (The salt caramels preferred at The White House? They're hers.)"

> **Reasons Seattle Wins At Life** (*The Huffington Post*). "Obama likes his chocolate Seattle-fied. Reportedly, our nation's commander-in-chief feeds his visitors the milk chocolate and smoked salt caramels from Fran's Chocolates. Michelle prefers the gray salt ones."

Nancy was doing everything she could to handle all of her client's publicity. "I felt like the Wizard of Oz behind the curtain," she said, "trying to make big noise for them in the media but nobody knew my name."

Nancy ran a Google search of her name one day and all she found was that she ran 10K races really slowly. This is not what she wanted her legacy to be. She was working really hard and making other people famous and decided she wanted people to know her name too.

"I didn't want to be known as a slow runner," she said. In 2006, she tried dabbling in information products to get her name known but was still having more success making other people famous.

Everything changed in 2008 when the economy tanked. Clients were calling one after the other asking to be let out of their contracts. They were hanging on for their own financial life and couldn't afford to pay her.

She had two house payments and was watching her business disintegrate right before her eyes. She was dismayed and upset because it was all out of her control. "I checked into Pity Party Hotel and had myself a good ugly cry," she said. When she felt like she didn't have any more tears left to cry, a friend said something that changed her life.

"Didn't you always want to write a book?" she asked. "Oh sure, I've thought about it," Nancy replied. "Well, I dare you," the friend said. "I dare you to write a book about how to write a better bio and I dare you to do it in three weeks so it is ready for the workshop you are scheduled to run."

Nancy thought about what her friend said. *What do I have to lose.* "Ok, I accept," she answered. She wrote a forty-seven-page book and had the cover made at Kinko's. Across the title was the word "draft."

Three weeks later Nancy delivered her scheduled workshop on public relations. At the end she asked the audience if anyone was struggling with their bio. Every hand went up. She agreed to gift every audience member a copy if they would promise to give her feedback within the week so she could make the book better.

Audience members were thrilled, reporting that it was the best part of the workshop and exactly what they needed. Every person honored their commitment and gave her feedback and also suggested she sell it.

She priced the e-book at twenty-seven dollars, sent out a notice to her newsletter list of eleven hundred people and then took the dog for a walk. When she returned she said the orders on her computer looked like a slot machine at Las Vegas.

That experience put her on a new trajectory. Someone dared her, she accepted the challenge, she pulled it together, she got it done. It started opening doors for her and money started coming in. The book she put together in three weeks with a cover from Kinko's encouraged her to think that maybe she was on to something.

Today, she has turned a twenty-seven-dollar e-book into a $197 experience and for those who would like a different level of mentoring also offers group or private coaching programs.

She has catapulted herself to the number one ranking in Google for Business Bio Expert and shares the stage with luminaries to reach larger and larger audiences. No one thinks she's a slow runner anymore. She put on a helmet and started playing for her own team.

Where are You in the Line-Up?

There are three different kinds of people in the world, and during my lifetime I have been all of them. How about you?

There are people who sit on the sidelines and wait for life to happen. They're close to the field and they think about jumping in, but never really do it. They go to work, they go home, and wait for the next day to arrive.

These people don't really get involved. They show up and do what people ask them to do and that's about it. Nothing is really good and nothing is really bad. It is just life. Often, this group thinks more successful people are just lucky. This is how I spent my eleven years as a secretary.

Sometimes these people take themselves out of the game entirely, usually out of fear of failure. They can move from the sideline to sitting on the bleachers. Afraid that they don't know the right answers, they would rather not put themselves out on the field. Feelings of uncertainty and self-doubt rule, and sometimes ruin their lives.

Some of us are in the game, but, for many different reasons, play only half-heartedly. Maybe we don't really know what's expected of us. We would like to be all in but hold ourselves back a little bit. Sometimes out of fear, and sometimes out of confusion—of not knowing exactly what steps to take—we hesitate.

I was at this point many times where I was in, but not all in. I was not playing a starring role in my own life. When I first opened my business, I didn't know what I was doing and I didn't know what to do. I held back hoping that the business was going to take off on its own. It didn't. I had to jump in for the business to start moving.

And then there are the people who are all in—the ones who put on their helmets and get in the game. These are the people who are playing to win. These are the people who are willing to do whatever it takes to accomplish the mission. These are the people that say *I will* and not *I'll try*.

I mentioned before, I started writing this book five years ago. I had multiple starts and stops. I would write a chapter and think, *not bad*. The next day I would read it and say, *no way*. I felt like I was trying to write the book for years. I never told anybody because I knew I wasn't all in.

One day, I said, *enough already*. My husband, who has written two books, shared his secret formula for writing: (a) sit down, (b) write. I followed the secret formula and at the same time put a presentation together and put myself on the speaking circuit. And I started announcing to everyone that I was writing. *And now you're reading.*

Where are you? Maybe you're in the bleachers watching everyone else play. Or maybe you're on the sidelines, a little closer to the field but not ready to step out. Maybe you're already on the field but playing without purpose, just hoping for the participation trophy. Or maybe you're suited up and playing to win.

It takes courage to step out onto the field. Do you need a helmet?

The Take-Away

If you want to be successful, you have to play to win. You can sit in the stands and watch, you can stand along the sidelines and give your opinion, you can wander aimlessly on the field hoping for the participation trophy or you can put on a helmet and get in the game. Are you willing to do whatever it takes to accomplish your goal? Are you ready to play to win?

CHAPTER 7
Embrace Embarrassment

*The rate at which a person can
mature is directly proportional to the
embarrassment he can tolerate.*

— Douglas Engelbart

Some days are pretty and some days are messy. And
sometimes you're ready and sometimes you're not, but
unless you're hiding under a blanket fort in your living room,
you have to show up to all of them. That means sometimes
you look perfect and sometimes you feel perfect and other
times you just feel inadequate, stupid, and embarrassed.

Starting Medical School and Feeling Vulnerable

Medical schools across the country are loaded with students
who all came from the top of their undergraduate class.
Mount Sinai was no different. The day I started, I found
myself sitting in a classroom with 114 other students who,
just like me, had excellent records and were all used to being
at the top of their class.

Now, 115 people cannot all be at the top. Someone has to be at the bottom. I realized very early on it was probably going to be me. I believed that for two reasons. The reality of my situation was I was about to deliver a baby and my life was going to change drastically.

No matter how smart and organized you are, there are still only twenty-four hours in every day. But more importantly, I walked into that situation with an inferior mindset. The day I started, I already felt like a fraud.

It had taken me two years to get into medical school. The year before, I had been rejected from every medical school in the country. I had piles of rejection letters. I hid them away in humiliation before I threw them away en-masse. The first rejection letters didn't really bother me because I knew it was all part of the process, but when it became apparent no one wanted me humiliation set in.

I had to tell everyone I didn't make the cut. Those rejections shook me to my core. It made me question the grades I got for the past three years. I graduated with a bachelor of science in biology, at the top of my class, and it wasn't enough. I had two Bs on my transcript. Besides those two, I earned all As, and still it wasn't enough.

What did my good grades really mean? Was I smart? Was I really able to earn those As? Did I deserve them? Or was I fooling myself? I worked my butt off to be at the top of my class. Maybe I was just a hard worker. Maybe I wasn't really smart.

The second time around, after going through the application process all over again, Mount Sinai was the only school that showed any interest in me. But it wasn't an outright acceptance. I was put on the waiting list meaning an applicant who was their first choice had to decline acceptance in order for them to start picking people off the waiting list.

So I walked into the classroom on that first day already feeling like I was not on an equal playing field. I wasn't anybody's first choice. I know I wasn't the only person accepted from the waiting list, but nobody talked about it. I felt like the only one. Even though I saw my name on my identification badge and sat at my assigned desk, I kept waiting for someone in administration to realize they made a mistake.

Everyone would have you believe that they were smarter than you and that they had it all together. Now I found myself sitting in the classroom as a brand new exhausted mother and a first-year medical student. Life was whizzing by me faster than I could imagine.

I knew if I didn't understand the concept in the classroom, I would fall behind quickly. I didn't have the luxury to go home in the evening and spend time figuring concepts out. Many of my colleagues were going home to the dorm and forming small study groups. I was going home to a crying infant, so I had to understand the concept in the classroom. There was no time or energy to pore over books in the evening for me.

No one wanted to admit in front of 114 other people that they didn't understand a concept, but that's exactly what I had to do on a daily basis. I used to sit in the back of the room and I would watch everyone sit in lecture hall nodding their heads looking like *yeah, I got it, let's move on.* I would be sitting there thinking *what the heck are you talking about?*

So I was always the one who would raise my hand and say, "Excuse me, I don't understand that. Could you go over it again?" From my vantage point in the back of the room I could tell that I was exasperating some people and it made me feel stupid, but I had to do it.

The difference was that they were all able to go home after school and, in the privacy of their own group, with people that they trusted, work on it together. I had to be vulnerable and bare my soul in front of 114 strangers to say I didn't understand. In the end, becoming a doctor was more important than feeling stupid, inadequate, or embarrassed.

Trying on My New Title

When I first graduated from medical school, I was uncomfortable referring to myself as Dr. O'Malley. I felt like an imposter. I didn't feel like I knew as much as my medical school colleagues because I didn't have the time to study as long as they did. After all, I was raising a child.

I passed, and I graduated, but I still felt inadequate. After graduation, it took me months to refer to myself as Dr. O'Malley. One of the first times I tried on the title lead to a humiliating experience that set me back even further.

I was at the reception desk of the hair salon checking out after my services. The perfectly coiffed twenty-year-old receptionist referred to me as Miss O'Malley. "Well, it's not Miss," I answered demurely. "Oh, I'm sorry Mrs. O'Malley," she said, and proceeded to tally my bill. "Well, it's not exactly Mrs. either," I said. Then I added, with a smile on my face and in my voice, "It's Doctor O'Malley."

I was feeling proud of my accomplishment and was finally ready to share. She took a few seconds, looked me in the eye and replied with an edge in her voice, "Well, if you're not married, you're still a Miss." I was dumbfounded. I couldn't even speak and to make matters worse the desk was crowded with other women. I left humiliated.

That five-second interaction confirmed all my feelings of inadequacy as well as making me feel like I was bragging and needed to be brought back down. It was many more months before I referred to myself as Dr. O'Malley again.

Inadequacy is an Equal Opportunity Player

Time may heal all wounds but it has little effect on feelings of inadequacy. You need a different remedy. I don't know what the remedy is and even if really there is one. After all, if there were a magic bullet, therapists would be out of business.

For me, I needed to be pushed aside many times and for many years until I finally got angry enough to recognize my own value and worth. It was only after I identified what I brought to the table that I stopped feeling uncomfortable in my profession and even in my own skin. Similar to the strategy I used to quit smoking, I again used anger as a catalyst for positive change. It took me years.

Becoming an Entrepreneur

The day I opened my medical spa, I had four years of undergraduate work, four years of medical school, four years of internship and emergency room residency, one year on staff in an interim hospital, and five years as a doctor in the emergency room under my belt.

I knew skin and head and neck anatomy inside and out. I had worked with a needle in my hand every day for the past ten years and had successfully sutured many complex facial lacerations. Still, it wasn't enough.

There were commercials on television warning consumers to only trust their face to a dermatologist or a plastic surgeon. Women would call and ask, "Is she a dermatologist or a plastic surgeon?" Before I even finished my sentence, they would hang up. Many of them without even saying thank you or good-bye.

It was demoralizing and it went on for years. I had finally reached a point where I felt my own worth and value as a physician, yet here I was again feeling like the new grad at the hair salon reception desk all over again.

It's hard enough to get a business off the ground, but when your medical colleagues are trying to discredit you, it's a double whammy. When it became apparent that I was not going to build a business from an ad in the newspaper, I started joining networking groups and giving presentations.

I would get a knot in my stomach before I set out to a networking meeting. I didn't know anyone and I just wanted to hug the wall. Sticking my hand out to a stranger in a crowded room and saying, "Hi, I'm Dr. O'Malley" was not in my comfort zone, for a variety of reasons.

Finding My Voice

I have a New York accent. I never thought much of it but it became a source of embarrassment when other people started pointing it out to me. In conversation, people would actually repeat something I said with an exaggerated New York accent, and then add, "You sound just like Rhoda!" For those of you too young to remember, Rhoda was a fictional character from New York on *The Mary Tyler Moore Show* played by Valerie Harper.

It went on for years until it progressed to, "You remind me of the Nanny! Say that again." The Nanny was a fictional character played by Fran Drescher in a television show of the same name. Everyone would laugh and I would smile all the time thinking to myself, *what the hell is wrong with this person?*

I once had a colleague at work come up to me on a Monday morning to let me know that she had been to a wedding on Long Island over the weekend and those people sounded much worse than I did.

It took me a long time to have the courage to stand up in front of a group and give a presentation. There was the fear of public speaking, the fear of not having an adequate message, and most of all, the fear that my New York accent made me sound unprofessional. Years of being chided created self-doubt that almost derailed my speaking career.

The first time I gave a presentation, my mouth was so dry I went through two bottles of water. I could hardly hear what I was saying because my own heart was beating so loudly in my ears.

It took many years to realize I have something to say and if you don't like the way I say it, you don't have to listen— New York accent or no New York accent. Now when people comment on my accent, I smile and say, "It's part of my charm."

Being comfortable reaching out to strangers and standing up speaking in front of a crowd are not like riding a bicycle. You need to do it over and over again to stop feeling uncomfortable. So if either one of these strikes fear in you—there's no other way than showing up and working through those feelings.

Laughter is the Best Medicine

Sometimes you find yourself in an embarrassing situation and the only remedy is to laugh. I remember just such a situation when I was in my early twenties.

I was driving my first car, a four-door, lime-green something-or-other. Even in the 1970s there weren't many lime green cars. I had done some grocery shopping and had two brown bags loaded with supplies. I walked to my car, which was parked on the busy street a few doors down from the grocery store.

I was juggling my pocket book, two bags of groceries, and trying to get my car key into the door in the rain. In the seventies you had two car keys, one for the ignition and the other for the trunk. So I was standing alongside my car trying to get either key into the lock and getting frustrated.

A man approached me and asked, "Lady, what are you doing?" I looked at him and said with an air of indignation, "I'm trying to get into my car." "No," he said, "You're trying to get into my car. Your car is over there." Unbelievably, my exact car was parked right behind his. Two lime green cars—what were the chances? All I could do was laugh.

Kathy's Story

Some situations can be classified as downright humiliating. Kathy's story is a prime example. She had joined the health care industry in an administrative capacity after college graduation. As she rose to a managerial position, Kathy found herself in male-dominated meetings. In the early 1980s, Kathy was the only woman in charge of an assisted living facility in her community.

She held a position on the board of examiners and was part of the team that regulated the administrators of all facilities in her state. Through diligence and hard work, Kathy eventually rose to vice-chairman of the committee. In March 1982, the chairman of the board announced that he would be retiring in six months. Historically, the vice-chairman would assume the chairman position.

After years of hard work, Kathy was astounded to learn that there was tremendous push back to her ascending to the top position. The male-dominated board of directors did not want a woman at the lead and let it be known. Kathy couldn't believe this was happening and was prepared to do battle. It never came to a battle and in September, Kathy assumed the role as chairman of the board.

Much had happened in that six-month period and Kathy gave birth to her first child just before her new position started. The day of her first meeting, she was running around the house, getting everything together before she left. Like all first-time mothers, Kathy was consumed with having everything perfect for her new baby girl.

Although she was very organized, this was more difficult than she had imagined. The baby wasn't on a schedule and that meant Kathy wasn't on one either. But here she was, in the car dressed in a suit, make-up on, agenda in-hand, ready to assume her rightful position as chairman.

As she walked into the male-dominated room and took her place at the head of the table, she could feel her breasts filling up with milk. "If there was ever a rock and a hard place, this was it," Kathy said, "I forgot to pump." As the meeting progressed, Kathy could feel her engorged breasts starting to leak.

By the middle of the meeting, her breasts were leaking milk and soaking not only her blouse but her jacket as well. She knew she had no choice but to be embarrassed and keep on going. Three-quarters of the men sitting at the table did not want her to be there in the first place. Had she ended the meeting because of her situation, she would have no credibility.

That day, she felt the embarrassment to achieve her goal. Not only did she prove that she was qualified to be chairman, but she opened the door for women to follow.

If you're not willing to be uncomfortable and show the world your imperfect work or your imperfect self, you run the risk of getting stuck. Some of us wait for the stars to line up perfectly before we're willing to announce ourselves. The truth is, it will never be the right time, there will never be enough money, and you will never have enough education to get it perfect.

If you're consumed with getting everything right, you run the risk that life will go on without you. You become a self-fulfilling prophecy. If the tape in your head is, *I knew my work wasn't good enough or I knew I wasn't good enough,* at some point the opportunity passes and you are left with your feelings of inadequacy and not much else. The victory went to someone else.

Janice's Story

Janice had a coaching and mentoring program that was transitioning from one-on-one to group coaching. She was reaching more and more people and was excited to not only be of service to others, but to be building a reputable business for herself.

She was often a guest on webinars and teleseminars for other professionals and had been offering her own for almost a year, even though she admitted that technology was the bane of her existence. She had planned this session for a month. It was going to be offered on two consecutive days— Monday, to her smaller group of private coaching clients, and Tuesday, to a much larger audience.

At the beginning of the call, all six private clients were chatting with each other and Janice on an open line. When it came time to start the session, Janice said, "Okay, I'm going to mute everybody and we'll get started." That was the last anyone heard of Janice's voice. The slides were visible on the webinar but there was absolutely no sound on the phone or the computer.

At the end of the hour, Janice unmuted what she thought was her audience and found out that she had muted herself as well. "I was so embarrassed," she said. "I couldn't believe I did that."

The first thing she did was apologize to everyone—
who could now hear her—and the next thing she did was
burst out laughing. And everyone who was still waiting
patiently on the call laughed with her as she explained,
"Had this happened at another time in my life I would have
immediately gone to, 'I'm so stupid, I'm not good enough
or smart enough' but thankfully this was a small group and
tomorrow when I give this presentation to a larger group, I
won't make this mistake again." She offered a gift to thank her
clients for their time and everyone hung up laughing.

We all make blunders. It's when people find out your
blunder, that you feel open to judgment, ridicule, and criticism.
My advice is to learn the lesson and have a laugh. True growth
comes from stepping outside of your comfort zone. It doesn't
matter who you are or how big or small your comfort zone is.
You can't grow in an enclosed space. We've all seen the videos
of models who fall down on the runway and get up and keep
on walking. So, be a model, keep on walking.

The Take-Away

Every day isn't perfect. Some days are just a big mess and you
wish they could just pass you by. They can't. It's not pleasant
to feel embarrassed or inadequate. Sometimes it's over small
things and sometimes it's a big deal. And sometimes we do it
to ourselves and sometimes others do it purposefully to take
us down a peg. If you're feeling embarrassed over something
small, make a joke out of it and have a good laugh. If others
are judging or criticizing you, take a step back to figure out
why. If there's a lesson for you, learn it and keep on moving.
Always bring your "A" game.

CHAPTER 8
Ask for Help

The nine most terrifying words in the English language are: I'm from the government and I'm here to help.

— Ronald Reagan

Once you decide that you're all in and you're proudly wearing your helmet, things can get overwhelming. My advice to you is to take any help that is offered, and if you need it, and no one is offering, ask. Don't stand on ceremony, don't let self-limiting beliefs cloud your goal. Just ask. People have always asked me how I got through medical school with a baby and my answer was always the same. With everyone's help.

Learning Not to Ask for Help

When I was growing up, parenting was different. You asked your children for help doing things around the house. As the oldest of five children, I got asked to do things. There were four babies behind me and there was no nanny or housekeeper. There was only my mother. She was clearly outnumbered.

If my mother asked me to do something she didn't expect me to ask her for help. If she could have stopped what she was doing and helped me, she wouldn't have had to ask me to do it in the first place. I heard many times in my young life, "Don't be helpless." As a result, I grew up with a mindset of not asking for help. You just figure it out.

It's ironic because the message I got was if I couldn't do it myself then I was not strong or independent. However, I never viewed my mother as not being strong or independent because she asked me to do things for her. I think that message carries through for a lot of us. We feel inadequate if we have to ask for help but we are more than willing to help others.

It sometimes worked against me because if I couldn't figure something out, I would just walk away rather than ask. I would convince myself that I really wasn't interested in the first place.

I became the Queen of Self-Sufficiency. I could get it done without you. Maybe it would take me a little longer, but I'd eventually figure it out. I prided myself on not relying on people. And that worked great for me until I got to medical school with a baby and I needed help, big time.

The day I started medical school I was thirty-five years old and six months pregnant, without a husband. It was an unplanned pregnancy and the father of my unborn child decided it wasn't for him. I decided everything I wanted in life came at the same time and I wasn't willing to give anything up. It became apparent early on I was in over my head and I had to ask for help. It was out of character for me. But if I was going to make it through, there was no way I was going to make it through on my own.

Who taught you not to ask for help? Was it your mother too? Maybe it was an older sister or brother who got exasperated every time you asked for something. Maybe it was your first boss who made you feel like you weren't qualified to do the work.

For some of us it was a teacher. I remember in my first year of medical school, I had approached an instructor to help me with a concept I just couldn't grasp. I was probably eight months pregnant by that time and I could feel the sense of disappointment from some faculty members who feared I would drop out—that a medical school seat had been wasted on me. I could feel he was one of them.

He wasn't very helpful in that encounter, in fact he was downright rude and the encounter left me feeling stupid because I couldn't grasp the concept on my own and fearful that he thought I was stupid too. I never approached another instructor for help again. I did, however, find allies.

Learning to Ask for Help

For the first time in my life, I relied heavily on anyone who crossed my path. I took help from my mother, my father, my sisters, my brothers, girlfriends, and medical school colleagues. I would have taken help from strangers on the street if they offered.

The first two years were a blur. I went through eight babysitters, a two-month stint in day care, and countless times when my parents came at the last minute to pick up my son because another babysitter quit without notice.

The call would usually come at eight o'clock on a Sunday evening from the friend or cousin of the babysitter informing me there was a family emergency and she would not be at my door the following morning. I would have to call my parents who would get in the car and drive an hour from Long Island to New York City and take my son home with them until I could line up another babysitter.

It always seemed to happen one week before final exams. That meant I couldn't take time to interview a new candidate until my studying and finals were over. Sometimes, finding the right candidate dragged on for months. It was stressful and humiliating. Not only did it bring up feelings within me that I wasn't coping well, but also made me feel like a burden to my parents.

Everyone in medical school was offering to babysit and I handed my baby off to anyone who volunteered. There were three young guys who would offer to come over and watch Ryan. He was three months old at the time. I was so exhausted that I agreed.

I left my new baby in the care of three twenty-four-year-olds on more than one occasion. I didn't have a cell phone—no one did. It was 1987. There were no cell phones, no text messages. All I knew was I needed help and they were offering.

When you ask for help you can sometimes step away from a stressful situation and re-charge yourself. That's how it worked for me. Medical school and motherhood were two twenty-four-hour jobs that I had to combine into one and it was exhausting. The school didn't care that I had a baby and that baby didn't care that I was a medical student. I would have never made it through without the help of my parents and classmates.

Even though my classmates didn't think of themselves as helping me, they did. They volunteered to babysit because it was something fun for them to do. I don't think they realized what they were doing for me.

Sometimes we don't ask for help because it makes us feel stupid or we are afraid the person will say no. The encounter that I had with the medical school instructor illustrates those points. I wasn't able to get past those feelings at the time, but it was truly just a waste of my emotions.

Not only did I ask for help through medical school but also well into my emergency room career. I believe that asking for help made me a better doctor. The crime isn't not knowing all the answers, the crime is *not knowing where and when* to look them up.

When I first started my career, I found myself more than once on an overnight shift as the only doctor with two nurses. When I needed more brainpower, I called the pharmacist. He was a very smart man and knew how to treat many diseases better than I did at the beginning of my career.

I asked for help many times over the years in the emergency room. There were many evenings when I would call the doctor on call and ask if they would give me their thoughts about a particular patient I was treating. I would always start the phone conversation the same way: "This is not your patient and you do not have to take the time to talk to me but something has me stumped and since two heads are better than one I was hoping I could discuss this case with you." My colleagues would put down their dinner forks to be of service. And in the end, everybody benefited.

There have also been times when I was reluctant to ask for help. One incident occurred within a few months of my working as a brand new emergency room doctor. It was Thanksgiving Day and I assumed everyone would be at home with family and it would be a quiet shift. I was wrong. It was bedlam.

People kept coming and coming and they were sicker and sicker as the shift progressed. The nurse in charge suggested that I call in another doctor to relieve the burden. I refused for a few reasons. First I was brand new to the hospital and I didn't want the chairman of my department to think that I couldn't handle the workload. Also, I kept thinking that I could handle it.

When the nurse in charge made the decision herself to call the chairman of the department, I was caring for close to thirty people by myself. She made the decision to ask for help for me because she deemed that the emergency room was not safe at that point. She was right. I was relieved when she made that call.

Asking for Help with My New Business

When I left to start my own business, I once again found myself needing a lot of help. No one in my family had ever owned a business. I didn't even have a lemonade stand as a child.

People I knew went to work and came home and I was one of them my entire life. I had no idea what I was doing and no idea how to run a business or the true costs involved. My husband, who was my boyfriend at the time had his own consulting business and was a big help to me both emotionally and financially.

When I made the decision to leave mainstream medicine and start my medical spa, I had allocated every penny. I made lists of what it cost me to run my home and what it would cost to run the business, and decided that I had enough money to keep it all going for six months.

I was very naïve because in all of my calculations I never factored in advertising costs and I truly believed that in six months the business would be up and running and sustaining itself. Don't ask me why.

I didn't allocate very well because within three months, were it not for the financial support of my husband and my mother, I would have been forced to close the doors. Since I started my medical career twelve years behind the traditional student, I never had time to build a nest egg or a retirement fund. I didn't have money to see me through the rough patch.

It was demoralizing having to ask. I was fifty years old and needed financial help. I'm so glad that I did but more than that, I'm so grateful I have people in my support system who are able to help me out.

Reaching Out Helped Me Grow My Business

The truth is, you don't make it on your own and you don't make it without help. In business, I heard many times to delegate tasks that take time away from what you do best. I thought that was enough, but it's not.

If you really want your business to succeed, you really need help. More help than just delegating responsibilities that you don't want to do. For years I thought that meant finding someone to answer the phone and make appointments, finding a good accountant, and so on. I can tell you that it not enough.

You need a soul mate if you really want to take your business to the next level. You need someone who loves your business as much as you do, someone who has as much of an interest in your industry as you do, and someone who regards your business as his or her own.

You need someone with whom you can collaborate on new ideas and someone who will help you without being asked. That's how you're really going to succeed. Steve Jobs had Steve Wozniak, Bill Gates had Paul Allen and I have Diane Zorich. She has made all the difference. If you can find someone who loves you and who loves what you do, it will really pay off.

It's not just finding someone who can do the things that you don't want to do, it's finding someone to do the things that you can't do that will bring your business to greater heights. Diane brought a level of business savvy that enabled me to reach heights I never dreamed possible.

Oftentimes when we start a new venture we think we should be able to do it all. When I first started, I prided myself on not paying someone to do what I could do myself. This is a hard trap not to fall in to when you are just starting and you don't have the money to pay someone else. Believe me, I know firsthand.

I knew how to add and subtract—why did I need an accountant? I knew how to dust and mop—why did I need a cleaning lady? I knew how to make appointments—why did I need a receptionist?

I also prided myself on my ability to learn new things. I learned how to market my business very early in my career, sending out newsletters and joining networking groups. I learned how to track my expenses on a spreadsheet. These are skills that are not obvious to you when you are an employee. I set out to learn everything there was to know about running a business.

At the same time, I was also on a quest to learn everything there was to know about my industry. As a result, even though I reached a point where I had a receptionist, the entire business was run by me. It was exhausting.

I had reached such a frenetic point in my journey trying to do everything that I described myself as *living in the blender*. Sometimes I was on chop and sometimes on puree, but I was always spinning. You cannot and should not be doing it all on your own. Like the blender that never shuts off, you too will eventually burn out.

Diane saved me. She took over the entire business part of my spa and enabled me to just be the doctor. In the beginning it was difficult for me to let go of that control. And believe me, it's not like I was doing a bang-up job of handling everything, but I knew what I knew and I was afraid to let go.

When Diane first came she would ask, "Why are you doing that? That's my job." Little by little, I let go of the reins. One day I realized I was no longer waking up at three o'clock in the morning wondering if front desk activities had been completed. I no longer lived in the blender. Thanks to Diane, we are now working smarter not harder. Profits are up and work hours are down. We laugh a lot. She is my teammate, my confidant, and my friend in the truest sense of the word. We are a true partnership. Find your Diane.

Sometimes in the corporate world people are most reluctant to ask for help. Not only for all the emotional reasons already mentioned but also because of concerns of losing your job if you show incompetence. In a corporate environment, like medical school, you need allies. That's where you go for help—to someone you can trust. And just maybe under the two-heads-are-better-than-one theory of life, a better plan may be born.

Admitting we need help, showing vulnerability, and revealing that life has gotten out of control is hard for many of us. It doesn't matter how you got here—it matters where you're going and sometimes you need help to get there. I am living proof.

Pay it Forward

And while we're on the subject of asking for help, have a spirit of generosity. Pay it forward by helping someone else. I learned this lesson in childhood, before consignment stores and eBay.

I would watch my mother give everything she had. If she had a piece of furniture that she didn't need and you did, she gave it to you. If your children needed clothes and we had outgrown ours, she gave them to you. She never charged anybody for anything. She was just happy to help.

In business, I have followed this since the beginning and it has really paid off for me. Don't worry about getting paid for everything you do or say. Don't hold on to everything. In my business at Sonas Med Spa, I give a lot away. I write a newsletter every other week that just gives information. I don't ask you to come in and buy anything. I just write an article about a topic of importance and share.

On my website, sonasmedspa.com. I have a twenty-page e-book on aging that is free for download. I sat down and wrote it. It took me hours. It's yours. In my free consults I have been known to sit for thirty to forty-five minutes at a time answering every question. I let you know all your options—even ones I cannot help you with, and let you know who in the area can.

Before this book was published I wrote a tips booklet. *48 Tips to Turn Try into Triumph*, is available for download on trytotriumph.com. It's also free. The forty-eight ideas outlined in the booklet are designed to lay out a blueprint to get you started pursuing your own big dreams.

I can tell you that my business has really benefited from being totally honest and having a spirit of generosity. I have found when people realize the amount of information you are willing to give them without being paid, people trust you and will come to you for their needs. And they'll tell their friends.

My advice is, put your pride aside and take the help you need to get the job done. No one climbs Mount Everest alone. If they did, Sherpas would be out of business. It doesn't matter if it's emotional support, intellectual advice, or financial assistance. Ask for help and be helpful—it's a win-win.

The Take-Away

Asking for help can be an emotional experience, and a reluctance to ask can hold us back. When we ask for help, we may feel weak. We may feel like a failure. Or we may feel disorganized and incompetent. Sometimes we don't ask for help because it makes us feel stupid or we are afraid that the person will say no. We would rather not ask for help than risk feeling embarrassed. If you find that you are missing opportunities because of your reluctance to ask someone to help you, I recommend putting your pride aside. Let your goal trump your humiliation.

CHAPTER 9
Figure Out the Rules

You have to learn the rules of the game. And then you have to play better than anyone else.

— Anonymous

Every situation in life has rules. There are rules for climbing the corporate ladder, rules for dating, rules for starting a business, and for many other life challenges. When we are children, one of the first things we learn is rules. The lesson doesn't always come with the word rules, but we learn them and are expected to follow them. For young children, one of the most basic rules is using an inside voice or an outside voice, followed, hopefully, by no hitting. I remember when my son was as young as three explaining that he couldn't run and yell inside the bank, but he could run and yell as loud as he wanted when we got outside. Those were the rules of the bank.

Sometimes rules are unspoken and sometimes they are right in your face. It is important to figure out the rules so that you can give yourself a fighting chance—so you can compete on a level playing field with others who already understand the game. To be clear, I'm not talking about following the rules. Rather, about understanding the rules so you know which ones you can break and which ones you can't.

My National Board Exam Experience

In order to graduate from Mount Sinai, I was required to pass a two-part national licensing exam. Those were the rules. Part one was a two-day exam and was given after the first two years of classroom work. Part two was given before graduation. If you did not pass part one you were not eligible to continue with school until you did. You were allowed two attempts, one in the spring and the other in the fall. After two failed attempts you had to sit out of school for a year. And if you could not pass the exam on the third and final try, you were expelled. Yikes!

By the end of my second year of medical school, life was spinning out of control. Ryan was two years old and I was exhausted. Although I was passing my classes, I felt like I was struggling to keep up. I did not have the luxury of time to figure things out in the evenings like my medical school colleagues because, when I went home, I was caring for a two year old. Unbelievably, my baby wanted my undivided attention at night!

This was a brutal exam, eight hours a day, two days in a row. It's computerized now but when I took it, you spent sixteen hours hunched over a desk filling in circles with your number two pencil. Standardized exams and I never got along. Some people breeze through them. But for me, no matter what the exam—college entrance, medical school admission, just to name a few—after months of preparation, I was always left staring at five choices and surprised that the answer was actually there on the paper. Sometimes even more humiliating was that the answer could be all of the above or none of the above. My score was always the same—middle of the pack.

Each exam solidified for me that I was not a good test taker and each brought more and more dread. That day, I sat down for this exam with double the terror. These stakes were really high. I could be stopped here. All these years, all this time, all this effort, and I could be stopped here. The sixteen hours were a blur and I walked out thinking that I either just got a perfect score or zero. I failed the exam by five points. The exam was graded in five-point increments meaning that I failed the exam by one question. One question! I was devastated.

Two years of running at the speed of light, two years of juggling medical school and single motherhood, two years of sleepless nights and eating on the run, two days of grueling test taking, and I missed it by one question. Now I had to do it all over again. When the scores came out, my classmates were high fiving each other and planning celebrations. I was mortified and demoralized.

I was able to keep it a secret for a little while but that's the kind of news that spreads quicker than you would like. It was the spring of my second year. I spent that summer preparing for it and re-took the exam in the fall. Unbelievably, I got the exact same score. I failed by one question. How could this be? What was I going to do?

True to their word, Mount Sinai would not let me continue and I was forced to sit out the year. What a mess. My financial aid was cut off because I was not technically a student. I had a two-year-old son, a babysitter, and New York City apartment and no money. After four years of undergraduate work and two years of medical school, I owed more than $60,000 and now my whole life was derailed by one question.

I went to the dean and begged to be let back in. He wouldn't budge. After I stopped crying, I sat down, pulled myself together, and put myself on a schedule. I was on a mission. The first thing I did was to sign up for Kaplan study courses. Stanley H. Kaplan Company (now called Kaplan Inc.) is a test preparation center that offers instruction for taking many standardized tests, including college and graduate school admissions, and programs to prepare professionals for a variety of licensing exams. I had utilized the center to prepare for the medical school admission exam so this was familiar territory to me. I made it my full time job.

The next thing I did was to join a gym. Every day for the next nine months I started the day at 9:00 a.m. with a swim in the pool and then pored over tapes and mock exams at the center until 5:00 p.m. Then I went home to be a good mother. I used money left over from my previous year's financial aid package to survive. Mount Sinai owned the building in which we were living and I am embarrassed to say I did not pay my rent for a year. There was only so much money to go around. Thankfully, we never got an eviction notice.

I didn't know how I cracked the code to pass that exam and I didn't care. I just wanted to get on with my life. Years later when I was a doctor in the emergency room there was one last board exam to take. With that humiliation fresh in my mind, I went to a class designed to help doctors pass the emergency medicine boards. I was taken aback to realize that I had been playing the wrong game.

My focus had been on making the right clinical judgments—on being a good doctor. I made every question more complicated that it was. The instructor explained that this exam had very little to do with the practice of medicine. It was a fact-based exam. The fact was buried in the clinical scenario of each question, for instance, what is the number one cause of this disease, which age group is most likely to contract that disease, and so on.

The day I took my last standardized exam I was able to dissect each question to figure out what exactly was being asked. What fact were they looking for? I did not get bogged down in the scenario, nor did I try to imagine how I would handle each hypothetical situation. I knew I was looking for a fact. And I almost always found it.

I'm sure all the other exams that terrorized me were also fact-based exams. Had I understood that, life would have been much easier. But I didn't know that. I was playing by a set of rules I made up instead of the rules of the game. I was playing by the set of rules I followed to be a doctor. They worked in the emergency room but they were never going to work to pass a standardized exam. And, as I looked back on part one of the national board exam—the one that almost got me thrown out of school—I most likely memorized facts at the Kaplan test preparation center and didn't even know it.

It came as an epiphany that all I needed to do was memorize 730 facts and I could pass the exam. I memorized the facts, and I passed. I lost a year of my life, but I learned an important lesson—figure out the rules.

Bill Reilly's Story

Bill Reilly's experience with police department exams illustrates the importance of figuring out the rules, but with an entirely different path to success. Initially, Bill got a degree in business and worked in a corporate environment. He knew early that it wasn't for him. "I hated it," he said, and at age twenty-three he joined the Hartford Police Department in Connecticut.

As a police officer, he was assigned to the patrol division, which is what the layperson would refer to as the cop on the beat. Five years later he was decorated for protecting a family from a knife-wielding attacker and transferred to the street crimes unit.

His first opportunity for promotion came after being on the job for seven years. The first level of promotion in the police department is sergeant. In order to be promoted to sergeant, an officer needs a certain amount of time on the job and a certain score on the exam.

There were 220 hopefuls sitting with Bill on exam day. In order to prepare for the written exam, candidates studied textbooks and policies. Those who met a certain threshold on the written exam were invited to take the oral exam. "About 50 percent of us were invited to take the orals," Bill said.

In order to prepare for the oral exam, his studying had to switch from memorizing textbooks to understanding how policies, procedures, and laws integrate. With that information he could talk about the decisions he would make when faced with certain situations in the field. He needed to learn how to apply concepts, not memorize facts for the oral exam.

In 1990, the Hartford Police Department had eight volumes of policies and procedures. There were more than one thousand pages that had to be processed. The volumes of information were overwhelming. Initially, Bill approached each volume individually, hoping to conquer one before moving on to another.

Each policy would identify what the responsibility of a sergeant was—a sergeant's response to a bank robbery had a certain type of procedure, the response to a hostage situation another type of procedure, and so on. It was at this point when he was trying to remember large volumes of information from all the different policies that he started to see the commonality and a pattern emerged. "I was just trying to make the complex simple," he told me.

Bill realized in every situation, the steps were the same. Although every scenario was worded differently, the first step was to be on scene and get involved. The second step was to take stock of the situation before you take any action, and so on.

When he spread the policies out, he saw that more often than not, this pattern existed. For the oral exam, Bill memorized eight different actions he believed covered all the steps necessary in any situation. It worked! He was ranked first on the promotion list. And he did it again, and again.

Bill holds the distinction of being the only member of the Hartford Police Department to ever be promoted as the highest-ranking candidate on competitive testing for sergeant, lieutenant, captain, and assistant chief. He figured out the rules to pass that first exam and applied them consistently to rise up the ranks in his police career.

Shortly after his retirement, Bill founded Finest's Professional Development, a coaching company dedicated to the professional advancement and development of police officers. For more than twenty years, Bill has personally delivered training programs to thousands of police professionals across the United States.

His signature program, *Oral Boards Made Easy*, not only helps these professionals get promoted, but gives them the tools to use the information in their new leadership positions as well. All this came to be because he figured out the rules.

My Early Business Experience

Some children are very enterprising—running lemonade stands in front of the house, selling Girl Scout cookies door to door. I wasn't one of them. There were no entrepreneurs in my family and I didn't know anyone who owned a business. I should be embarrassed to admit this, but when I was a child for a long time I didn't realize that people did own businesses. I just thought people worked for the company. It never occurred to me that someone actually owned the company.

There were a lot of rules I had to learn and very quickly when I left the emergency room and opened my business at age fifty. At one point very early on I was starting to run out of money so I decided to ask my bank what was involved in acquiring a business loan. The loan officer said he would need to see my "P and L." And I said, "What's that?" Profit and Loss—seems simple once someone tells you. I had a lot to learn.

I didn't know what I was doing. I didn't know what the rules were. I didn't even know there were rules. I didn't know anything. I had allocated money for house expenses and what I thought would be business expenses: rent, telephone, utilities. I did not know to allocate money for advertising. This wasn't even on my radar screen. I was in the emergency room for nearly ten years. We didn't advertise in the emergency room. We didn't even lock the door. A good day was one when no one showed up. I just assumed that I was going to open the business and women would just show up.

Don't ask me why—maybe it was blind optimism. It's not like I had ever started a business or knew anybody who had. I chose a location that was two doors down from a hair salon because I truly believed that would assure me a constant stream of business. I didn't know how that was going to happen and I didn't know the rules about building a business. Apparently it doesn't happen overnight, no matter where you are located.

I didn't even know the difference between advertising and marketing. I learned you can pay someone to advertise your business but marketing requires you to get out and press the flesh. I learned those rules quickly.

My first tip off was watching women get out of their cars and walk right past my business to the hair salon without even realizing I was there. I was sitting at the reception desk of a business that had a large picture window with a huge Medical Spa sign and I felt invisible. After I got over my surprise and disappointment, I started getting creative.

I realized just because I had an ad in the newspaper and huge lettering above my door, it wasn't enough to get me noticed, let alone launched. I started giving presentations about aging successfully and sending out monthly newsletters. I researched organizations like the chamber of commerce and started joining organizations with other entrepreneurs. I figured out the rules to make myself a successful business owner. And I followed them.

Breaking the Rules

As a doctor who helps women stay beautiful from the inside out, I can tell you there are rules to follow if you want to look as young as you can for as long as you can. They're simple: stay out of the sun, don't go tanning, and don't smoke. I can also tell you that by the time women get into their fifties, the ones who followed those rules are for the most part much happier than the ones who didn't.

I once had a consultation with a young woman in her early thirties who was already a long-time sun worshiper. Her summers were spent on the beach and her winters in the tanning bed. She came to me because she was starting to notice some changes and wanted to know what she could do about it.

I explained the dangers of her lifestyle and what the sun and tanning booth were doing to her skin. I explained how making changes now would alter the course of her aging. "You could get a spray tan or use an over the counter product," I said. "But the tanning booth is causing severe damage." This was not an acceptable alternative because she argued products made her skin turn orange.

"You should be wearing sunscreen everyday," I pressed on. Again, she said this was not going to work because sunscreen made her break out. She thanked me for my time and decided that she was not willing to change her lifestyle at this time. "When things get bad enough, I'll just get a facelift." In the end she decided to break the rules, but at least she knew what they were.

Renee's Story

One of the greatest lessons of Renee's life came when she figured out the rules of the family court system. At age twenty-five she married Gary and shortly thereafter became pregnant. When her daughter was three months old, Gary, who was always a little hot headed, hit her in the face. Renee picked up her daughter, left the apartment, and filed for divorce. Gary never paid a penny in child support and never had any interest in seeing his daughter. Two years later, out of the blue, Gary decided he wanted custody of their baby girl, Jessica. Renee went to court thinking this would be a slam-dunk. After all, how could the court award custody of a baby girl to a man with a history of violence toward women and who had shown absolutely no regard for his own daughter for two years.

She was very impassioned on the witness stand and turned out to be her own worst enemy. At one point, the judge told her if she did not calm down, she would be in contempt of court and custody would be awarded to the father. It seemed the rules of this court favored the father's rights. That day, Gary received unsupervised weekly visitation with Jessica, and Renee had no choice but to comply. Renee was astounded. What about the truth? What about common sense? It was never her intention to keep Gary from his daughter and she would have agreed to supervised visitation. It turned out the truth had nothing to do with anything. He had rights.

The next two years were a nightmare. Jessica would return from visits with her father angry, sullen, and withdrawn. Renee was walking a tightrope—not wanting to traumatize her daughter further and not knowing what was happening during her visits. She spoke with one attorney after another who all told her there was nothing that could be done. Those were the rules.

Gary wasn't paying child support but would show up to court and say that he had. The *he said, she said* always worked in his favor. He would miss multiple court dates and be given another without any reprimand. He would lie on the witness stand and his girlfriend would lie as well, supporting his story. At one point, he even gave the court a phony social security number.

Renee finally found an attorney who knew how the rules of the court could work in her favor. It took almost a year, but Renee was awarded child support that was to be paid through the child support collection unit rather than paid to her directly. The day the rules changed and Gary was ordered to pay support through the court, he never contacted her again.

Corporate Rules

Understanding the rules is imperative in a corporate environment. As a leader, you need to understand the rules of engagement and know how to work through them in order to be successful.

There are different sets of unwritten rules in different companies. Maybe your company has a culture where people are encouraged to have out-in-the-open conflict at meetings. Being vocal is an indication of your willingness to get things done and earns you respect.

Perhaps you work for a company where meetings are subdued and roundtable conflict is frowned upon. A culture where everyone agrees, but they really don't and it is up to you to go back to your team members and resolve the problem behind closed doors.

Once you figure out the unwritten rules of your corporation, you will have an inside view into how decisions get made and what kind of performance is rewarded or valued. You'll also be able to figure out how to adapt to that environment, or decide if you want to adapt at all.

Ryan's Workplace Transition

When my son graduated from college and started looking for a job, he initially thought that he could follow the same rules that he followed through college. He had a beard and always seemed to need a haircut. The voicemail message on his cell phone featured a mumbling, barely audible voice saying something to the effect of, "I'm not here. Leave a message. Later."

No *hello*, no *have a nice day*, nothing. And he was having a very difficult time finding a job. I said, "Shave the beard. It's fine for college but is not going to get you a job." He replied that the beard made him look older and therefore a better candidate. He insisted that he could trim his beard and make it look presentable. There were plenty of men in the workforce who had beards, he argued.

Then I started on the voicemail. What businessperson is going to leave you a message when you don't even announce who you are? Getting messages had never been a problem for him so this was also a hard sell. "Young girls in college might have left you a lot of messages," I argued, "but potential employers are not going to leave you messages."

We went around and around on this for a long time but he finally figured out he was no longer playing by college rules. He changed his voicemail message and shaved his beard. He learned a beard doesn't take you as far in business as it does on a college campus, and prospective employers expect to be wished good day before they leave you a message. When he made the choice to follow the rules of the interview game, he gained more control and stopped leaving the outcome to chance.

A Book of Rules

In 1995, Ellen Fein and Sherrie Schneider wrote the book, *The Rules*. It outlined rules for dating and the best approach to finding a husband. The premise was that women who played hard to get got their man, while women who made themselves available got less in the end. The uproar was palpable. Women's groups were outraged arguing the rules were archaic and were setting women back to the 1950s without control of their lives.

I'm not here to tell you what to do but I'll tell you my story. After two failed marriages and a string of failed relationships I reached a point in my life where I decided if this was as good as it got, life was good. I was an emergency room doctor, I owned my own home, and I had a beautiful son, loving family, and great girlfriends. If a man came along that would be nice, and if he didn't, that would be okay too.

On-line dating was a new phenomenon, not the common occurrence that it is today. I had tried it twice without success. I had reached out to some men and some had reached out to me. My subscription to the site was due to expire and I was not planning on renewing. I had had enough.

A man reached out to me a week before my profile was due to come down. We had two or three e-mail exchanges and he asked to get together. I didn't have my picture posted and I had no intention of putting one up. He still wanted to get together. I just wanted to have one last date and be done with online dating.

I didn't make a fuss about his e-mails or getting together with him. He still wanted to get together. After our first date, a girlfriend told me I was going to marry him. I told her she was crazy. It turns out we were both right. I married him and she's a little crazy, but that's why I love her.

I've heard it said that rules were made to be broken. I say no they're not. You can bend them a little, you can make them your own, and you can even decide not to follow the rules. But when you know what the rules are, you know what you're dealing with, and you are on a level playing field with everyone else.

To get through medical school with a baby, I had to make my own set of rules that would enable me to make it through. I couldn't abandon the school's rules, but I couldn't follow them exactly either. I just didn't have the time or the energy. Somehow, I figured out the most important parts of both jobs and concentrated my energy straight down the middle. Peripheral rules got jettisoned. It worked for me.

By now I hope you are starting to look at situations in your own life differently. Look for the rules. It took me a long time to realize that there are silent rules everywhere. Once you figure them out you gain more control. You start to realize that other people aren't just lucky, they have figured out the rules.

When I figured it out, life changed. I absolutely gained control of the standardized testing that terrorized me for years. I was able to gain control of my face and look younger and help thousands of women do the same in my cosmetic practice. My son gained control of the interview process. He has grown the beard back but it is not an issue because he is now evaluated on his merit, not on his initial presentation. Interview rules are over and workplace rules have taken their place.

If you feel like you are ready to break the cycle, look for the rules. Once you find them, you can stop leaving outcomes to chance. Whether you decide to follow them or modify them, knowing the rules will help you stop wasting time and get control of your life.

The Take-Away

Every situation has rules, sometimes they're unspoken and sometimes they are clearly delineated. It is important to figure out the rules so that you can give yourself a fighting chance—so you can compete on a level playing field with others who already understand the game. This strategy is not about following the rules. Rather, it is about understanding the rules so you know which ones you can break, and which ones you can't.

CHAPTER 10
Make a Friend of Fear

Everything you want is on the other side of fear.

— Jack Canfield

One of the scariest moments of my medical career came weeks after graduation, during my first overnight on-call experience as an intern. A hospital is a hustling, bustling place until about ten o'clock at night. Empty corridors take on an eerie feeling when you're part of the skeleton crew caring for patients until daybreak.

The nurse paged me at 2:00 a.m. to let me know one of my patients was having chest pain. As I was running down the darkened corridor to his room I was saying to myself, "This man needs a doctor!" And then I realized, *I am his doctor.* A chill ran through me. I was no longer a secretary. I was no longer a medical student. I was now the doctor and I felt like I didn't know what I was doing.

By the time I got to his bedside I was having chest pain myself, although mine was caused by anxiety. I did the only two or three things I knew to do for him and thankfully his pain resolved. I'd like to report I felt a sense of pride and accomplishment, but all I really felt was relief. However, the next time I got called to a patient's bedside for chest pain, I was a little more confident.

Things are scary but sometimes you have to do it anyway. I was afraid a great deal in the emergency room. It didn't matter that I had twelve years of training and knew what I was supposed to do—it was still scary. Sometimes in business, you have to make scary decisions as well.

During the planning stages of opening my medical spa, I was terrified. I had no business experience and I didn't know what I was doing. I was gearing up to make to big step, but was looking for a safety net. I had discussed opening the business with a colleague who had agreed to go into business with me.

Nothing was formalized or in writing. I had already given my notice and she was planning on giving notice at her job as well. I was relieved to have someone with whom to share expenses and make business decisions, since I had never undertaken any entrepreneurial venture.

I had found office space and had an appointment to meet with the owner of the building to sign the lease. There would be no turning back once the lease was signed. The meeting was set for 5:00 p.m. At 4:15 p.m., she called to let me know that she had changed her mind about going into business and couldn't take on the lease.

I was in a tailspin. I had figured out my expenses down to the penny and now they were going to be double. I had a mortgage. I had a son in private school. All the money was allocated! I put in a call to my then boyfriend and now husband with this devastating news. *What now? What do I do? How can I do this alone?*

He was out of the office but I got his assistant on the phone. I started spilling out the whole story. I was rambling and hyperventilating at the same time. "This man is expecting me there at 5:00 p.m. and she's not going to do this with me and I don't know what to do. This is a big expense." I was going on and on and Anna said to me very calmly, "Susan, go sign the lease. You can do it."

I got in the car and signed the lease. I think my hand was shaking but I did it and it was the right thing to do. Did you ever let an opportunity pass because you were afraid to take a risk? Afraid you would fail?

I could have not faced that fear. I could have called that man and said, "You know what, I can't take the space. My partner backed out and I just can't do it alone." And believe me, I thought about backing out. That would have changed my whole career. That would have changed the next ten years and beyond for me. I wouldn't have a successful medical spa. I wouldn't be writing this book. Chances are I'd still be in the clinic or perhaps back in the emergency room.

Everybody is afraid at one time or another. Maybe you are afraid of being too successful because you don't want people to think you're full of yourself. Maybe you are afraid of failure because you don't want others to think you weren't strong enough or smart enough to get the job done. Maybe your fear is more localized and you're afraid of public speaking, or afraid of being fired, or afraid of looking like the bad guy. Maybe you're afraid of being alone or being abandoned.

Madeline's Story

Madeline was forty-eight years old when her fifty-nine-year-old husband died of cancer. They had been married twenty-four years and she had seen him through a three-year illness.

After he died, she found herself drinking wine and crying herself to sleep. "I can't do this forever," she thought and so she started accepting invitations to get together with friends.

About six months later she met Steve at a friend's barbecue. When they first started dating she confided that it was really just a diversion for her loneliness. But she grew attached quickly. About a year into their relationship, she could feel Steve pulling away. The more he pulled away, the harder Madeline fought for the relationship. She knew he wasn't treating her well but she was afraid to be alone. More importantly, she didn't want to go through losing someone again.

When it ended, Madeline sought out the company of a therapist rather than another male companion. She was able to come to terms with her fears of being abandoned, and more importantly, of being alone.

Fear can pass, or it can stay and incapacitate you. Sometimes the threat is real and sometimes it is imagined, but the feeling is the same. I'd love to tell you I have the magic bullet for getting over your fears, but I don't. I can tell you that avoiding the situation will not make fears go away. Unless, of course, you're willing to let avoidance steal your dreams. Then the situation will go away, along with your hopes and dreams.

Conflict

While we're on the subject of avoidance, I'd like to take a minute and talk about conflict. I'm not a big fan of conflict and chances are you're not either. Unfortunately avoiding conflict doesn't make the problem go away.

Many times over the years, a situation would arise that I didn't like. I just wasn't up for the fight and so would convince myself that whatever it was wasn't really that important anyway. Here's what happens when you take that approach. Little by little, year after year, you lose a little part of yourself. It leads to feelings of weakness, sadness and sometimes anger.

You have to get in the ring. You don't always have to have a knock out. You don't always have to be in the center under the bright lights. Sometimes you can hug the ropes, but you have to get in the ring.

If you're in a corporate environment, avoiding conflict will kill your career. If you're the leader, your approach to a direct conversation with team members involving negative feedback will either enhance or cripple your team. And if you find yourself on the receiving end of negative feedback in a corporate scenario, my advice is to separate your emotion from the feedback. The feedback is being given to move the company or project forward, not to tell you you're a bad person.

Cindy Myer's Story

Cindy Myer's life turned upside down in a weekend when she went from stay-at-home mom to chief executive officer. For seventeen years she'd been a full-time wife and mother of two daughters, living happily in New Jersey, and had taken very little interest in her husband's business, Ridgewood Moving Services.

He died suddenly and quite unexpectedly of a heart attack in June 2005, leaving her in charge. "We buried Rob on Saturday and I was in the office on Monday," she said. The family business would be her only source of income and she wanted to send a message to her daughters. "We have choices in life and you should never give up even if you don't know what the heck you're doing."

The male-dominated field did not welcome her and the fifteen-person staff was less than cooperative. Over the next few months, Cindy had to learn the moving and storage business from scratch. She discovered that her husband did not have systems in place.

There was no procedural structure to assigning moves and no paper trail for income and expenses. "My signature was on the checks and I wanted to see where the money was going," she said. What she discovered was horrifying. Drivers were doing moves on their own time using Ridgewood's equipment. Trucks were missing and supply boxes were disappearing. "That's money flying out the window," she said.

She explained to her workers that using company equipment was stealing and she would be forced to fire anyone who continued. Drivers ignored her and the same problems persisted. At one point, Cindy needed to involve the police to get a driver to return one of her trucks.

The business was turning into a nightmare. More labor problems surfaced and Ridgewood Moving Services was now losing money. "I'd put on a big show at the office and then go home and cry," said Cindy. She was scared to death but believed this business could be successful and she could pave the way for other women to break into this male-dominated field.

Against the advice of experts, Cindy invested her husband's life insurance into the failing business. This was a huge gamble because if the business failed, she would have no money with which to raise her two daughters. She then joined an entrepreneurial association, the Women Presidents' Organization. Members gave her advice that helped her move her business forward—fire fast and hire slow.

According to Cindy, the day she fired the last of the original employees, two years after taking over, was the first day she was able to exhale. Since that point, the business has grown exponentially, and Cindy, who was once shunned by male colleagues, now sits on the executive board of the New Jersey Warehousemen and Movers Association.

She was scared every day for a long time. She was gambling her daughters' future, but Cindy worked through her fear and despite having minimal business experience was able to not only rescue her late husband's business from near bankruptcy, but turn it around as well.

What if It's the Wrong Decision?

Some of us are not risk takers. We want all the information before we're willing to make a decision. Well, what a perfect world that would be! It takes tremendous courage to put yourself out there and make a critical decision when you don't have all the facts.

Fear can prevent us from taking risks and stepping outside of our comfort zone. What if you fail? What if you make the wrong decision? In business, there are successful people with products or messages inferior to yours. They're no better than you. It's because they had the courage to try.

So if you're afraid to take a risk, start small and work your way up. You have to take a risk to move yourself forward.

Sometimes decisions are crucial and other times we convince ourselves that they are crucial. When I was an emergency room doctor, it could be crucial. Many times I was treating a critically ill patient who couldn't communicate with me. Literally, their life hung on my ability to make the right decision—and make it immediately with a paucity of information.

In those situations, I would gather up all the information I had and combine it with my years of training and make the best decision I could. Most of us will never be in those kinds of situations but it doesn't feel any less critical to you. Hopefully, when you realize it's not life or death, it will be easier for you to take a risk.

What's the Worst That Could Happen?

I have found it helps to work through the worst-case scenario to calm your nerves. As part of my emergency room training, I spent time in the cardiac intensive care unit. These patients are the sickest of the sick in any hospital. They are surrounded by monitors, tubes, intravenous lines, machines, alarms—you get the picture.

When it came my turn to be in charge of the unit on an overnight shift, I was filled with dread. As the five o'clock hour drew near and the other doctors were starting to leave, a knot was forming in my stomach. I went to the chairman of the department and begged to be let off the hook. He asked, "What's the worst thing that can happen tonight?" I responded, "Someone could die." "And what would you do?" he asked calmly. "I would start CPR and run the code." He smiled, "Then what are you worried about?"

The same line of thinking helped me make a big leap at the beginning of my medical career. I had trained in New York and relied heavily on my parents to take care of Ryan with my sporadic hospital schedule.

When training was over, I had no interest in working in New York hospitals. I found a hospital in Connecticut that really resonated with me and applied for the job. This was a big move for me and I was very nervous. I was leaving behind my safety net of childcare.

I rented a house and employed a nanny from South Africa to live with us. I signed a one-year contract at the hospital and off we went. It was a bold move and I was clearly out of my comfort zone, but I knew in my heart if it didn't work out I could always move back to New York. I've now lived in Connecticut since 1996.

If you're in the corporate arena and are contemplating a move to another company or a move that involves relocation, I advise you to use the worst-case scenario to help clarify your decision. What's the worst that could happen? You make a bold move and it doesn't work out? Set a fallback position for yourself. *I can always go back to—whatever that is for you.* Do you really think you wouldn't find another job?

Finding Your Voice

If you surround yourself with positive people it makes scary situations more bearable. In business you have to be willing to take risks or you're not going to go very far. Maybe you don't want to go very far. Me—I want to go far. I've taken many risks and worked through a lot of fear. When you work through fear, it helps you find your voice.

When I first opened my medical spa, I felt like an outsider looking in. The public was swayed by television ads telling them not to trust someone like me, and therefore didn't welcome me. My colleagues were trying to discredit me because we had taken different paths after obtaining the same credentials. For years, I felt like a little kid begging for a seat at the adult table.

It has taken me many years to find my voice and to find my place in my industry. It has taken me a long time to be comfortable knowing that I belong here and deserve to be here and that I can be considered a leader in my field.

That didn't come from not being afraid. It came from being afraid on a daily basis—being afraid about how I'm going to pay the bills, being afraid that I didn't know enough to be in business, being perceived as not having enough to offer in my business, being afraid of what other people in my field are doing. You look at others in your industry and you see only what they want you to see.

The cosmetic industry is very isolating. People would have you believe that they're all doing very well. So here's another lesson that I've learned and am still learning: do not compare yourself and your business to other people. You can fall into a trap thinking that you're not doing as well. They may in fact all be doing very well but it's hard to know. It doesn't matter, though, because you can only control yourself.

We have a tendency to look at others and think they have it all together. Well, supermodels get pimples and major league baseball players strike out. Did you ever hear of a supermodel who passed up posing on the cover of a magazine because she had a pimple and was afraid the public would think she wasn't pretty? Or a baseball player who let someone else up to bat because he struck out last time he was at home plate and was afraid he would cause the team to lose? Of course not!

Celebrate Everything

Once you work through your fear, it's important to celebrate your achievements. I have a difficult time and don't always practice what I preach but I'm getting better. When something is unattainable to me, I will work my butt off until I figure out how to do it. Once I figure it out, I look back on it and think *well that was easy—anybody could do it.*

No it is not. Once you know the answer, then everything is easy. Not acknowledging my achievements is something I did in college, in medical school, and in business, and I advise you not to do the same. In college, I would pore over physics concepts for days feeling stupid and not qualified to be in the class. Once I figured it out I would immediately shift into *why, of course—I can't believe I didn't see that all along.*

I would set financial goals in business and when I reached them I would move the bar rather than celebrate the goal. If you're doing the same thing, all I can say is please stop. Celebrate accomplishments. Celebrate easy things. Celebrate hard things. Celebrate goals. I continue to work on this.

One last bit of advice I'll leave you with is copy good practices and don't compare yourself to others. When you compare yourself to someone else or your business to another, you only see what they want you to see. You never get the full picture. It can leave you feeling inadequate and like a failure.

If you look at others in your industry and think that some idea seems to be working very well, then tweak it to make it your own. If it worked for them it will work for you too. Though, that being said, have the good grace not to copy your next door neighbor.

We're all trying to get to the top. I learned a long time ago that the top is not a peak, it's a plateau and there's plenty of room for everyone. I try and take my cue from the hairdressers. There is a hairdresser on every corner and yet no one is going out of business. Why? Because there's plenty of hair to go around. So find your voice through the fear, surround yourself with positive people and celebrate your accomplishments. I'll see you at the top.

The Take-Away

Life is scary but sometimes you have to do things anyway. Everybody is afraid at one time or another and it can prevent us from taking risks and stepping outside of our comfort zone. Some of us would prefer to wait until we have all the information before we make a decision.

All the stars will never be aligned perfectly and sometimes you have to make a decision with what you have.

It's risky and sometimes scary. When you work through fear, it helps you find your voice. Also, once you work through your fear, it's important to celebrate your achievements. Remember, once you know the answer, everything is easy.

CHAPTER 11
Be Willing to Make Mistakes

Experience is what you get when you didn't get what you wanted.

— Randy Pausch

As an emergency room doctor for ten years, I treated thousands of people who had been in motor vehicle accidents—everything from minor fender benders to life-changing crashes. Some people walked away with only bandages and some were admitted to the intensive care unit, or even worse, not admitted at all. I treated people on suburban Long Island, in the Bronx, in Queens, and in Connecticut—from all walks of life and driving every different car imaginable. No matter what the location, how big or small the vehicle, or how life altering the accident, they all had one thing in common—It was always the other person's fault.

Not once did anyone ever come to the emergency room and say, "I hit him. I can't believe I hit him. I was driving too close and didn't have time to stop." Or "I took my eyes off the road for a second to change the radio station." Never once did someone take the blame and I treated thousands.

Now I realize this may be an extreme case because there is always a possibility of litigation, but still, thousands of people? Either I was the luckiest emergency room doctor in the country because I never treated the person who caused the accident, or someone wasn't taking responsibility. There's more than the fear of a lawsuit at work here.

We sometimes have trouble admitting our mistakes. Admitting mistakes can conjure up a lot of emotional feelings, from being embarrassed or ashamed, to perhaps not being "enough" whether it be smart enough, good enough, thin enough.

My Experience at a New Hospital

A few years into my emergency room career, I changed hospitals and found myself working in a new place. I was there only a few weeks and was figuring out the rhythm of the emergency room. I was still getting to know everyone and ascertaining how everyone worked together and how the place ran.

One day shortly after I started my shift, one of my physician colleagues approached me with a piece of paper in his hand. He had worked there for years and wanted to let me know about the protocol that was followed at this hospital when a mistake had been made. If you're an emergency room physician, you know no good comes after the sentence, "Remember that patient you sent home?" A chill ran through me.

He proceeded to tell me how he had taken care of a patient I had seen a few days prior. He said I had given the wrong diagnosis and she returned to the emergency room very ill and he had admitted her to the hospital. Apparently, the form he was delivering to me was to be filled out for cases such as these. I was horrified.

My first thought was, *is this woman ok? Did I do something to jeopardize her health?* I felt very badly that I had perhaps misdiagnosed someone, but at that point, there was nothing I could do about it. I was relieved to know that she was at least admitted to the hospital and getting the proper care.

I was also embarrassed that a new colleague was coming to me pointing out mistakes when I was brand new to the hospital. I took pride in my work as an emergency room physician. I'm not saying I never made a mistake—we all do—but when you're a doctor and you make a mistake the stakes are much higher. For me, that meant the sense of responsibility was greater as well.

I immediately went to the office of the director of the emergency room. Being new to the job, I hardly knew this man, but I sat across his desk and said, "I want you to know I screwed up a case." He looked at me puzzled and asked, "What?" Again, I repeated, "I want you to know I screwed up a case." He answered, "I'm here eighteen years and no physician has ever come in here and said they screwed up a case." He went on to add that, if anything, people work to deflect any mistakes that they make.

I showed him the paper that I had been given and wanted him to know about it from me. It turned out, when I sat down for an extended conversation, it was not protocol for one physician to come up to another physician with this form.

And just for the record, thankfully I did not make some grave error. I never found out this doctor's motivation, but my suspicion is he was driven by his own emotions or ambitions and it had nothing to do with me. I tell this story as an illustration—if you make it wrong, make it right. We all make mistakes.

I also tell this story because I think it has a valuable lesson for those of us in the corporate arena. There are a lot of people in the workplace that spend their time sabotaging others in order to erode the confidence of colleagues they view as competitors. It is usually because of their own ambitions and objectives within the company.

In my situation, I chose to stay focused and communicate with my supervisor, rather than challenge my colleague. As a new employee, I did not want to deal with the politics of the workplace. At that point, I wasn't even sure what the politics were. Depending on your corporate culture, this may or may not be the solution for you.

My Big Blunders

"If a thing is worth doing, it is worth doing badly." I didn't come up with it. G.K. Chesterton, a Christian philosopher said it in 1910, and it's worth repeating. When I opened my business in 2002, I picked the wrong name, I was in the wrong location, and I bought the wrong equipment. Other than that, I was off to a great start.

After much thought and consideration, I named my new business, The Aesthetic Care Center, A Medical Spa. I believe it was the first medical spa in Connecticut. Med spas were only just popping up in places like New York and Los Angeles. They were cutting-edge facilities run by dermatologists or plastic surgeons, and they offered anti-aging treatments and skin care.

I was new to the field of aesthetic medicine and wasn't trained to do as many procedures, but my thought was I would offer more of a total body approach. I had a skin tightening procedure, a cellulite treatment, skin care products, a nutritionist, facials, massage, yoga, and Pilates. Even though it was not the same medical spa that you would find in New York City, I thought I had enough offerings to be unique and was excited to be one of the first to bring this type of business to life in Connecticut. I thought wrong. Women in New York and Los Angeles might have known what a med-spa was, but Connecticut women did not.

Women would look up at the large lettering above my business, open the front door and ask: "A medical spa? What's a medical spa? Do you do physical therapy here?" As if I wasn't demoralized enough sitting at the reception desk myself, it was crushing to answer the same question time after time.

What was even worse was, when I explained what I did at the spa, many did not seem to understand. So here's my advice. If you are going to be the trendsetter or the trailblazer in your industry, you should have an established name or enough money to sustain your business until you are an established name. Learn from my mistake.

And back to the name: The Aesthetic Care Center, A Medical Spa. I loved the word aesthetic. It sounded so sophisticated. I was heavily invested in that word and that name. It was a mistake.

First of all, as we already discussed, nobody knew what a medical spa was, and secondly, no one knew how to spell the word aesthetic. This should have been the tip off for me, but it wasn't. Shortly after opening, I was noticing a pattern. Women would constantly have to ask me how to spell the word aesthetic so they could write me a check. So let me say it as bluntly as I can, when someone has their checkbook open and has to ask you how to spell the name of your business, you goofed.

Instead, I spelled it out for years on end, like a teacher giving a lesson. Almost like a jingle. I don't know what it was in me that couldn't let it go. I think I couldn't admit it to myself. This was my first attempt at business and money was really tight.

I had invested in the large sign above the building, the lettering on the door and the stationery. How could I have made such a serious blunder? I didn't have the money to change the signs and I didn't know what else to call the business anyway. And I still loved the word. I held on to it long after I knew it was a mistake.

Three years later, when I changed locations, was a perfect opportunity to get rid of that word. My new location was a forty-five-minute drive away. Although I did retain some clients, I knew most of my ladies would not be making the trip, so this new location would be like starting the business all over again. It would be a brand new start.

So what did I do? I contorted the name of my new business around the same word that wasn't working in the first place. And yet I knew enough to get rid of the medical spa part of it. So now, it was Shoreline Aesthetic Care. After all, I moved to a town that is located along the Connecticut shoreline. It made perfect sense to me.

I still loved the word and I was hoping against hope that it was the ladies in my first location who had the problem and not me. Guess what? It was me. I spent the next four years like I spent the previous three, spelling out the word aesthetic. By now, I was able to afford a part-time receptionist so I didn't have to be reminded on a daily basis.

At one point, I was lucky enough to win a branding contest and my prize was a new logo. After many failed attempts at capturing the perfect logo for my business, the owner stepped in to solve the problem. "The name of your business is all wrong. It sounds like you're selling ropes."

I knew she was right and I knew this was the perfect opportunity to fix it. This time, I did some research rather than pulling a name out of a hat. Medical spas were a known brand now. Women knew what they were and what services they provided. I decided to re-incorporate med spa back into my name.

Then I did an Internet search of med spas across the country and found most of them had one thing in common. The name was one word, not three. When my husband came across the word "sonas", I knew immediately this was the new name of my business. Sonas is the Gaelic word for happiness—a perfect fit for me—and Sonas Med Spa was born.

Making mistakes is fine. We all make mistakes. Mistakes are going to happen, but if you do make a mistake, admit it. And fix it. If you make it wrong, make it right. I held on to that name for four more years after I changed locations. That's a total of seven years. So that was actually one mistake on top of another. Two wrongs don't make a right.

Mistakes That Impact Others

A while ago, I had a problem with an ad that I ran in a local publication. I give this company a lot of money. I run a lot of ads. When I'm advertising my services in a newspaper ad, and the ad looks terrible, it reflects badly on my business. Remember, I sell beauty.

The ad had many problems, so we weren't being nitpicky about it. My assistant called up to complain. Let's not forget, a lot of money crosses hands. The reaction that she got was a very defensive one.

"Mistakes happen," she was told. And she was offered an explanation. The person on the other end of the phone topped it off with, "You have to understand, this is newsprint." Well, I don't have to understand anything. I don't care why it happened. I know why it happened.

It happened because someone used color copy to run a black and white ad. It happened because someone was asleep at the switch at the newspaper. It happened because someone made a mistake.

What a different experience that phone call could have been had someone on the other end of the phone said I'm sorry that it happened. You are a valued customer and I'm sorry you are not happy with our performance. I would like to make it up to you. Let me make it right.

Because of the reaction we got, we decided to explore other advertising options. I had been a loyal customer for more than six years and was one of their top customers. Now I am exploring other options. No one won in this situation.

The truth is that newsprint is unreliable. Sometimes it comes out crystal clear and other times it looks like you've been in an earthquake. That's fine, but that's not my problem.

I do a lot of cosmetic work for many women. Not everybody is happy. Most are but not everybody is happy. I tell everybody right at the beginning that everybody gets a different result because we're all different. As a matter of fact, what I say exactly is, "If I took two women and put them on the same diet and exercise routine for two months, I'd have two different results. If I knew why, I'd be rich."

Women go into all kinds of procedures knowing that. But when somebody isn't happy, I do my best to make them happy. The last thing I say is *well, you have to understand we're all different.* If that costs me money, so be it. That's what you do.

Figuring out the Why

Why don't we admit mistakes? Sometimes people are afraid they will look weak in front of others. This can turn into a compounded problem very quickly. In the corporate arena, if you made the mistake but won't admit it then what you are saying is that it must have been someone else on your team.

And if not someone on your team, then it must be the customer's fault. If you're the other person on the team or the customer on the receiving end of that one, you're not happy. Admitting mistakes is a sign of courage, not weakness.

I made a very costly mistake in business a few years ago that thankfully didn't impact anybody but me. I purchased a used laser hair removal machine for $25,000. As I was increasing my service offerings, I thought I would have a double line of women wanting hair removal but taking on the $25,000 debt did not increase my business much at all.

I didn't research different types of machines. I didn't research the market. I made a decision in a vacuum. It was a mistake. Because I funded it on credit, it cost me much more than that. My credit cards got moved around like a shell game for years.

I wound up paying for that mistake long after I realized it was a mistake. I never added up what I really paid for the machine. I couldn't bear to know. I was able to sell it a few years later for $10,000. I took the money. At least I didn't hang on to it for seven years like I did the word aesthetic.

Often times, admitting you made a mistake can bring up feelings of shame or feelings of vulnerability. The "not good enough" list is a long list—not smart enough, not strong enough, not thin enough—and weakness is at the top of the list. Whether you feel weak or are afraid others will perceive you as weak, neither one is a good feeling. It attaches itself to your sense of worthiness.

Perfection Paralysis

I have been trying to write this book for five years. I had multiple starts and stops. I would write for days on end and then have a sense of horror when I went back to read it. I couldn't possibly show this to anyone, so I put it away and would start over another time. Meanwhile, others who I thought had much less to offer were being published. So here's my imperfect book.

For more than a decade, Dr. Brené Brown, a professor at the University of Houston's Graduate College of Social Work has studied vulnerability, shame, and courage. In her book, *The Gifts of Imperfection: Let Go of Who You Think You're Supposed to Be and Embrace Who You Are*, Dr. Brown has this to say about perfectionism: "Understanding the difference between healthy striving and perfectionism is critical to laying down the shield and picking up your life. Research shows that perfectionism hampers success. In fact, it's often the path to depression, anxiety, addiction, and life paralysis."

As a leader, it is imperative to accept imperfection, not only in yourself but in your team members or peers. To be clear, I'm not advocating mediocrity. Sometimes, done is better than perfect. In business, in order to keep things moving, you have to make decisions quickly. If you're hung up on perfection, the project will never get done and goals and objectives will never be reached.

The truth is we're all imperfect. Are you being true to yourself or are you trying to be who you think the world expects you to be? Oscar Wilde is often credited saying, "Be yourself. Everyone else is already taken." The world doesn't come to an end if you make one mistake, ten mistakes, one hundred mistakes—okay maybe you should reevaluate if you make that many mistakes.

You'll never be original if you're not prepared to make mistakes or be wrong. You need to be willing to be embarrassed. It's not easy to feel embarrassed. When I'm in that position, I have found that laughing at myself help a lot.

Sometimes business or life decisions that you make are wrong. Every decision you make isn't going to be the right decision. You have to be willing to make mistakes. A mistake is just an opportunity to learn and grow, so learn from it and don't make that one again. I have found in my life that I keep making the same mistake until I learn the lesson. The mistake shows up in different forms, but the lesson is the same.

Making decisions can sometimes be risky. You have to take a chance and be willing to make the wrong choice. I'll tell you this: Reward doesn't always follow risk but it never follows indecision. And if you don't believe me, remember my seven years of, "How do you spell aesthetic?"

The Take-Away

We all make mistakes. Why do we have trouble admitting our mistakes? Admitting mistakes can conjure up negative emotions, from being embarrassed or ashamed to perhaps not feeling smart enough or good enough. Sometimes people are afraid that if they admit they made a mistake, they will look weak in front of others.

Others are consumed with making everything perfect and will hold back until they get it just right. Now is better than perfect. If you make it wrong, make it right. A mistake is just an opportunity to learn and grow.

CHAPTER 12
Be Your Own Champion

Speak your mind even if your voice shakes.
— Maggie Kuhn

Do you find it easy to stand up for yourself? I have always been a better champion for others than for myself, but I am learning. Being a champion for others is what helped make me a great emergency room doctor. I would, and did, go to the mat for you.

A Life-Saving Decision

During one of my emergency room shifts, a distressing call came in from the paramedics. They were at the diner a few blocks away with a forty-two-year-old man who was in the process of having a stroke.

A stroke victim can be treated with clot buster medication, but time is of the essence. There is a three-hour window and then it is too late for any intervention. Before any medication can be given, the patient must receive a CT scan of his head, which takes time as well.

I called the radiologist and explained the situation. He told me that he was in the process of scanning another patient and would be done in about an hour. He had a full schedule that day but would take my patient next. "That's not good enough. I need you to take your patient off the table and scan this man immediately. We can save his life and we're running out of time." He protested and so did I. I won.

My patient was scanned immediately and was able to receive the appropriate medication. Later that afternoon, the neurologist who admitted him to the hospital came down to the emergency room to give me an update. "You saved a life today," he said. The forty-two-year-old man was returned to his wife, his children, and society, because I was his champion.

Okay Changed My Life

When I left mainstream medicine, I had to learn how to advocate for myself. My first opportunity was my transition to the entrepreneurial world and the catalyst was the word "okay." I had left the emergency room and was working in an occupational health clinic where I treated work-related injuries. During my year at the clinic, I had treated two patients with life-threatening conditions.

One person had fallen off a ladder and sustained a collapsed lung. The day prior, he had been seen in an emergency room and discharged home in that perilous condition. The other was a city worker who was delirious from working in the street during sweltering summer heat. Neither of these people had any business being in a clinic and could have died.

When it came time for my year-end review, the director of the clinic sat me down in his office. "You're doing okay," he said. My evaluation was based solely on the three-tiered system set up by the hospital—excellent, okay, or you're fired.

My quick thinking and emergency medicine skills that saved the lives of two individuals were not part of the equation. I received an insulting raise that worked out to be somewhere in the neighborhood of fifty dollars per week before taxes.

I found out during this meeting that receiving an "excellent" review would not have gotten me a much higher raise and that almost everyone gets a middle-of-the-road review. In that moment I knew that I had to leave.

I had turned fifty years old and was starting to feel restless. I wanted to do something on my own, but I didn't know what. I knew I was too tired to return to a career in the emergency room. I just couldn't work around the clock anymore. I didn't have a plan, but I knew I had to make a change.

My head was spinning during that meeting. I was feeling undervalued and underappreciated. I was feeling trapped which was very distressing considering the amount of time, money, and sweat equity it took to get me to this stage of my life. I was disappointed and just plain angry.

I listened quietly to his presentation, thanked him and got up and left. That evening I had extensive conversations with my mother and then boyfriend and secured a back-up financial plan. Because I had started medical school later than most traditional students, I had less time to save sufficient funds on my own.

Two days later, I returned to his office and tendered my resignation. I didn't have plans yet of opening up the medical spa. I didn't know where I belonged, but I knew it wasn't there.

When I looked back on that time, I realized that "okay" changed my life. Had my director handled that situation differently, I might still be there to this day. Had he said, "You're doing a great job and we are so lucky to have you on our team but unfortunately my hands are tied when it comes to compensation," or, "I realize that your raise is not a lot of money but I just want you to know how much I appreciate you and I recognize the contribution you have made to our clinic," I would have stayed.

I would have felt compelled to stay. I would have felt obligated to stay. But when he told me I was doing okay, he actually set me free. In all my years of working in all walks of life, no one had ever said, "you're doing okay" during a review.

As you examine your own life, you will realize that sometimes it's wise to play out a situation and other times you need to stand up for yourself and make a change. In this situation, I didn't feel appreciated. I am many things, but I am not okay. I think Diane's story illustrates this perfectly.

Diane's Story

In 2002, Diane left the corporate rat race behind at the age of forty-two, and decided to become a realtor. This was the perfect position for her and she loved it. She enjoyed working with people and helping them solve their problems and find their dream home.

No surprise that she outshined many of her competitors and was financially successful as well. In 2008, Diane saw the economy turning and knew it was a matter of time before her financial situation would drastically change. With a heavy heart, she started exploring other options.

When she was a little girl she always wanted to be a doctor. Medicine still held her interest after all these years so, in 2009, she decided to become an emergency medicine technician. She approached her studies with the zeal and determination that were the fabric of her being, and rose to the top of the class quickly.

As such, she was one of two people in the class who were offered seats in the paramedic program. She jumped at the chance, and in 2010, found herself as the only woman in an elite, well-known program. She was excited to be preparing for a profession, which would enable her to help people in need and be of service to her community.

Diane plunged into her studies often studying eight to ten hours a day. Within a few months of the yearlong program, she was starting to become disillusioned. Having run human resource departments in her corporate career, as well as her own successful business, Diane was extremely organized and recognized the shortcomings of the program.

The syllabus did not match the lessons and, as such, the class subjects and readings were out of sync for weeks, leaving students confused. Labs were inadequately staffed and much of the equipment was in bad condition. Students would show up to the hospital for their required clinical rotations and no one knew they were coming.

Of greatest concern was the behavior of the education coordinator of the program. It was not only Diane's observation, but also many of her classmates', that this educator treated students poorly, often acting in a belligerent, condescending, and rude manner, making it difficult to learn the material and skills vital to become a successful paramedic.

Students were raising concerns to the administration regarding all of these issues but nothing was ever addressed. It came to her attention that students of previous years had also voiced the same concerns.

"I find this program to be lacking in leadership, organization, and to be an overall administrative mess," she confided one day. "I can't believe this is happening." She knew she couldn't continue and made one of the most difficult decisions of her life. She withdrew from the program. She had never quit anything and walking away after six months of hard work, effort and dedication, made her feel like a failure.

Diane explained her decision and her reasoning in a lengthy letter to the director and program coordinator and asked for an exit interview and a full refund of her tuition. She knew this was the only way to raise her concerns so they would be part of the official record.

It was clear that students of previous years had complained without any resolution. She had invested almost $5,000 and the program had failed her. But more importantly, she knew the program was failing everyone.

She wrote letters for months that all went unanswered. Everyone advised her to move on and forget it. In her last piece of correspondence before she hired an attorney, Diane wrote, "It is my hope that exposing these issues publically and officially would necessitate corrective actions rather than rhetoric, so that future students would not be subjected to the lack of support and administrative deficiencies that I experienced." She ended with, "I just wish someone else had the courage and fortitude to do this, because then I would still be continuing with my education right now."

Three months later, Diane received her exit interview and her tuition was refunded in full. More importantly, the education coordinator who had wreaked havoc on so many students was removed from his position. In the end, not only was Diane her own champion, but also a champion for others who have followed.

Learning to Be a Business Owner

I opened my medical spa in December of 2002. Initially, I was trying to be everything for everybody. Business was slow and I was scared. If someone made a fuss about the price of a service, I immediately lowered my price. I wanted to keep everybody happy and I was afraid that I would lose a sale. Less money is better than no money, I rationalized.

Charging for my time was an uncomfortable feeling for me. I had spent many years in the emergency room giving everything I had. I gave my time, I gave my brainpower, I gave my sympathy and, as patients were leaving, I filled up a plastic bag with supplies and gave that too. The first time I said, "That will be one hundred dollars," I thought the sky would fall in.

Things had changed from my being an employee of a hospital to the owner of a business, but I hadn't made the shift in my mind. I was so accustomed to focusing on other people, that I didn't understand the importance of focusing on myself. I learned the lesson in the spring of 2003.

My hours were 10:00 a.m. to 5:00 p.m., but many times I would bend them to oblige women who insisted that they just couldn't make it during those hours. I was trying to accommodate everyone's schedule and put my own schedule last on the list.

One day a woman called for an appointment but could only come at 8:30 a.m. Please could I come in early for her? Since I was the one sitting at the front desk and making the appointment myself, it was difficult for me so say no. I agreed.

Another woman called and wanted an appointment the same day but could only come at 6:00 p.m. after work. Please, please she begged. Although I didn't want to do it, I denied my feelings and made the appointment.

Do I have to tell you what happened that day? I got to the spa at 8:15 in the morning and sat there until 6:30 at night and no one showed up. That was a turning point for me.

Up to that point, I had been operating from a position of fear. It was one hundred times harder than I thought to get a business off the ground. I was running out of money and I was extremely nervous. I had signed a lease. I had invested in equipment. And, if the financial obligations weren't enough, the humiliation factor was looming large. *I couldn't fail within six months! I had to make this work!*

The embarrassment of sitting alone in the spa for eleven hours that day caused me to make a mindset shift. I went to my boyfriend and my mother and secured the loans we initially discussed to relieve the financial pressure. And I started to honor myself. It was hard but I stuck to the schedule I set. And I stuck to the prices I set.

Shortly thereafter, I was put to the test. I offered a cellulite treatment that was sold in a package for one hundred dollars per treatment but separately for $125. After giving the treatment to a new patient, she decided that she didn't want the package. She took a one-hundred-dollar bill out of her purse and held in in her hand.

I explained that for one treatment, the price was $125, which was clearly stated in my brochure. She took the one hundred dollar bill and threw it across the counter at me. I looked at her and looked down at the money on the counter. Finances were tight and I really needed the money. I slowly pushed it back towards her and said, "I don't think this is going to work." It was a defining moment for me.

Put Yourself on the List

It's not easy to ask for what you need or what you want. Most of us advocate better for our children or our friends than we advocate for ourselves. When you put yourself on the list, you run the risk that people won't like what you have to say.

In my med spa, I've had women keep secret their Botox treatments from their pre-teen daughters, saying, "She would kill me. She hates Botox." I once asked a patient what would happen if her young daughter found out. "She won't talk to me," was the answer. It is astounding to me that grown women are willing to hide their wants and needs because they are afraid of being abandoned emotionally by their pre-teen daughters. I totally understand the concept of not wanting your young daughter to think that her worth is defined by her appearance, but that's not the issue here.

A woman once came to me for a consultation. She was
turning fifty and was feeling discouraged and depressed about
her changing face. She was interested in a Botox treatment to
relax her stress and worry lines. It was just what she needed.
At the end of the consultation she said, "I really want to do this
but I have to save up because I need to take care of my kids."
'How old are your kids?" I asked. "Twenty-two and twenty-six,"
she said. *At what point do you get what you want?* When you're
not important enough to make the list, your children and
sometimes your spouse get that message.

There are many times in life when you put the needs of
others before your own. Many times your children and your
spouse need to come first. But when you keep yourself on the
back burner you run the risk of losing your identity. Shows
featuring makeovers demonstrate this point. How many
times have you seen a makeover candidate lamenting that
she put everyone else in front of herself for so long that she
doesn't recognize herself anymore. You become John's wife or
Suzy's mother or Evelyn's daughter, not really having a sense
of your own identity. It becomes harder to stand up and be
counted when you can't even define who you are.

Beth's Story

People exploit you when you don't stand your ground, even
your children. Beth was a stay-at-home mom and her entire
life revolved around her three children, her husband and
the house. She did everything for everyone. She washed
clothes, cooked meals, and scrubbed bathrooms. She ironed

sheets and underwear and shuffled children between after-school activities.

Growing up, her three girls never made a bed or cooked a meal. Now, not only do they not know how, but they have no interest. Why should they? Although grown, everyone still lives at home and Beth feels like a doormat. After twenty-eight years of this scenario, I believe it will take some serious intervention for Beth to become her own champion.

Advocating for Myself

When I was qualifying for membership in the National Speakers Association, I was again put to the test. In order to qualify, you need twenty paid speaking engagements in a one-year span. I had set my speaking fee relatively low because I was more focused on achieving the goal of twenty engagements rather than making money.

A woman approached me after one of my talks and expressed interest in booking me for her organization. We spoke by telephone the next day and the first thing she said was, "We don't pay our speakers." I listened as she described her organization and needs for a speaker. I was interested in the engagement as they were the perfect audience for my message.

As a speaker and an author, your goal is to get your message in front of as many people as possible. I explained that although I do a lot of pro bono work, I was in the midst of qualifying for NSA membership and as such I needed to be paid. "Unfortunately, I can't," she said and we hung up. The following day she called me again. Remarkably, she discussed the situation with her board of directors and was able to get my fee approved.

As a child, I shied away from confrontation due to my childhood experience. As a result, I grew up with low self-esteem making it very difficult to stand up for myself. It took me a long time to learn to empower myself and become my own champion. Truth is, I'm still working on it.

If I could give you any advice about standing up for yourself and flexing your advocacy muscle, it would be to take the emotion out of the conversation. This is easier said than done when you feel unappreciated or taken for granted. People aren't mind readers. If you don't tell someone what's bothering you, they won't know. If they don't know, you can't blame them. So if you are sinking further down your own priority list, just remember it's never too late to become your own champion.

The Take-Away

Some of us are better advocates for others than we are for ourselves. It's not easy asking for what you want or need. You run the risk that people won't like what you have to say. If you have made it commonplace to put everyone's needs ahead of your own you run the risk of losing your identity—you can identify with being someone's wife or someone's mother but not being yourself. Also, when you don't stand up for yourself it makes it easy for your good nature to be exploited.

CHAPTER 13
Never Surrender

The difference between try and triumph is just a little "umph."

— **Marvin Phillips**

I learned perseverance from my mother. I didn't know what it was and I didn't know it had a name. All I knew was my mother would never take no for an answer. It was exhausting.

By the time I was six years old, we had been to multiple dentists trying to fix my two front teeth. My mother was now twenty-seven with another baby, running our household, and working as a secretary. She didn't have a college degree or medical training. She didn't know what the answer was, but she knew pulling out the two front teeth of a six-year-old girl was not it. So we visited more and more dentists year after year.

After years of searching, my mother's perseverance finally paid off and she found someone with an idea. I owe my smile to perseverance. I owe my smile to my mother. Where would I be if my mother denied her instincts and let a dentist pull out my two front teeth? I shudder to think.

I can't imagine the determination it took for my young mother to search for years without giving in. She was a warrior and an advocate for her family, but as a child, the message was lost on me. It was just too much.

My mother battled everyone. She battled with store clerks to return items after the seven-day grace period passed, she battled with butchers for a better cut of meat at the price she could afford, she battled with dentists who told her she only had one option. I would be thinking, *they said no. Why can't the answer just be no?*

I didn't see my mother's strong will and focus on moving her family forward, as a positive trait. As a result, I shied away from confrontation. I found it easier to accept unpleasant or unjust situations rather than fight for my rights. I wasn't up for the fight.

Clearly in my twenties I had no perseverance. No drive. I floated from one dead-end job to another, not putting forth any effort to take control of my life. When I finally got my act together and returned to college, I worked hard to get good grades but true perseverance didn't come out until after graduation. I just didn't have it in me until I was almost shut out of my dream.

Applying to Medical School

In January 1985, I was finishing up my bachelor's degree and awaiting the results of my many medical school applications. Six months later, I got my answers. Did you ever get a rejection letter?

By June 1985, I was rejected by every medical school in the United States—at the time, forty-two schools. I didn't see that one coming. I graduated at the top of my class with a bachelor of science in biology, and it wasn't enough. All that sacrifice, all those years, and I found myself shut out. To say I was disappointed or disillusioned doesn't even begin to describe what I was feeling.

It took a while, but after I stopped feeling sorry for myself, it was time to make some plans. I decided to apply again. It was worth one more try. I still wanted, more than ever, to be a doctor.

Applying to medical school is a yearlong process that takes stamina and determination. There are multiple applications and each one has multiple essay questions. I didn't want to go through it again, but I knew I had to.

The same feelings came back to me from my twenties when I would look around every position in the company and ask, "Do I want that job?" I didn't want another job. I wanted this job. I couldn't believe it had taken me all those years to figure out what job I wanted, and now I couldn't have it. I had to try one more time.

Life changed that year. I returned to school for some additional courses while I went through the application process a second time. Now, I had more free time and even found a boyfriend.

Again, rejection letters were starting to come in, but there was still hope. I had been placed on the waiting list at Mount Sinai. And then a big surprise—an unexpected pregnancy left me with a baby on the way.

I was thirty-five years old and had wanted to be a mother for many years. I just never thought the opportunity would present itself while I was in the midst of the medical school application process and without a husband.

After the shock wore off, my new boyfriend made his position clear. He would never tell me what to do and this was clearly my decision, but he didn't want any part of it. He thought he would be further along in his life at this point, and didn't envision a child yet.

Just because I got pregnant once, didn't mean it would ever happen again. I was scared to death, but knew having this baby was the only decision for me. And for many of us, it's never the right time and there's never enough money and not enough space and yet it all works out. I just held on to the belief that it would work out somehow.

In order to make it work, I moved back in with my parents. My family was very excited to welcome their first grandchild. Let me just say this—It's one thing to have a support system and a cheering section, it's another to have medical insurance and an income.

My life was in such turmoil that I needed to get assistance from welfare in order to be able to birth my son. I was in limbo. No one was going to hire a pregnant me and I still didn't know where I stood with medical school.

I was accepted to Mount Sinai School of Medicine three weeks before school started. The call came in on a Friday evening. It was a hot, July day in New York, and my five-month-pregnant body was not happy. I was lying on the living room floor with my feet up on the couch hoping to relieve ankle swelling when the kitchen phone rang.

In 1986, phones were still attached to walls. I knew my parents were both upstairs with an extension line and was hoping one of them would answer the phone. One ring, two rings, three rings, annoyed, I rolled myself over, got up off the floor and answered the phone at the same time as my mother. "Hello," we said in stereo.

A man on the other end of the line asked to speak to me. I recognized the voice but couldn't place it. In that instant, I was going through everyone in my mind, mentally flipping through a Rolodex. It came flooding to me at the exact time he announced himself and I went weak in the knees, placing an added burden on my swollen ankles!

"This is Jay Cohen," he said. *Jay Cohen, the director of admissions at Mount Sinai?* screamed through my brain. "You know why I'm calling," he said with a smile in his voice. "Jay," I said, "I need to hear the words." And in that instant he said the words that changed my life. "Susan, the Mount Sinai School of Medicine would like to extend an invitation to you to join their graduating class of 1990. Are you still interested?" After I stopped crying, I choked out a "yes!" Baby or no baby, I knew I had to keep moving forward. I had no idea what was in store.

I had three weeks to pull it together. I couldn't live in the dorm because I was now pregnant. I didn't have furniture. I didn't even have maternity clothes that were appropriate to be worn in public. There was a lot that needed to be sorted out in a short period of time.

My mother and I hit every tag sale on Long Island. Within weeks I had a beautifully furnished apartment, proving that beauty truly is in the eye of the beholder. My baby's crib was old and worn and cost me twenty-five dollars. I bought a new mattress and new bedding and it was beautiful to me. Ryan slept in it until he was two years old and the slats starting falling out on one side. I turned that side to the wall until I could afford a twin-sized bed.

My two bedroom dressers were purchased for seventy-five dollars. Circa 1950, they were considered old and worn in the eighties. They are beautifully crafted and what are now considered "vintage." Those two pieces have been incorporated into my spa and serve as a constant reminder of what you can accomplish when you set your mind to it.

My beautiful son, Ryan, was born on a Sunday morning two days before the start of Christmas vacation. I technically missed two days of school to deliver a baby. I came back in January as a brand new mother and got back in step with my medical school colleagues. They were refreshed from vacation and ready to start a new semester. I was exhausted.

One Day at a Time

Medical school is one of the most demanding educational experiences in the world. Motherhood is one of the most physically and emotionally demanding experiences in the world. I combined them. I don't know how because a lot of it is a blur. I know I said I did it with everybody's help, but I was the one in the pit day after day, hour after hour.

There were times when I barely got through the day. I never made plans. People would make plans for tomorrow or next week. I could only make plans for the day. I couldn't even look to tomorrow, it was too overwhelming. There were some days where I felt like I was getting through hour by hour. I remember sitting next to someone in the classroom one day when Ryan was a few months old. I looked at this girl and said, "I can't wait until tomorrow." She got all excited,

"What's tomorrow?" I answered, "It won't be today. I have had enough of today." It was sad, but true.

Did you ever want to just walk away? Have you ever been so sick and tired that you just wanted to close the door, put the key on the porch and walk away? There were plenty of times that I wanted to quit. In my second year of medical school, my good friend completed her MBA training from Harvard. She graduated and tripled her income.

I still had two years to go and had a two-year-old who was getting angry that I wasn't home with him. I was despondent. I could have walked away at that point and I actually gave it serious consideration. But even after my earning a bachelor of science in biology and two years of medical school at Mount Sinai, I wasn't trained to do much.

I owed more than $60,000 and had a son that was relying on me for a life. I was so exhausted that I could have easily just walked away. It was perseverance alone that kept me going.

My mother gave me some great advice. "Susan, no matter how crazy the day gets, that day will end, and tomorrow will be a brand new day." And that got me through many a hard day. I knew the day was going to end and I would have a new chance at craziness the next day. It's a great lesson for life because every day is a new opportunity to make brand new decisions and re-evaluate the decisions you made the day before.

So how do you eat an elephant? One bite at a time. I'm sure you've heard this saying. The lesson is to break up your larger goal into smaller, more easily accomplished parts. I had never heard this saying when I was combining medical school and motherhood, but I can tell you first hand that it works.

When I knew that all I had to do was make it through that day, I had the strength and the stamina to do it. I once heard Don Imus refer to his sobriety in the same fashion. He explained that if he thought he could never drink again for the rest of his life, it would have been too overwhelming and he would never been able to accomplish it. Instead, his goal was to not drink for one day. He was able to manage one day at a time. As of 2013, he has been sober for twenty-six years.

I never allowed myself to look ahead the four years to graduation day. But on that day, one of the proudest of my life, as I held on to Ryan with one hand and accepted my diploma with the other, it was much easier to look back.

Perseverance is the vital component to every success story. I was far from the smartest person in my medical school class, but I made it through and am successful today because I wouldn't give up. It's hard to have the stamina to face a workload that seems insurmountable or obstacles that seem to grow in front of your eyes. I wish I could tell you it was easy. All I can say is, it's worth it.

Taking a Lesson From a Stranger

When I drive to work in the summer mornings, I sometimes pass an elderly gentleman taking a walk just before the entrance ramp to the highway. He walks with a cane and a limp. From his gait, I suspect he is recovering from a stroke.

One morning, as I passed him, he stopped walking and just stood motionless in the same spot. There was traffic behind me so I could only see him in my rear view mirror and I had no choice but to get on the highway. I got off the next exit and circled back to make sure he was okay.

I found him sitting on a small fence at the corner of the street. My suspicions were confirmed when I asked if he needed me to drive him home. A previous stroke had left him with speech impairments so he couldn't really have a conversation, but he gave me a smile and a thumbs up. He was clearly determined to continue his walk. What an inspiration, I thought to myself.

But the true power of his perseverance revealed itself to me on another morning. I couldn't believe my eyes when I passed him by on a cold January morning walking his same route. If there were ever a time when an elderly stroke victim could take a break it would be a January morning in Connecticut. This man is bound and determined to regain as much mobility as he can. What perseverance. We can all take a lesson.

Breaking New Ground

When I started my business in 2002, I was very naïve. I never dreamed my qualifications and accomplishments wouldn't be enough. Botox cosmetic procedures had just been approved and I wanted to offer them as one of my services. I called Allergan, the manufacturer, and explained I had opened a medical spa in Connecticut and would like to offer Botox to my patients.

She asked, "Are you a dermatologist or a plastic surgeon?" I proudly explained my background was in emergency medicine and she politely said, "I'm sorry, Doctor, but you don't qualify for our product."

I was astounded. How could it be that I didn't qualify? Clearly I had performed much more invasive procedures in the emergency room over the years than injecting Botox into small forehead muscles. To compound my confusion, I knew nurses who worked for plastic surgeons were the ones doing the injections in many practices, freeing up the surgeon to be in the operating room. How could a nurse be qualified but I wasn't?

The reality was this decision had nothing to do with my qualifications as a physician. This was a decision of exclusivity. I wasn't part of what was coined the "core" group of physicians deemed qualified—dermatologists, plastic surgeons, and ophthalmologists. I was trying desperately to move my business forward and I knew this was a service I needed to offer in order to be competitive. My medical spa business would have no credibility without this service.

At the same time, I was also facing an uphill battle with my insurance company. Medical malpractice carriers did not want to insure me to perform any cosmetic procedures because I was out of my specialty. If I went back to the emergency room, I would have no problem getting coverage for invasive procedures, but no one wanted to take a chance that an emergency-trained physician could inject a medication into specific forehead muscles. *Getting this business launched had more obstacles than I thought.*

I called Allergan once a month for three years. Every month a very polite young lady would tell me the same thing. I'm not qualified. I refused to believe it. I tried everything— explaining my qualifications, explaining my extensive medical training, asking to speak to supervisors, but none of it worked. I never got past the gatekeeper.

One day a man answered the phone. I guess he had never come across this request because he was confused and thought I was a consumer looking for a doctor in my area. When I explained that I *was* the doctor and I was trying to learn how to inject Botox, he was very apologetic and gave me another number to call, instructing me to ask for the telephone number of the sales representative in my area.

Here was my big chance. One phone call later I was writing down the number of the local representative. I remember staring at that name and number in total disbelief. Three years of perseverance finally paid off.

Today, Botox is one of my biggest revenue generators. My medical spa is thriving, and I have helped thousands of women get rid of unwanted wrinkles because I refused to give up when someone said, "No."

Also, after three years of fighting with the insurance company, I finally stopped asking politely for additional coverage. I wrote a letter asking that Botox be added to my list of services. I enclosed my training certificate and, voila— coverage! Three years of fighting ended, just like that.

Where would I be if I had given up at the two-year mark? Where would I be if my mother listened to the second dentist, or the third, or the fourth? Where would I be if I listened to forty-two medical schools the first time around? I went on to be an emergency room physician. Over the years, I treated thousands of patients and saved hundreds of lives. Where would all those people be? And where will you be tomorrow based on the decisions you make today?

A Final Thought

As I come to the end of this book, I would like to leave you with one last thought. Sometimes, even when you've done everything you possibly can, you will still find yourself living in turmoil.

When I was giving examples about figuring out the rules of the game, I spoke about my difficulty passing the national board exam. As you know, I did crack the code and I did pass the exam, but there was more to that story. When it came time for my third and final attempt, I was too humiliated to take the exam at Mount Sinai with the students of the next class. I made arrangements to take it at Stony Brook University Hospital on Long Island rather than in the city. My sister lived about thirty minutes away, so I could sleep at her house and take the exam where no one knew me.

When I woke up the morning of the exam, it was pouring raining. It was the kind of rain that comes down so hard you could barely see the car in front of you. It was like going through a carwash. The windshield wipers could hardly keep up.

Even though I allowed time for the weather, I was stuck in bumper-to-bumper traffic and arrived at the hospital with only minutes to spare. The campus is large and confusing and I was lost and panicked, not to mention soaked.

The test started at 8:30 a.m., and if you weren't signed in and seated by then you were not eligible to take the exam. They closed the doors. That meant if I didn't get to that room in time, I was out of medical school.

I was running all over the hospital, flagging down security guards and anyone who would point me in the right direction. I was shaking and crying. *Dear God, please, after preparing for a year, please don't let my dream slip away because of traffic and rain.* A security guard not only pointed me in the right direction but walked me to the room as well. Actually, we ran. I signed in at 8:27 a.m.

By the time I got to my seat, the test had already started. People were already furiously answering questions. I could hear pages turning. I composed myself, took a deep breath and opened the booklet. I knew the answer to the first question, and the second, and the third. I knew in that instant I was going to pass that exam. I did pass and with flying colors. And my life changed.

My final thought to you is simply this: When all seems lost, sit down, take a deep breath, and answer the first question.

The Take-Away

If you want something badly enough you have to be willing to do whatever it takes to get it. Period.

Epilogue

Everything will be all right in the end. If it's not all right, it is not yet the end.

— Patel, Hotel Manager, The Best Exotic Marigold Hotel

For years I minimized my greatness and hid my story. I viewed every accomplishment and every defeat as an isolated incident. Writing this book has helped me realize the power of my story, because it belongs to every woman. My experiences are unique to me, but my story belongs to all of us.

If you know what it's like to fall down and get back up, my story is your story. If you know what it's like to persevere through exhaustion to accomplish a goal, my story is your story. If you know what it's like to question your own worth, or to have a dream so big you are embarrassed to share it with anybody, my story is your story.

When you let the world see you at your worst and at your best without making excuses, no one can hurt you. You have told them everything and so have nothing to hide. This is what I have accomplished so far. What's in store for you?

Go share your story.

Acknowledgements

Silent gratitude isn't much use to anyone.
— G.B. Stern

When you start writing a book, you think the project belongs just to you and eventually, an editor. By the time you're finished writing the book, you realize it's you, the editor, and a long list of people. People who gave you ideas; people who gave you encouragement; people who checked on your progress—which gave you encouragement; people who corrected your first draft; people who corrected your second draft; people who let you speak for their organizations. And so on, and so on. Here are my people and my heartfelt thanks.

Thank you Paul Fedorko for helping me put together my first book proposal and getting me truly excited that I could really take what was swirling around in my head and put it into someone's hands. In the relay race of book writing, you handed off the first baton and got me off to a running start.

A special thank you goes to Henry DeVries, Devin DeVries, Joni McPherson and the entire team at at Indie Books International for helping me cross the finish line, book in hand. I so appreciate your hard work, dedication to my project, and attention to detail. Your editorial suggestions substantially improved my manuscript and your sense of humor helped me brainstorm a title that eluded me for a year. I have a better book because of you.

I would like to thank Jillian Murphy and Colleen Marr for editing my first draft. In its infancy, my manuscript was short and raw. Your thoughtful comments and keen eye for typos helped give me a firm foundation from which to build.

Special thanks to Mary Jane Fortin, Dr. Madeline Heilman, Kathy McShane, and Randye Kaye for reading my manuscript and offering advance praise. Approval from women of your caliber means the world to me. Thank you so much for taking time out of your busy schedules to read my manuscript, offer thoughtful suggestions, and align yourself with my message. Girls rule!

I appreciate the many contributions made by Susan Keane Baker. As a past president of the National Speakers Association – CT (NSA) she started a Speakers Mastermind group to help individuals qualify for membership. Thank you for believing in me and recommending me as a speaker on more than one occasion. But most of all, thank you for poring over my second draft on a coast to coast red eye, when you could have gotten some much needed sleep. Your encouragement helped reassure me that I had a powerful message worthy to be shared with the world.

I so appreciate the encouragement and support of Kathy McShane while qualifying for membership in the NSA. We started as accountability buddies in the Speakers Mastermind and quickly grew into friends. I am especially thankful for that.

Victoria Vinton, your talent and creativity helped me put together my tips booklet and now book cover. You made both projects fun, no matter how many tweaks were involved. You are a gifted graphic designer, making the world a better place —one creative design at a time.

Thank you to my fellow board members at the Madison Chamber of Commerce for following my progress, encouraging my journey, showing up to my speaking engagements and for the overall high praise you have all heaped upon me. I'm so happy to be a member of the best board of directors in the world! A special thank you goes to Eileen Banisch, Craig Bernard, Kathy Dann and Carlene Weis for arranging speaking engagements to help me get my message out. You guys rock!

Jessica Brigham, thank you for helping me make sense of WordPress so I could get my Try to Triumph website up and running. And for being the cheeriest 24/7 tech support person ever. But most of all, thank you for taking the most beautiful picture of me for my book cover. I'm so glad we share that bond.

Nancy Juetten, my mentor and now my friend, I couldn't have done it without you. First you changed my bio and then you changed my life. With your guidance, I took a five chapter idea and turned it into a thirteen chapter book. Your generosity of spirit is overwhelming. You truly practice what you preach—lift as you climb. With your love, support and guidance, my star is rising. Thank you, my friend.

Laura Ardito and Trish Messina, my two dearest friends from birth—literally. We have shared a lifetime— childhood sleep-overs, boyfriends, marriages, divorces, births, deaths, child rearing, child launching, advanced degrees, entrepreneurship, successes, failures, and everything in-between. Ours is a friendship that has withstood it all and will be with me to my last day. You've kept my secrets, forgiven my mistakes, and championed my successes. You've seen me at my best and at my worst and loved me every step. I couldn't love you two more if I tried.

Diane Zorich—my greatest supporter, my confidant, my friend. Thank you for everything you do and everything you are. Thank you for bringing my business to a different level. Thank you for your wisdom and your compassion. Thank you for your fierce loyalty. Thank you for telling me when I'm wrong and validating me when I'm right. Thank you for helping me see myself through your eyes. Thank you for being my friend in the truest sense of the word. You'll never get rid of me.

They say you can't pick your family. Mom, Dad, Danny, Kathleen, Kelly, and Robert, if I got to pick, I would pick you all. Thank you Dad for sending me feathers from heaven to let me know you are still by my side. I miss you every day. Mom, thank you for your love and support throughout my entire life, but especially through medical school. I would have never made it through with a baby, without you.

Danny, Kathleen, Kelly, and Robert—we are all so different and yet the same, bound by family memories. Thank you all for your love and support; encouraging me through medical school; babysitting when I needed a break; helping me find humor in overnight shifts; supporting me through the scary new business start-up years. Every small piece of support brought me to this place today.

Thank you Danny for being my partner in crime long ago, when we were the only two children in the family, and I was the only one who could read. We will have that bond forever. Your love and support helped me navigate a divorce, when I thought I'd never be happy again. Kathleen, thank you for being there through the child rearing years. There were summers when Ryan slept at your house more than he slept at our own. Thank you for loving him, as if he were your third son.

Kelly—it has been a gift to share so much with you. How many sisters can say they went to the same college, same medical school and now both have cosmetic practices? I think we might be it! Your love, friendship and sense of humor helped me get through many difficult days. Thank you for always being there for me—for being a shoulder to cry on, a friend to laugh with, and for sharing inside jokes no one else would get.

Thank you, Robert, for being a good uncle. You were there for Ryan from the start, even teaching him to shave, perhaps a little early at five. But the pictures are still good for a laugh today. You were a father figure in the early years, when Ryan didn't have one. I will appreciate that forever.

Thank you my beautiful son, Ryan, for choosing me as your mom. I fell in love with you before I even saw your face. You were my first true love, and I was yours. You were my reason. The reason I persevered through exhaustion to finish medical school, the reason I tried to be a better person, the reason I aimed high every day. You have been one of the greatest joys of my life. Thank you for your unwavering love and support, and for being the best son in the world.

My last and deepest thanks go to my husband, Dennis Perkins, my pack of two. The last fifteen years with you have been the best years of my life. From the beginning, you enveloped me with generosity, wisdom, humor, encouragement, and true love. Thank you for believing in me when I said I wanted to write a book and encouraging me through many bad attempts. Thank you for being my biggest cheerleader and supporter, every day. You helped me find my voice and speak out loud. Thank you for finding me and for choosing to spend the rest of your life with me. I didn't know what love was, until you loved me. You are my inspiration, my motivation, and my salvation.

How to Get in Touch

Dr. Susan O'Malley has turned the success strategies outlined in her book into an inspirational keynote presentation. She travels from Madison, CT to bring her "How to Turn Try into Triumph" message to appreciative audiences, and looks forward to the opportunity to deliver her motivational message to you.

Dr. O'Malley delivers personalized, practical content, while outlining a simple process anyone can apply to create their own unstoppable results. Her story of overcoming obstacles speaks to anyone who has pursued a seemingly impossible goal.

She welcomes invitations to share her content via teleseminar, webinar and to live audiences that are serious about taking bold steps forward to realize success on their own terms. To learn more about Dr. O'Malley or to book her to speak at your next event, please visit www.sonasmedspa.com and www.trytotriumph.com.

She can also be reached by phone at (203) 245-2227 or email at somalleymd@sonasmedspa.com.

Novels by Trisha R. Thomas

Nappily Ever After
Roadrunner
Would I Lie to You
Nappily Married
Nappily Faithful
Nappily In Bloom
Un-Nappily In Love
Nappily About Us

First Paperback Edition
Published by Face Press

Nappily entangled

Trisha R. Thomas

Face Press

Los Angeles, CA

Chapter one

THIRTEEN YEARS EARLIER Sirena Lassiter and Jake 'JayP' Parson had made beautiful music together, resulting in a hit record and the birth of a healthy baby boy named Christopher. She'd left the latter out of her résumé. She'd also failed to mention this fact to Jay, not revealing the truth until only a few short years ago.

She'd kept it from him even after they'd reunited with another hit record and a movie they'd starred in together. He was the co-star, she liked to point out. Just teasing. He'd always be the star of her heart. She'd always love him, even though he vowed to never forgive her.

It was understandable. Any man would be angry. He'd missed out on raising his son for ten long years. But now Jay had custody of him. He and his annoying wife, Venus, were raising Christopher together, as if Sirena were dead and gone. They should be thanking her everyday instead of pretending she was invisible.

Not a single letter, no phone call, nothing. She'd given Jay a son. Who cared if the birth announcement was a decade late? If it hadn't been for Christopher, he and his wife probably never would've had their own children. They'd had trouble being fruitful and multiplying.

It was a biological fact. Research proved once a family had the child they'd always wanted in the home, they easily conceived with a second, or third, as if fertility had never been an issue. Jake wanted a son. Now he had two for the price of one.

They could thank her for that, but she knew they wouldn't. They could keep Christopher. She'd take the cash instead. The money Jay had stolen from her in royalties while she'd been away would do just fine.

At least that's what she understood when she approached the music label. Apparently there'd been a mix up in the accounting record. Her royalties were being sent to another address on file. It took them a week to get back to her.

"Ms. Lassiter, we have the address where the last checks were sent," the office lady said in a nasal tone. She read it off.

"That's not my address," Sirena blurted. "Don't know how you messed this up, but I want my money."

"So you've never lived at this address?"

"Never. Not even close."

"And you have no idea who the address belongs to?"

Sirena stayed quiet. She knew exactly who the address belonged to. She'd spent enough time there, parked in front of their grand Gingerbread house, watching and imagining what her life would've been as Jay's first lady instead of Venus.

"It's not my fault you sent the checks to the wrong address. I want my royalty payments, or you will hear from my lawyer."

"Ms. Lassiter, our apologies. We'll get to the bottom of this and let you know what we can do to fix it."

"Fixing it only requires one thing, money in my pocket. This is a travesty. How're you just going to give my hard earned royalties to somebody else?" Jay had taken enough from her. First her son, and now every dollar she'd earned for the last three years.

"I assure you, we'll get to the bottom of this," the woman said with confidence.

"Fine, you have one week." She had no real choice in the matter. She couldn't afford a lawyer and she certainly couldn't knock on Jay's door and demand what was owed to her, seeing as how she couldn't come within five hundred feet of the Parson's home, or make any contact whatsoever with Venus and her brood, or she'd be violating her parole.

Something as innocent as shopping in the same grocery store as Miss Holier-Than-Thou was an extreme no-no. But Sirena had a good reason.

She'd gone inside the over priced gourmet market purely out of necessity. Yes, she would admit she had no business being in their high priced enclave of the rich and barely famous. She could see how it would look if she'd been caught. They'd think she was following Venus again, when really it was an unsuspecting Christopher she'd been interested in. The past few weeks had been spent watching him at his football practice, all purely innocent.

It was dangerous but worth every minute. Her boy had grown up so much; handsome and strong like his father. She got to see him hang out with his friends and knew which girl made him turn on his megawatt smile, all from a distance of course.

After sitting for hours in her car nursing a bottled water, she had to use the restroom and there was nowhere else to go. The store in the exclusive neighborhood was a whole lot better than the mini-marts where she was staying, so why not pick up a few essentials? She perused the aisles without a care in the world, lost in the fancy organic offerings. The beauty section was her favorite.

So much to choose from. One of the bottles caught her eye. She read the ingredients before flipping it over to see the price. Steep for such a small amount. More than any of her other products. Weren't they all making the same glorious claims on every colorful package, promising soft, silky, shiny hair?

The big block letters going down the side simply read COURAGE. On another, the word was UNITY. On another, it read WISDOM. She unscrewed the top and sniffed. She poured a tiny amount on her fingertips. Nice. For a few seconds she felt light headed.

She smiled and recapped the bottle before plopping it into her basket. She could officially call herself a product junkie, a user, an addict who'd do anything for the right mix of manageability. She couldn't resist carrying it to the checkout stand with nothing else than an apple in her cart. Even the damn apple cost two dollars.

As she was paying at the register that's when she saw Venus browsing through a magazine.

Sirena didn't bother with a bag and bolted for the exit. "Oh, excuse me." She bumped into an older man and held out her hands in apology. She hadn't seen him, desperate to clear the door before Venus looked up.

"It wasn't your fault." The white haired gentleman paused with a twinkle in his eye. "I wasn't seeing straight. Can I just say, you smell delicious?" The scent from the bottle still hung in the air.

Her hand went to her chest, overwhelmed from hearing her first compliment from a man in years. "It's not me. I mean, not yet. But thank you." She hugged the bottle feeling some kind of kinship. "You have a nice day."

"You too, dear."

Her rapid heartbeat made her think she was about to have a stroke. It took her several minutes to calm down before starting her car and making a clean getaway. She'd hoped it was a clean get-away. It took several minutes of checking the rearview mirror until she was sure the police weren't behind her.

Once she'd gotten safely back home there were no regrets. She was grateful she'd gone there, even after being nearly caught. Watching Christopher, seeing who his friends were, and catching the occasional smile cross his lips, had all been worth it.

The other reward for risking her freedom was the bottle she held in her hands. The sweet aroma called COURAGE Moisturizing Conditioner made her forget about what could've happened if Venus saw her.

Sirena had very little money for such luxuries. The court required her to pay restitution to her victim—as if Venus needed her chump change. Wasn't she married to a successful man who'd given her the right to sit at home and do nothing but have babies?

Sirena had already paid her penance to society. Two and a half long years. But no, what little money she earned calling people on the phone to ask them if they needed steam cleaning on their pet stained carpet was split between the poor little rich girl and her rent at the halfway house. She hated living there but had nowhere else to go.

The day she was released from the Georgia Women's Correctional Center she had to beg her cousin to pick her up. When she saw Shay's blue rusted out Ford pull up to the gate blasting music with the windows down, relief crawled over her. Who else did she have? No one.

Shay hopped out the car and threw her arms around Sirena. "Oh my goodness, you look a hot mess. They don't let you get relaxers in prison?"

"No. Those ladies would be trying to blind and poison each other. You know how strong those chemicals are."

"So you have to walk around looking like that everyday? Well, I'm just glad you're free. Seriously though, our first stop should be the salon. You need to get a relaxer on that kinky mess like yesterday." Shay drove with two hands on the wheel and hardly looked in Sirena's direction or she would've seen her mouth twisted with disgust. Talking to her like they were besties after letting nearly three years pass without so much as a birthday card. Her cousin had only visited once the whole time she was gone, and now she wanted to act like she cared one iota about Sirena's appearance or wellbeing.

It was a hot August day while they drove with the windows down. She almost wished the prison had kept her until the days turned cooler. Of course Shay's car had no air conditioning. They drove the hour-long ride listening to the radio and not talking. Hearing the new music from artists she thought would never survive, gave her renewed inspiration. *Good for them. Good for me too.* It was possible she could get a record deal and get back into the studio again.

"Still one of the most requested hits here at Hot 102.8," the radio host announced. "JayP featuring Sirena, *Call Me.*" The song intro kicked in with a strong bass and Sirena's voice flowing in with the hook.

Sirena shook her head with disbelief. The local radio stations didn't reach past the prison walls. "Wow. This song Jay and I recorded before everything happened, most requested—I had no idea."

"That's everybody's jam. I thought you knew," Shay said over the loud whistling wind blowing against their faces from the open windows. With the steady heat, it was doing them no good.

"Maybe if someone told me I would've known. Seems everyone was too busy living their lives."

"Sorry about that, cousin, but the gas alone to make this ride was a grip. Times have been seriously tight. Now that you're out, maybe I can work for you again." Shay snapped her gum. She'd been Sirena's assistant when she was a shining star. The minute Sirena's light dimmed, friends and relatives made themselves scarce. When she couldn't afford to keep overpaying Shay for doing pretty much of nothing, she'd disappeared too.

"For now I just want to chill. I'm not trying to hustle my way back in the limelight. I have other things more important on my mind." Sirena had thanked Shay for the ride and was grateful to be free. Afterwards, she hadn't called anyone or asked for any favors. The time would come soon enough.

Until then she ignored the cracked tiles on her bathroom walls and the rusty water coming out the spout that would've ordinarily made her squeal. This was home for now. She was happy to bask in the small joys, things she couldn't have when she was locked up like a warm shower without twenty other women beside her.

She unscrewed the top on her new purchase and inhaled the scent before pouring a small amount in her palm. She felt sensual like she was lying naked on a beach with the warmth of the sun and the cool breeze of the ocean. Her entire body tingled with the fragrance.

She stuck her head under the pulsating water before massaging the ingredients into her wild curls. A few brief seconds later her eyelids were fluttering with joy. Her imagination was powerful these days transporting her anywhere she wanted to be, something she learned in prison. Your dreams were all you had.

The warm shower raced over her head and body. In an instant she was kissing him, the man who'd almost made her happy, feeling his caress around her waist while she massaged his wide shoulders.

"I'm back. I promise to be good," she said out loud turning her face up to the jets with her eyes closed. The water sprayed hard but she deserved it. She'd been a bad girl. "You know I wasn't in my right mind. I'm better now."

His image was fading. Another face came into view. This man wasn't the one she wanted to see. His passionate kiss wasn't the one she wanted to feel. Her heartbeat quickened imagining his voice in her ear. "Damn, you taste good."

Within seconds she was seized with an overpowering pulse through her body. An orgasm she had no control over. *None*. She placed her hands on the walls for stability. The water continued to roll over her face. The waves still rippling at her core. It took a few minutes before she could let go. She felt for the shower knob with her eyes still closed, twisting until it turned off.

The air was thick with steam. The mirror covered with fog. She shivered from his memory, fresh and open as if they'd truly just made love. As much as she tried to hate him, she equally craved his touch.

He wanted to visit, he'd said in his letters, but it wasn't the smartest thing to do. He was taking a risk by writing her. Even with signing the letters under a different name, there were ways of tracing these things. He had too much to lose. That was the part that made her want to hate him even more. If you really cared about someone, nothing else mattered.

She was ready to climb into bed with nothing on but the towel she'd used to dry herself when someone knocked on the door. She already knew it was the jailer, that's what she called him for being unnecessarily interested in every single thing she did.

The bulky man stood a polite distance away. "Someone heard talking. You realize it's after seven. No phone, no TV, no music."

Sirena pushed the door open for him to get a good view, dropping the towel for shock value. "I don't have a TV, a phone, or a radio."

"No singing or chanting, nothing. All right. Silence after seven. It's a simple rule."

She put her finger to her lips. "Then you should stop talking."

He stepped toward her filling in the doorway with his wide shoulders. "Don't start with me. You follow the rules and we won't have any problems. Understood?"

"Yes," Sirena said. "Perfectly." She closed the door slowly to show him she wasn't afraid of him. She wanted to shout from the rooftops like Diana Ross that she was coming out to take over the world. There was so much to do. She believed her life could start fresh and new but first she had to deal with a few loose ends.

Chapter two

"I'M NOT LETTING some other man raise my kids. So you can forget it," Jake said with a pleading expression in the mirror.

Too much, pull back, he told himself before trying again. "I'm not letting some other man raise my kids. So you can forget it." This time it felt right. He'd been sitting on set for the last hour going over his scene and didn't mind. Getting his emotion on point for his character would only be in his favor. He understood how Blackmon should feel. Jake could only imagine the same devastation if his wife confessed to having an affair, then asked for a divorce.

Thank God, he would never know. Venus loved him unconditionally. She'd proven it consistently over the years of their relationship. Lately she seemed preoccupied. Understandable with a new business. He'd been very supportive of her new venture, appreciative there was something to keep her busy while he worked over two thousand miles away in Los Angeles. Working was what a man was supposed to do. Providing for his family was his number one priority. He just so happened to enjoy his work. Acting was a dream come true. Sure he'd started out with music. Either way he was expressing the art of entertainment. He didn't want to trade in one for the other so he kept his music alive with writing and logging in notes and melodies on his off hours. He could honestly say he was living life at full tilt.

Out of fairness, he offered whatever encouragement he could in his wife's journey. Venus always supported him throughout his career. She held down the fort while he was free to soar. It hadn't always been that way. His star status had taken a few dips and dives. More lows than highs. He'd lost count. What mattered was that he'd survived the lean times.

A short stint as the face or in this case, the body of Calvin Klein, kept him in the black for a good long time. Private school for Mya, a huge home in the suburbs, dance, piano, and the art of tea lessons added up. He remembered seeing himself half naked on a hundred foot tall billboard on 5th Avenue in downtown Manhattan. His six-pack abs had only needed the slightest airbrushing. He'd worked hard on that body. He'd been proud to look up and know he was worth every penny he'd been paid. After that it was hocking chips, soda, and beer in thirty-second commercials.

Next was the reality show, the last stop to losing what was left of his dignity. America wanted to know what the ex-hip-hop star was up to. Letting an entire film crew scuff up his shiny wood floors every day to film his wife and children was the point of his new low. Not quite rock bottom but close enough to snap some sense into him. If he wanted to get back in the light he had to come out of the darkness. He had to pick up the phone, get on a plane to Hollywood, and knock on some doors. The same doors that shut him out only a few years earlier might be willing to budge.

If he had a dollar for every hour he waited, standing, sitting, or pacing for a director or agent to see him, he could've been rich already. Eventually, Gayle Friedman, a young new executive called him back to read for the role of Jeremiah Blackmon, a lawyer who played on the good side yet always found himself cleaning up the dirt of his clients.

He understood Jeremiah Blackmon's flaws, the things he had to do for the sake of keeping a roof over his family's head. Jake understood all too well the sacrifice of a good man's conscience. Losing sleep over decisions made even though everyone would benefit in the long run, at least the people that mattered.

"Jay, you're up." The production assistant with a short red pixy cut and shiny red framed glasses stood next to him while he faced the mirror. Jake wished he could remember her name. "You look great. You always look great, come on," she said lifting off the linen bib that the make up artist had left around his neck.

"Be right there." He checked his phone one more time to make sure he hadn't missed his wife's call. It was three o'clock.

They had an agreement that unless it was impossible, they would talk at the same time everyday. One of the important rules posted on signs everywhere in the studio, NO CELL PHONES meant if Venus didn't call in the next few minutes they wouldn't talk at all. The three-hour difference put a cramp in their communication big time. Venus hadn't called him back after he'd text and called. He wanted to check on Christopher's love life, but mostly he wanted to tell her how many lines he had in this week's script.

The hour-long drama had been picked up for another season and it looked like the writers and execs were securing his character's place in the thick of things. His storyline was rich with scandal and mayhem. He knew things were looking up when the Armani suits arrived in his trailer, custom fit to his athletic build. In a separate box were shirts and ties in vibrant shades with the scene numbers attached. Today was the purple shirt and light lilac tie underneath the charcoal gray three-button suit. He felt like a million bucks right then.

He tossed the phone back in the drawer and put himself back in Blackmon's shoes. The man was fighting for his marriage, his home, and his family. A custom suit wasn't going to make that kind of pain go away but he'd damn well look good while he navigated the waters.

The scene went smoothly. The director, Josh Bein, threw a loose arm over Jake's shoulder. "You're on all cylinders, brother. I wish everyone came prepared like you."

"Thanks, man. I appreciate the feedback. I'm just trying to be a rock star like you." Jake gave him a light nudge.

"In that case, you might want to hang out with some of us tonight. We're going to the Chateau. There's a couple of people you should definitely meet. Can't hurt to press the flesh."

Jake knew about the private club where the seriously high level executives hung out. The people who made the deals and decided a show's fate took their meetings there over aged whiskey and cigars.

"I'll put your name on the guest list."

"Yeah, definitely." Jake nodded appreciation. "I'll be there." Getting an invite to the exclusive Chateau was a big deal, something else he'd planned to share with his wife when she finally called.

When he got back to his trailer, his cell phone remained a blank screen. No missed calls. He dialed Christopher's cell phone, though there was a good chance he was going to wake him up.

"Yep, yep," he answered. "I made a touchdown, dad," he said groggily.

"Outstanding. I'm proud of you," Jake said. "I wish I could've been there."

"Me too," Christopher said turning solemn. "So maybe you can see me play this weekend."

Jake waited a breath before responding as if he had to think about it. "This weekend. I can't come this weekend, buddy. But I promise the minute I get a couple of days open I'm going to be there. So, is everything okay?" His inquiry was rushed. Kids weren't as sensitive about getting to the point like adults. They preferred to get on to the next thing.

"Yeah. Bliss and Mom went somewhere. Jezzy's here with all of us."

"Do me a favor and check on the twins and Mya anyway. Make sure the place is locked up, the back door especially."

"I always do, dad. You know I got this," Christopher said, reminding Jake he was the man in charge when his father wasn't home.

"Thanks, buddy. I love you and I'll talk to you soon."

"Love you too. See you this weekend."

"I'll try," Jake said before hanging up. He told himself to relax. Worrying about what he had little control over was bad on the skin. Stress was a death sentence in this business. Make-up could only cover so much. So far, he was a make-up artist's dream. A little dust of powder on his milk chocolate skin and he was ready for High Def in primetime.

The drive down Sunset Avenue was best enjoyed with his convertible top down. He pushed the button while the canvas folded automatically over his head and buried itself neatly in the compartment. The Porsche was a gift to himself for his birthday. That was one of the things he hadn't yet told Venus about, only because he knew what she'd say, boy-gone-wild asking for trouble.

True. He had gone without the things he enjoyed for too long; he couldn't see depriving himself any longer. Life was too short.

He wove up the narrow winding hill of Laurel Canyon as the sun started to set behind the mountains. The air was sweeter up here; he couldn't even pretend it wasn't. He'd tried to talk Venus into moving back to Los Angeles where they'd met, fell in love instantly, and started a family all in the same short year. He was born and raised in Cali.

The only reason they'd moved to Atlanta was to get away from a bad business deal, a homicide accusation, and affordability of a life without wondering how to pay their bills. Los Angeles was expensive. Triple the cost of the average city then multiply it times two. But things were different now. He could enjoy the fruits of his labor with sunshine and trips to the beach.

The kids would love it. At some point, Jake knew there'd be no more discussion in the matter. Just as he pressed the gas so effortlessly to get up the hill, he'd have to put his foot down about moving his family back to Cali. Going back to Cali, he hummed the song.

His phone rang through the speakers interrupting his singing. He answered without recognizing the number. "Hello."

"Mr. Parson, I'm calling from the accounting office of Revel Records. You remember we spoke earlier in the week about the missing royalty payments for Sirena Lassiter? Well the bank has confirmed those checks were deposited into an account with you as the holder." The woman's voice on the other end sounded like an autobot, one of those machines that called and spoke about the new candidates running for office.

"Okay. What can I do for you?" Jake still wasn't admitting to anything. He drove slower, easing his foot off the gas. He eventually pulled over completely.

"Miss Lassiter continues to inquire about her royalty payments which are due to her. We'd like to have a check for her to pick up as soon as possible before legal action is taken."

Jake rolled his eyes. That wasn't going to happen. Sirena was locked away for a long time for kidnapping his wife. She could make plenty of phone calls from behind her concrete walls but she wasn't going to be collecting on her share of missing royalty payments, he could guarantee that much.

"I'll look into it and get back to you," Jake said pulling his Porsche back onto the road. He wondered when, if ever, he was going to be free of Sirena Lassiter.

"So you have no idea where the royalty payments have gone?"

"I'll have to check with my accountant. Like I said, I'll investigate and give you a call back."

"I'd appreciate it, Mr. Parson. Have a nice day."

He was having a nice day, until that phone call reminding him of why he was concerned lately about Venus and the children. He didn't trust what Sirena was capable of, even from behind bars. She'd tried to hire someone before to do her dirty work, the last thing he wanted to do was give her any money to work with. He didn't believe she could be rehabilitated, at least not so soon.

When she was out of prison the money would be waiting for her. Maybe she'd appreciate it in twenty-five years. For now, she had no use for it.

VENUS
Chapter three

BLISS AND I HAD spent all night handing out samples of Two Sisters Organic Hair products to thousands of women at the Thrive Alive Conference. The hours were long but our business was growing and we were having a great time.

The doorbell rang. Another shipment was ready to go. I swung the door open to see George, the delivery guy, in his usual blue shirt and beige shorts, who liked to remind me he could rescue me from my life of suffering. Take me away from all this hard work and make an honest woman out of me. We'd ride away in his blue and white van and live happily ever after. Only problem, I was already an honest woman, married ten years, and knocking on wood for another ten. I wasn't greedy.

"Miss V, how you doing?" He smiled while holding his electronic tablet in hand. "You ready to make me the happiest man on earth?"

"Hey George," I smiled. "I don't think your wife would be too happy about that proposition. What do you think?"

Silence. George couldn't hide the shock and surprise sending both his eyebrows high on his usually mellow face by now wondering how I'd found out about the Missus. He wore no wedding band to speak of. A hint of wedded bliss had never passed his lips in all of his brief conversations on life, weather, and promises to sweep me off my feet. Then how did I know about his wife and his one and a half kids at home?

His usual flirty demeanor changed into professional status. He kept his brown eyes down while he scanned the packages into the system. "Anything else?"

The sudden coolness could've come from the cloud cover but I was guessing the temperature drop was from the iciness he was giving off.

"Feels like it might rain," I offered hoping to lighten the mood. He stayed sullen and silent.

Bliss arrived scooting past George as he was leaving. I took one of the recyclable shopping bags out of her arms to help.

"You let the cat out of the bag?" Bliss asked, already knowing the answer.

"You should've seen his face. I feel so guilty. He was so hurt."

"Oh please." Bliss tossed her braid over her shoulder with a dismissive air. "That'll teach him to stop acting a fool on customer's doorsteps. We're trying to run a business. And what about those poor lonely women who actually fall for his sweet talk? Trust me, you did the women of Georgie-porgie's route a favor. Kiss the girls and make them cry is his motto."

"I hope he doesn't stay mad a me. I was only joking with him. I didn't know he was going to get so defensive." The flirting was harmless, even kind of fun. Where else was I going to get attention from another man since my husband was too far away to do the honors? A girl needed compliments.

"Look at these Mangos on sale, two for a dollar." Bliss inhaled the sunset colored side of the fruit. "And look, the coconuts are ready to burst." She shook one. Juice sloshed around inside the hard shell. "You hear that? These will compliment my secret ingredient nicely."

"Ahuh."

She snapped to get my attention. "Come on. Who cares if his feelings are hurt? He's a big boy. And you know what our grandmother would say, don't stick your hand in the bees nest if you don't want to get stung. That's what his ass gets for always looking for free honey."

"We're not bees. We're human beings. And trust me, George was a long way away from getting any honey," I said before following her orders and sniffing the fruit.

Bliss had liked George. Unfortunately he made the mistake of rubbing her hand, touching her during one of his flirtatious sessions. She was able to read someone by merely a graze of skin. "Come on, stop with the gloomy mood," Bliss ordered after an awkward silence while slicing mango and peaches.

"You didn't see his face."

"You're seriously still thinking about George? Trust me, he's not thinking about you. You were guessing and he took the bait." Bliss turned away not wanting to admit what she saw in her mystical state was hardly a guess. She saw things. She called it spirit whispering. Like the Dog Whisperer, except she could communicate with other's through their higher spirit.

At first, I didn't want to believe it was possible for anyone to have such a gift, or curse in some instances. But I'd seen it first hand. She could read someone's thoughts and even impose new ones with her own.

Knowing what was on the mind of those around you was a scary proposition. Especially when they didn't have the best intentions. She claimed we all had an ability to trust the voice in our head and heart, but most of us shut it off out of fear. In some cases out of selfishness, caring about your own thoughts and ignoring everyone else's.

None of it was considered concrete information. If she had that kind of perfect vision we'd be rich already. So far we were making enough to keep moving forward. Organic ingredients were expensive. Websites, advertising, packaging, and our labor, which so far was free, all added up on the ledger.

"We already have a pantry full of coconuts. Where are we supposed to store more?" I said holding a chest full of the brown scratchy fruit. I walked to the cabinets and exposed the space where a normal kitchen stored food. In this kitchen a real meal hadn't been prepared in months, many months. Here we chopped, mushed, and blended the fruit and oils to a fine smooth texture for hair shampoos, conditioners, and hair moisturizer.

The idea of starting the natural hair products came after watching Bliss mix a concoction in the blender, a recipe for shampoo good enough to eat, had she not added the raw egg. I used it on my hair, the children's hair, and even dropped a bit of it into Jake's bottle of shampoo. The results were too amazing to ignore. Shiny clean hair without the residue, or being stripped dry.

I felt like one of those ads on late night television with demonstrations and touch and feel testimonials. *Moisturize, moisturize, moisturize.*

Whenever anyone asked about how I'd grown my natural hair, which was a huge conversation starter no matter where I went, I told anyone who was listening about the miracle formula my sister had created. I talked Bliss into making a batch that I could pour into a few plastic bottles and sell. Between my book club, carpoolers, and dance class moms, she had no choice but to make more. As quickly as she made it, I sold it.

Then one of the mothers asked, "What's the name of your product line?"

Right then and there the perfect name popped into my head. "Two Sisters," I answered with confidence, because that's what we were.

Bliss and I had found each other late in life. One short year earlier I hadn't known she existed. My father had an affair that resulted in a baby girl being born. I couldn't believe my sweet, lovable, solid father could do something so out of character. He supported Bliss and her mother but had never spoken of them, at least not to Timothy, my older brother, or me.

The secret was kept until Bliss showed up on my doorstep one spring morning out of the blue, announcing our kinship. I thought she was just another crazed fan since we were starring in our own reality show. I left no stone unturned having her investigated. Turns out she was authentic. Our Grandma Sarah had raised her and kept her secretly away from the rest of our family.

It took a minute or two to digest the information. All I could do was let the past be the past. Besides, I had a new sister. It really didn't get any better than that.

Our bond was immediate and strong as if we'd shared sad stories and triumphs all of our lives. And now we were in business together. The long struggling hours were compensated by late night laughter or a good emotional cry. More laughter than tears, definitely. We learned about each other and ourselves.

Her analysis, I was a classic need-to-pleaser. After much denial I finally agreed. I wasn't sure when the transition happened. Some kind of biological shift, I assumed, after surviving a couple of near death experiences. A kidnapping or two will do that to you. I'd gone from being the most self-absorbed person on earth, to being excessively compassionate about others. Or in Bliss's observation, desperate to be kind and lovable lest you be punished with bad Karma.

So far, so good. My life was intact. I knocked my knuckles on the wooden cabinet door after I closed it, still holding the coconuts. "This is ridiculous. We need a place to operate the business. The kitchen just isn't going to cut it anymore."

Bliss rolled her eyes knowing exactly what I was thinking. "Oh please. We can't afford rent. Not yet."

"Hold that thought." I held up my phone knowing it was Jake calling. I'd broken protocol by not calling him back the day before. Routine and structure were important to him.

"Hello my wonderful husband."

"Hello my sexy, beautiful, smart, amazing wife who doesn't know how to call her husband back."

"That's all?"

He laughed. "Let's see what else. Did I say sexy?"

"Yes. Good enough. Sorry about yesterday. We had this huge event. Potential customers everywhere," I said, grasping the phone tightly between my face and shoulder while I continued to store gigantic fruits.

"That's great. How's everything with the kids?" He asked, ignoring anything about the business. To him it was a hobby and nothing more.

"The kids are fine," I assured him.

This was our ritual. I pretended to be happy and he pretended to care. I also pretended to keep a tight run of the household. He wasn't comfortable unless he had an update of what everyone was doing. Mya had dance and soccer. Chris had football practice, piano, math club, and debate team. The twins thankfully hadn't embarked on any skills or talents that required transportation as of yet.

Though at three and half years old they could do toddler commercials just with their laughter alone. Lauren was the biggest ham. If she saw anything resembling a camera lens pointed in her direction, she smiled, ready for action.

I'd wondered what kind of effect having been the subjects of a reality show would eventually have on my poor babies.

"Chris sent me a text. He's still having girl problems. Did you talk to him yet?" Jake asked in a conspiratorial whisper. "I don't want his grades slipping worrying about—"

"Michelle."

"Milan," he reminded me.

"Right. Milan. Got it covered. She's been threatening to break up with him," I said recapping the drama. "I can't believe Chris is falling for that. Don't worry, I've got it under control."

He sighed relief. It was hard for him being so far away from his brood. He was proud of the status of being a good father. Being a dedicated dad was the new Hollywood fad. You could get the cover on a magazine just for walking the kids to school these days.

Speaking of which, I closed my eyes and hoped he didn't mention moving to Los Angeles again. The series he starred in was long running. His role however could be a short story. There was no such thing as a contract that couldn't be broken. I didn't want to pack up our lives and move to Los Angeles only to find out Jeremiah Blackmon had been killed off in episode ten.

Uprooting the crew from our home seemed like moving a mountain with bare hands. And now that Bliss and I had Two Sisters up and running, the odds were even less likely.

I blew a kiss-kiss through the phone and hung up grateful we didn't have to talk about our long distance love dilemma. He didn't need to know I hadn't made up the bed in weeks, okay, months. It wasn't important that I hadn't picked up my own laundry off the floor after I'd regularly chastised him for leaving his socks and underwear in a trail.

I wanted to be a better person while Jake was gone. I'd committed to meeting Mya and Christopher's teachers at school, taking cupcakes on my Friday, and donating bags of used clothing for the fundraising yard sale. Yet, I'd been missing in action. I was that mom who showed up with sunglasses and her baseball cap pulled low on her head to avoid scrutiny for picking up her kids so late. And yes, my baked goods came from the grocery bakery.

"Hey mom," Christopher came through the back door. He kissed me on the cheek. He had an incredible growth spurt over the summer and was already taller than Jake. His biological mother was long and lean. I hoped that was the only trait he carried of hers. The woman was seriously unstable. Sirena Lassiter was in prison for kidnapping and attempting to kill me. Sure people fantasized about another person's downfall but who tried to actually carry out a plan? Psychopaths, that's who.

We never talked about her. I knew Christopher would never forget about Sirena, but she was not my favorite subject. Hopefully, she wouldn't be bothering us again, at least not until 2035.

Christopher went straight for the refrigerator.

"Hey, wash your hands."

"Why, there's probably nothing to eat anyway?" He grabbed the only thing in the cabinet that hadn't fallen off a tree. "Why do you buy these things? They taste like dog biscuits."

"That's because they are dog biscuits." Bliss came from behind him and snatched the box turning it around to face him. The clear picture on the front was a tongue-wagging puppy.

"Can a man get some real food around here?" Christopher stormed off while Bliss and I giggled. He took his role very seriously as the man of the house while his dad was gone.

"My poor children are starving. I'm going to the store. Maybe I'll even fire up the stove and cook something."

"Miracles are good for the soul," Bliss said sweetly.

"Ha-ha." I grabbed the keys and my purse and scooted out the door. If I moved fast enough I could get a basket full of shopping done before it was time to pick up Mya from dance practice.

Chapter four

SIRENA SAT OUTSIDE the gate and watched the lights of the Gingerbread house upstairs. The one that was Christopher's bedroom was her only concern. Now that he was most likely alone she could send him the message. She'd already retyped it several times, checking to make sure she didn't sound desperate. She re-read it again. She reiterated that she could get into trouble if anyone found out they were communicating. She reminded him that if he told Venus or Jake, there'd be repercussions. Sirena was depending on his maturity. She'd included the phrase, young man, at least three times just so he'd know what was expected of him. There were lives at stake, well hers anyway.

She shouldn't have to tell him this. She'd given birth to Christopher. She'd provided financially for his well being the first ten years of his life. She was his mother and he knew that she loved him, in her own way.

The judicial system had no right being involved in the lives of families, human beings. The system had no way of knowing the real relationship between a child and his parent. Judges and courts only saw black and white. No gray area.

She'd never tried to harm Christopher, so she didn't understand why she wasn't allowed to contact him. Women denied their maternal rights were a dime a dozen. At one time, Sirena would've heard the same story on the evening news and not looked twice, but now she understood the unfairness of it all. Not being able to control the simplest of things was pure torture.

Her finger hovered above the send button. Before she could press it, a knock outside her window sent her heart into overdrive. She pressed her hand to her chest. She lowered her window. "Oh, God. You? What are you doing here?"

The man reached inside the open window and unlocked her door. "Get out."

"I can't leave my car here."

"You should've thought of that before you did something this stupid." Detective Lucas Heights towered over her. She hadn't seen him since he'd sat in court and testified against her three years ago. She wondered how he was able to park directly behind her without her noticing? She'd have to be more careful.

His muscular arm reached in, pulling her out of the car. He led her by the arm to the shiny Marquis parked a few feet away. He opened the passenger side door and pushed her head-first, inside his car. Once she was locked in, he moved swiftly to the other side, starting the engine.

She faced him. "You've been following me all this time, waiting for me to make a mistake? Thanks for the vote of confidence."

"I guess we know where confidence will get you these days, back in jail. Why would you risk it?" He pulled off eventually making a U-turn at the end of the block. Sirena watched the Gingerbread house fade into darkness as they tore down the street headed to who-knew-where.

"I want to see my son."

"You think I believe that? You think anyone would believe that? When you kidnapped and tried to kill his stepmother, were you trying to see him then? No. It was all about jealousy. You wanted Jake and your silly plan was to get Venus out of the way. You weren't thinking about that boy, so why would anything be different now? What are you planning?"

"I've changed. I've been rehabilitated, haven't you heard?"

"The only reason you're not being carted off to jail right now is because I found you instead of one of a patroller. The rest of the world may not know that the great Sirena Lassiter is a free woman but trust me, APD got the memo and they're going to be checking around here periodically."

"Venus and Jay, do they know I'm out?"

"Lucky for you, there's no system in place to notify victims when their assailants are released. They wouldn't know unless they asked," Lucas said confidently. "And they wouldn't ask unless they had a reason to, which obviously you're trying to give them. Are you crazy?" He finally snapped with the question. "Do you want to go back to prison?"

Sirena reached over and gently squeezed her captor's thigh, close to the part of his body she knew would respond. "I guess it's a good thing you found me first. We all have our own motives, don't we?" She understood perfectly well his motives. Following her meant he still cared. She didn't want to admit she felt the same way. But just like last time, what was the point? He wasn't the man she wanted, especially after he'd betrayed her. He was the reason she went to prison. He'd ruined everything.

Three years ago Lucas tried to talk her out of her master plan. They'd met online, he pretended to be a hit man for hire, while the entire time he was working undercover, setting her up. Lucas made her believe he was going to help her, for a small fee of course. She'd sold her jewelry and anything that wasn't nailed down to come up with the $30,000 he'd asked for.

After a while she noticed Lucas was stalling. She figured he was taking his sweet time to continue his little game of making her do whatever he wanted. He still refused to follow through even after she'd done everything he asked, including sleeping with him whenever he demanded.

Did she really believe by getting rid of Venus, Jay would come rushing into her arms? Yes, at the time, she believed whole-heartedly that it was just that simple.

Finally, since nothing else would work to dissuade her, Lucas revealed his true feelings, that he'd fallen in love with her and didn't want to see her make a mistake she'd regret for the rest of her life. That day, Sirena could hardly maintain a straight face. She'd laughed and turned a blind eye to his sincerity. She wanted Venus gone and wasn't going to let some man who had no part in her future get in the way of the one who did, Jay.

There was nothing left but to take matters into her own hands. She'd do the deed herself. Her big chance was getting Venus alone.

Venus hadn't known what hit her. Sirena easily pushed her into the back of the car. What to do after she'd taken her wasn't as easy. When she saw Lucas following her, she was relieved. He could do the dirtier part of the job. After he caught up to her, the one thing he was saying didn't make sense. "Let her go," he kept saying. "I'm giving you one last chance."

During his lectures of walking away and second chances, Venus managed to get free, running to the edge of the highway. Sirena chased her until finally giving up. The next thing she knew she was in handcuffs being put into a police cruiser. She never thought she would ever forgive Lucas, even imagining ways to make him pay for what he'd done.

Until the letters started coming.

He wrote the sweetest words. Sometimes two and three letters per week, always signed by *L*. and nothing more. He could get into trouble if anyone knew he was in love with a prisoner. A woman he'd help set-up and arrest. But it was for her own good; he'd tried to convince her over, and over again. "Having a death on your conscience would have driven you mad."

Little did he know.They were more alike than he probably cared to admit. They both wanted what they couldn't have and were capable of doing whatever it took to get it. They both had something to hide that could get them into trouble. She had the letters to prove it. She'd use them as leverage if it became necessary.

"You have a lot to learn?" His hand gripped her jaw and squeezed while he drove effortlessly with the other. His dark eyes were intense, moving from her to the road then back again.

"And you're just the person to teach me," Sirena said into his open palm, ignoring the pain of his grip.

"There are a few things I'd like to teach you. It might take a few lessons." His perfect smile met with the moonlight coming in through the windshield.

"I'm a fast learner," Sirena said rubbing her jaw. She already knew what she had to do. She'd play along. This time she'd figure out a way to win.

Not like before when he'd played her like a puppet. From the first time he pressed his body against hers she couldn't stop thinking about him. She wouldn't let her body betray her again. That's what she told herself.

Later that night, when he'd plunged deep inside of her there was no way she could hold back. The heat surged through her. She let out a deep guttural moan, unable to subdue the pleasure he unleashed while he gripped her thighs and rammed every piece of fight right out of her. From that point, reliving the past seemed irrelevant.

Chapter five

THE PROBLEM WITH INSOMNIA was that even though you couldn't sleep, you were too tired to use the hours for anything productive. Blurry eyes made it hard to read the computer screen and check for new orders or feedback. I laid in the dark and thought about things I wanted to do the next day, or the things that bothered me and wished had gone differently, replaying events as if I could magically change them.

Like believing I'd seen Sirena standing only a few feet away from me. I had to double take. She had a different hairstyle and heavier, much heavier than the Sirena I remembered. There was something about her profile, the striking aristocratic vibe she gave off that made everyone bow down in her presence. It wasn't the strangest thing to happen. Seeing Sirena in my peripheral vision was common. I used to think I saw her all the time; in the car next to me, walking down the street, handing me my change at WalMart. There was no point talking about it, or bringing up the subject with Jake because we both knew she was in prison. My paranoia could get the best of me. Traumatic events were hard to let go.

I couldn't tell him that I'd been back to the store a few extra times, sitting around in the parking lot to see if she'd shown up again. If I saw the woman, what was my plan? Excuse me, are you the woman who tried to kill me? Long time no see.

Expressing my worries to Jake seemed frivolous, especially since he wasn't interested in anything except the children. Which reminded me, I'd promised I'd talk to Christopher about his girl problems and I hadn't said a word. I worked with a different strategy. Trust. I figured if the kids knew they had a safe place to land they'd come to me with the things that were on their mind without any prying or bait.

Jake had a different parenting style. He was direct and to the point. He didn't like to waste time. Speak. Define. Resolve. End of story.

He used the same method in our relationship. There was no beating around the bush. Are you happy? Are you sad? Either way he had one answer, I can fix everything. Then the second answer was, let's make love. For a long time, jumping on each other's bones fixed any disagreements we may have had. Just the sight of his bare chest could make me forget what ailed me. But since he wasn't around, whatever ailed me only festered.

I tossed and turned in the dark. I ached with loneliness. I wondered what exactly it would take to stop the hollowness I felt. I could never ask Jake to come home. Stay home. It wasn't an option. I thought about the military spouses who had to live this way for months, years, at a time. Surely I could make it for a few more weeks until the end of his taping season.

Besides, I'd made my bed and I was laying in it. I'd chosen not to join Jake in California. My decision, my consequences. I'd already experienced that side of life. I didn't care about the Hollywood parties I was missing. I certainly didn't want to worry about every piece of bread I put in my mouth, afraid I couldn't fit into a dress the next morning. I wasn't interested in who was dating who, and the constant rumors being circled. Part of my new resolve was to accept the things I could change and step over the rest.

A soft knock came from the other side of my bedroom door. I wanted it to be Mya or Christopher ready to confide in me their insecurities or worries from the day. What else was a mother for? It'd been a long time since Mya curled up in the bed with me. I missed those nights when she'd find her way under my shoulder. And those mornings I'd wake up and she'd be right beside me.

I sat up and clicked the lamp on next to me. "Come in."

The door slowly opened. I was a tiny bit disappointed to see it was Bliss.

"I have to show you something." She entered the room carrying her laptop as the screen light illuminated her face. "You have to see this. I couldn't wait till morning," Bliss said before plopping on the bed. She turned the computer to face us both.

I read the email. "This is insane. We've only been in business a year, less than a year, and somebody wants to talk to us about offers."

"Not somebody, Keen Inc.," Bliss said definitively. "They distribute half the beauty products on the shelf all over the country."

We both screamed with delight before realizing the rest of the house was sleeping.

I read the letter again not sure if it was a dream. "It says they want to meet to discuss an offer. Wait, what if they think we stole their product or something. What if they want to sue us or something? An offer could be a lot of things."

"Stop it. You're not going to ruin this moment for me," Bliss whispered. "I know what this means and so do you. Quit trying to ground everything. It's okay to take flight and dream a little. Okay?"

"Okay," I said, still not sure this wasn't an ambush. "You call and set up the meeting."

"We should probably call a lawyer," I said before I could stop myself.

"I'm calling this guy first thing in the morning. Not a lawyer. We're not being sued."

"I really think—"

Bliss straightened a stray curl from covering her eye. "Look at me. I don't know what's on your mind these days, but you've got to address it. Where's your happy face? This is huge for us. Come on."

I smiled and just as quickly went back to my flat expression. "You're right. I should be ecstatic. I am. I'm thrilled. This is amazing news." I sounded like a robotic drone programmed to say the right thing.

Big companies liked to shut down little companies all the time. A preemptive strike was to offer what seemed like a good deal to buy them out, only to pull the plug once they had full control. I'd worked many years in the corporate world before becoming Mrs. Jake Parson.

Bliss closed her computer. Without the light from her screen there was only the moon shining outside the window. We sank into the cool linens. Bliss leaned her head against mine. "Think happy thoughts, sister. Positive energy can fix anything. Now close your eyes. We've got to be rested and ready for this next chapter."

I squeezed my lids closed to humor her. I planned to open them right back after she fell asleep.

* * *

To my surprise, my lashes hadn't fluttered open until the sun came up the next morning.

Bliss was gone. I rolled over and pulled the other pillow close to my chest expecting to smell Jake's aftershave. Instead, the fragrant aroma of peaches and mango from the moisturizer we used filled my nostrils. As much as I loved the scent, I quickly saddened. I couldn't remember the last time Jake slept in our bed. For that matter, the last time we made love. I missed him. I missed us. *Happy thoughts.*

I made my way downstairs to find Bliss and our nanny, Jezzy having a sketchy conversation in broken English and Spanish. Jezzy was from Panama by way of the Caribbean. Bliss spoke a mix of Portuguese and Spanish she'd learned from her mother who was Brazilian but raised in Haiti. We were a regular United Nations.

Jezzy was an honorary member of the family. She'd started out as our housekeeper. Beyond the children's nursery the house wasn't getting much attention. Every time I went to check on the twins, she was holding court in their room, singing, and sweet talking them. She would be sitting in the middle of the floor facilitating their block building efforts while the actual nanny sat and read her romance novels. Jezzy said she missed her little brothers and sisters and the twins made her happy. I let the original nanny go and hoped she enjoyed her free time to read as much as she pleased.

I planted kisses on Lauren and Henry's foreheads, the only place on their faces that weren't covered in sticky cereal. They were little people with definite ideas of their own, one of which included hating to have their faces wiped. I poured a cup of coffee then parked myself on the barstool.

"You've got to try this," Bliss said standing next to me holding a wooden spoon.

Instead of a taste, I swiped a bit of the slush and rubbed it on the back of my hand. I sniffed. "Heaven. Wow. Smells good. Kind of sticky though." I loved the freshness. Strawberry was one of the most refreshing scents, also one of the hardest fruits to buy year round. Starting a product line using it would take some ingenuity.

"Yeah, I'm trying it out for a styling gel. All the successful brands have a styling gel. We'll call it SUCCESS."

"I don't think we can afford to add it yet. We need to keep our product line neat and tight for now."

"Take flight." Bliss flapped her arms like a bird to remind me to soar.

I ignored her.

She in turn rolled her eyes, tired of my pessimism.

Mya came in dressed for school with her backpack ready to go. Her sixth grade uniform included a white shirt, navy blue sweater and a plaid skirt that got shorter every week. Since starting middle school, she'd gone from amiable to surly, completely dissatisfied with her lot in life.

"Why is it impossible to find something to eat in this house? I'm starving." She cut her eyes toward me.

"Have a mango." Bliss plopped the whole fruit in front of Mya.

"What am I supposed to do with this?"

Bliss handed her a knife. "Peel and eat."

"Forget it. I'll eat at school."

"You rather have mystery meat and powdered eggs instead of a nutritious piece of fruit?" I asked with sincerity.

"Absolutely. This is uncivil," Mya growled.

"There's leftovers from last night," I said, proud of my dinner making effort. It wasn't my best lasagna but I wanted some credit for the attempt. All those trips to the grocery store had produced something positive. We'd even sat down together at the table, though no one had talked to one another, the plates were cleaned and their bellies were full.

"Who eats lasagna for breakfast?" Mya stood in front of the open refrigerator door.

Christopher swooped in from behind. His long arm reached past Mya and grabbed the plastic container. "Me. There's only enough for one person and I will be happy to take it off your hands."

"Okay, wait. I want some." She tried to take it back.

"No. You don't. You said you rather have breakfast at school. I heard you."

"Mom," Mya whined. "How long must we live this way?"

"All right, that's enough. You both are giving me a headache." I stood and picked up the car keys. "Mya, I will gladly drive you to any fast food venue of your choice so you can have the hot, hearty, breakfast you so richly deserve."

Bliss snickered. Jezzy covered her mouth to hide her grin.

Mya stayed quiet, unsure of what was so funny. Suddenly she wasn't getting the best end of the deal. "Never mind." She sat down and grabbed the knife and mango, and started peeling. "Daddy would never let us live like paupers."

"You have his number," I said before I could stop myself. It was getting that way between Mya and I. I had no idea when this feud had started. Why, how, or when I had become the number one enemy was a mystery. Her against me. I was constantly defending myself against her jabs. She sliced one piece of fruit then tossed the rest away.

"I'll drive," Jezzy announced. "Let go." I was sure there was a double meaning; *let's go* and *let go* of your bad attitude.

I placed the keys in Jezzy's soft palm. She had a driver's license and I paid handsomely for her insurance. She was getting no protest out of me.

"Wait for me," Christopher chimed.

"Since when you want to fight with all the people in this house?" She questioned as they headed out the back door. They rounded the corner past earshot. I wanted to hear Mya's answer, sure she didn't have one anyway. Her temperamental status was probably natural, something I'd passed down naturally. I hadn't forgotten about my own childhood. Being a preteen never got any easier.

Bliss faced me with an exasperated grin. "Time to make the call to Keene, Inc."

"Yeah. Go for it."

Bliss cut her eyes back at me.

"I'm being sincere. Really," I said. "This could be good for business."

Chapter six

JAKE DROVE TO THE studio lot and waited at the gate for Keith, the burly security guard to wave him through.

Keith leaned against the open window smelling of too much cologne in an attempt to wash out the smell of medicinal marijuana. "Wassup, man? You know this car needs to be mine. Let me know when you're through with it and I'll take it off your hands."

"The insurance payments alone would kill ya, bruh." Jake revved the engine of his prize Porsche.

"Hey, we all gotta die of something." Keith had an interesting perspective. More times than not his words of wisdom made Jake think hard about his own journey, what it took to get there. The orange gate lifted.

Jake glided through the open entry with a smile on his face. His phone vibrated as he parked.

"Hey there," Jake greeted his wife with a light breezy tone though he'd been frustrated with her lack of following the routine lately.

"I'm sorry I didn't get to call you but I have some exciting news."

Jake inhaled and tried not to sigh into the phone. "Yeah, what kind of news?"

"This huge company might be interested in buying Two Sisters," she squealed. "We're headed to Chicago to meet with the Vice President. Can you believe it?"

Jake was out of the car and walking into the studio but came to a dead stop. "What do you mean, you're headed to Chicago?"

"I mean, we're on our way right now."

"You're leaving the kids with Jezzy?"

"Jezzy is more than capable of taking care of everyone. Bliss and I are only going to be gone for one night. Relax, everything will be fine."

Not knowing what was going on in his household brought back feelings of Pin the Tail on the donkey as a boy. Having your eyes tied blindly and being spun in circles was the stupidest game ever invented.

"Is this a real company? A legit offer?"

"Yes. Keene Inc. is offering us a million dollars. Can you believe it?"

"For hair products?" Again Jake was spinning with confusion. He hadn't meant to sound so shocked, but he was.

"Hair is profitable. Natural or otherwise, hair will always be the first thing on a woman's to-do list," she said as if she'd been practicing. "It might be a great offer."

"So would you be selling or is someone interested in investing?" Jake asked as a businessman. Before he turned his full attention to acting, he'd ran a successful clothing line based off his popularity as a rapper, which was how they'd met when he'd hired her as his marketing consultant. Over the years, he'd learned if something sounded way too good to be true there was a problem.

"That's what we're going to meet about." She spoke hurriedly but Jake hadn't gotten enough answers.

"If it's a sell option, I think you should take it. You haven't been spending enough quality time with Lauren and Henry." The silence on the other end of the line told him he'd said too much.

"What do you mean I haven't been spending quality time with the twins? How would you know? You're never here."

Her natural instinct was to go in the opposite direction of whatever he offered as advice or opinion. It hadn't always been that way. At one time she hung on his every word. He was the master of the universe. That lasted all of one year into their marriage. Mya was just a baby and Venus quit working to be a stay at home mother like she'd always dreamed of being. Then one day she declared it was going-back-to-work-day. Her life was being wasted sitting at home watching Sesame Street.

The more Jake disagreed, the more determined she was to take a job, with her ex-boyfriend, no less. From that moment on, he'd learned to only hint and never ever strongly suggest anything.

"I guess I have a lot to think about," she calmed down.

"Absolutely. It's all your decision. No one can make this decision but you," Jake said, doing his best to back pedal from his earlier position. Thank goodness he hadn't mentioned the real benefit. If she sold the business, there'd be nothing more to keep her in Atlanta. She and Bliss could go their separate ways and she could move to Los Angeles with the children.

"I have to go. I don't want to miss my flight," she concluded with a bitter tone.

He wasn't sure when they'd said good-bye. He was suddenly holding the phone with nothing but dead air on the other end. He thought about calling back but wasn't sure where they'd left the conversation since he'd obviously blanked out somewhere.

"There he is," Josh hollered as they converged on the studio lot door. "There's the man." He greeted Jake with a grazing of the fingers, the new LA handshake. "I told you, right? Once you stepped into the Chateau your stock went up triple points. The VP of the network knows your name." He stuck up his thumb. "You're my official arm candy. The way those execs were falling all over you, was like a moth to a flame." Josh was beaming like a proud papa. "So, tonight, you in?"

The sunlight was peaking over the Hollywood hills. Jake put up a hand to shield his tired eyes from the sun. Having to be on set by six every morning made it harder to make it to work each day. He'd partied too much the night before and now Josh was talking about a replay.

"I don't think so, man."

"I got something for that exhaustion, brother." Josh gave his chest pocket a light pat.

"It's going to happen naturally or it's not going to happen. It's called a good night's sleep." Jake opened the large metal door to enter the filming set. The crew sat around as if they'd slept there all night. When they saw Josh enter they perked up and tried to look busy.

"Yeah, right. We'll revisit this discussion in six months. So, you in for tonight?"

Jake was still lost on the conversation he'd just had with his wife. Chaos. He didn't like chaos. Too much was off track. The last thing he needed to add to that was a nightly ritual of partying with his director.

But he couldn't tell him no, could he? He didn't want to sing the holier-than-thou song. Nothing worse than someone on their soap box. He had Yoga class tonight.
He'd started only two months ago. Women of course had been doing it for the last decade but now the male set were getting involved. Guys gathered, talking about downward dog and Hatha breathing techniques instead of who won the NBA championship.

Strength training be damned. It was all about core energy. Jake met with his instructor, Nahlia, on

Wednesday and Thursday evenings and Saturday mornings. He loved Nahlia and he meant that with the greatest respect. She knew her stuff. No matter how Jake balked or complained that he wasn't limber enough to do certain moves, she brought him to the other side. Next thing he knew, he was doing headstands and spider poses once cursed about.

The days were long enough, ten to twelve hours, most of it spent sitting around. The last thing he wanted was to extend it by spending more time with Josh. He'd much rather be in Nahlia's company.

She was pretty and smelled a whole lot better than Josh. She taught him meditation. Zoning out, was what Jake called it. He had the most honest moments with himself. Memories of events in his childhood, growing up with his mom and his brother. The hard times were what shaped Jake. Eating grilled cheese sandwiches for practically every meal since loafs of bread and five-pound blocks of cheese were what the government handed out for public assistance. They gave them uncut bologna too, but even back then Jake knew there was something foul in the process of making meat into a gigantic round sausage.

"So we ride again, brother." Josh concluded.

Jake nodded, yes, when he meant, hell no.

His phone vibrated one last time before he'd have to shut it down. A message from Nahlia. "See you tonight." He could almost hear her voice in his ear, whispering how to breathe or hold a pose.

That was the deal breaker. Nahlia one. Josh zero. He would be doing down dog tonight instead of sipping on Cognac and holding a stogie all night long. A woman's company was always preferred over a man's. Specifically the reason he'd married in the first place, to be in a real relationship where he didn't have to prove his love every minute of the day in exchange for sex.

Yet, here he was without his wife, which meant no sex, no intimacy, not even a kiss goodnight. Jake typed the reply, *Can't wait.*

Being with Nahlia was his only real outlet. She understood he was married and wanted to stay that way, even after he promised himself he wouldn't let things go too far again.

What happened between them that day was out of his control. At least he'd used a condom. He wasn't foolish enough to expose himself to the consequences of a brief night of sex. Though he knew what he felt for Nahlia was far more dangerous than just sex. If he were smart, he'd stop seeing her all together.

A light tap on his shoulder shook him. "You're due in wardrobe and make-up, Jay," his assistant said.

Thank goodness. "I'll be right there," he said, shutting off his phone. He also shut off the noise, the debate of right and wrong raging in his head. He wasn't ready to come face to face with the answer, not yet.

Chapter seven

NEXT THING I KNEW we were on a plane to Chicago. Bliss did her impression of wings flapping every time I looked at her filled with nervous anxiety. I felt like we were playing Business Barbie, dressed in our cutest outfits and heels. I couldn't remember the last time I'd worn a business suit.

We arrived on time for our meeting. Keen Inc. took up an entire thirty-story building. Bliss, who stood a few inches taller than me, wrapped an arm around my shoulders and whispered near my ear.

"We got this, sister."

I hadn't slept which was nothing unusual. I laid awake worrying about this meeting. I didn't want to make a fool of myself. My past life had been filled with marketing meetings and corporate sales blitz. The difference was none of those experiences had been my own product. This time my blood, sweat, and tears were at stake. I couldn't let on that I was completely overwhelmed.

A pretty woman stood before us wearing a pair of heels higher than I thought humanly possible. "Follow me." She walked remarkably well and even managed a pivot turn when we reached the conference room.

"Hello, Nigel Waters," the elegantly dressed man put out his hand for a shake.

"Bliss Johnston." Bliss offered an eager smile. She wore a fitted dress to show her lean shape and let her hair down. She ignored the man's approving gaze and took a seat at the conference table.

"Venus Johnston," I said putting out my hand next.

"You mean, Venus Johnston Parson, don't you?" A second well-dressed man, equally good looking, entered with a rushed gait landing in the center of our introduction. He absorbed all the energy in the room. His sparkling eyes landed deeper than I was comfortable. "You are still married to thee one and only Jay P, are you not?" he asked all while bringing my hand to his lips. "You're married to hip-hop royalty."

I forced a smile, though my mind was racing with possible scenarios. The first being there was a true fan in our midst. Jake had many admirers from his earlier hip hop music days. His acting was considered second fiddle to his glory days as a rapper.

I glanced in the direction of Bliss to see if she was still riding high on confidence, though I smelled a set-up.

Maybe Keen Inc. saw the opportunity to gain a free celebrity by having the wife of JayP on the roster.

I took my hand back. "And you are?"

"Single," he answered with a smirk.

"No. I meant your name."

"Oh, right. Marco DeVon, VP of Acquisitions. Also a long time fan of your husband's work, but no, that's not why you're here," he answered the unspoken question to get it out of the way.

"I appreciate that." I smiled, while still not convinced. "This is my sister and partner, Bliss Johnston."

"Hello." Bliss shook his hand with a firm grasp eagerly wanting to get past introductions and down to business. She faced me and nodded with an approving wink to let me know we were in friendly waters. I trusted her reaction more than my own tingly senses that whispered 'run while you still can.' A handshake for Bliss was like an instant view into a man's soul.

We were in good company, her eyes told me. Relax.

Marco DeVon pulled out my chair and lingered a few seconds behind me after I'd already been seated. "As you'll see in front of you is a folder with our offer. First let me start by saying, you're products are impeccably packaged. Very impressive for a small mom and pop shop." He sat directly across from me instead of at the head of the conference table.

"Sister and sister shop, we like to say," Bliss corrected him. "So what's the offer?" She was in high-octane mode after four cups of tea. Her knee bounced excessively. A shared sisterly trait. We also looked alike, she a taller version, but the same dimples and almond shaped eyes.

I placed a hand on my bouncing knee first, then hers, to say, slow down. Appearing too anxious was a huge mistake in any negotiation.

"Well here it is. We want to make a full purchase for the Two Sisters brand and products. Open the cover and see the number we're talking about. I think you'll be extremely happy."

Full purchase? The number, as he put it, happened to be close to a million dollars. This time it was both of us grabbing each other under the table.

"Of course we would keep you both on in consulting positions if you were interested."

As excited as I was about the exceptional offer, I closed the file and pretended to be unfazed. "Unfortunately, we're not able to make a decision right now. We'll need a few days to discuss it."

"I can give you one day," Marco DeVon said without breaking stride. He leaned back in his chair and tilted his head slightly. His nonchalance was real, unlike mine.

"We can make a decision in one day. No problem," Bliss spoke through gritted teeth.

"I'm sorry, but no. We'll need at least two days to have our lawyer check over the terms. I'm sure you understand."

Marco DeVon smiled. "Do you believe in past lives?" He directed the question at me as if no one else was in the room.

"Not lately." My response was meant to shut him down. Wherever he was headed with this interaction was not where I was prepared to go.

"I think we're meant to work together. I bet you know it too. But I'll give you 48 hours just so you can save face and make a carefully thought out decision. Nigel, make sure these ladies have whatever they need while they're in town."

"Oh, no, we're leaving this afternoon," I said quickly. "I'm sure we can use the wonderful delivery system to overnight the contracts, that is if we sign."

He leaned back in his white leather chair. He exuded confidence like a man who always got what he wanted. "I prefer to always sign contracts in person. That's just one of my pet peeves." He wasn't kidding. Quirks, pet peeves, he probably had more than a few. Obsessive personalities seemed to gravitate toward my direction.

"Mr. DeVon, Marco," I corrected before he could interject. "Chicago is lovely and all, but I have a house full of children. I can't be gone for more than a day or all hell will break loose in the Parson household."

"Say no more. I'll come to you. Atlanta is one of my favorite cities. What do you say, Nigel? Road trip?"

"Sounds like a good time to me," Nigel said zeroing his blue eyes on Bliss who'd also been quiet during the uncomfortable exchange.

"All righty then. See you in Atlanta. Thank you for your time." I stood up and straightened out my suit jacket and skirt that felt two sizes too small. Jake liked to remind me that songs were written about women like me with ity-bitty waists and nice round posteriors. I wished I could back out of the room at this point.

"It was a pleasure meeting you." The believer of past lives put out his hand for a good-bye shake. He pressed my palm between both his hands. Soft hands. Never lifted a wrench or a screwdriver hands and could probably make a girl cry with pleasure hands.

I pushed back my seat and marched out the conference door. I walked down the hall in my modest pointed toe heels as fast as my feet would carry my backside and me. The elevator button lit up before I touched it. Which only meant one thing; someone pushed it from the other side.

I turned around and expected to see Bliss. Instead, there he was, behind me.

"I really think we should have lunch before you head out on that plane," he said, smiling.

"We're running late. Hopefully we won't miss our flight."

If Bliss hadn't moseyed her way down the hall chatting with Nigel as if we had all the time in the world, holding The Keen Inc. folder pressed against her chest like a schoolgirl there was a chance we could've gotten away.

"What time is your flight?" Marco seemingly knew the answer before I could speak. He waited patiently with his hands clasped behind his back.

"5pm," I muttered, unable to blatantly lie to a direct question.

"You have plenty of time. After lunch, I'll have a car drive you straight to the airport."

Awesome, I thought. Absolutely, awesome.

I knew what I was getting myself into the minute he sat beside me at the restaurant. I was a sucker for a great smelling man. I'd been known to fall in love from his scent alone. My *Married with Kids* repellant usually kicked in but this time I couldn't stop myself from noticing his cologne. The light and airy mix with a hint of clove had pushed straight past my barrier.

Then there was all that maleness floating around. Opening doors, pulling out chairs, making sure my order was exactly what I'd asked for. I wasn't sure if it was all about Marco, or that he reminded me of my husband who I missed down to my core. I missed *us.* The 'then and now' of relationships had a way of changing drastically. The couple we used to be laughed a lot and lit up when the other walked into a room.

"So a house full of kids, what does that come out to? Two? Three?" Marco's eyebrows went up when I shook my head, no, for him to keep going. "Four? You have four children? Wow. You look absolutely amazing."

The compliments were the other problem. Every woman was a sucker for positive reinforcement. It didn't take much. I softened with each stroke like a needy kitty looking for affection.

Bliss sat across from me. Nigel sat next to her. They exchanged witty banter that I couldn't hear. They weren't paying any attention to Marco or me. Neither was anyone else in the restaurant but I still felt uncomfortable with the possibility of being seen. The married woman sitting with elbows occasionally grazing against a single good looking man. I was acutely aware of my surroundings. Early training from being stalked by paparazzi for a brief time made me paranoid. From the person pretending to take a picture of themselves with the camera pointed directly in our direction, or the couple sitting at the next table quiet as church mice so they could hear our entire conversation. Tell-all-photos showed up from the darndest places, the least likely of places.

"So, who's brilliant idea was it to name the products based on virtues?"

"Both of ours. Right Bliss?" I leaned forward and tried to divert Marco's attention off me, even if for only a few seconds. I needed a break from his intense dedication to details. First of course were my eyes, then my lips, then a sweep around my entire face, then back to the eyes.

I was smart enough to know I was being sized up for the kill, yet I was still flattered. I twisted my wedding ring around my finger nearly burning a hole in my skin.

"Yes, right," Bliss answered without having the faintest idea what the question was. She returned back to Nigel and whatever they had to discuss in each other's ear.

"The packaging is what caught our attention. We don't plan to change a thing," Marco added.

"Thank you. That's definitely a plus. Handing over our business this soon is going to be hard. I mean, if we decide to go that route. I honestly thought you were more interested in distribution, not taking over our entire product line."

"I promise, your hard work will be handled with gentle care. What would be really great, is if you came with the package," he said, letting the statement hang in the air before cleaning it up. "I meant you, coming on board with Keen, Inc. Maintaining your brand with the company."

"That's not going to happen. Remember, the house full of kids? I won't be moving to Chicago in this lifetime. Maybe Bliss could. She's not really tied down, no obligations," I said of my sister who had no idea I was offering her up as a sacrificial lamb. I pulled at my collar and took a sip of water.

"Bliss doesn't have your experience."

I gave him a perplexed stare. "I don't remember either one of us sending over résumés."

"I have my ways. Your work background is pretty extensive. I hope you don't mind me knowing."

"I don't blame you. I wouldn't make an offer such as this without knowing who I was getting into bed with either." This time it was me who'd made the Freudian slip. "I'm sorry. I meant, merge, acquire." I shook my head. I checked my wrist where there was no watch. "Oh look at the time."

Chapter eight

BLISS AND I SAT in the backseat of the car while the driver moved us slowly through five lane traffic. "I can't believe you fell for their schmoozing. I thought you could see through people, Bliss. You couldn't see we were being worked?" I chastised, though I was angrier with myself than with her.

I turned my head to stare out the window. "We missed our flight and we might miss this one too. I told Jake we'd be up and back. What time is it?"

"My phone is dead too," Bliss said feeling weary with all my complaining. "Don't worry, we're going to make the flight."

I puffed my cheeks out. "Oh really? What else does my future hold, great swami?"

"You and Marco DeVon," Bliss said quietly, then quickly changed her tune. "You two were quite friendly. Do you believe in past lives?" She mimicked before falling into a fit of giggles. "I could see you fighting it all the way."

"I wasn't going to be rude. He's holding our million dollars hostage."

"And you, in the palm of his hand."

I rubbed my temples. My phone rested in my lap with a black screen. I'd made one last phone call to Jezzy before the battery flatlined. Everyone was fine, she said, not to worry.

That didn't stop me. I was good at worrying, it came natural. Why wouldn't I do what I was good at?

"Admit you had fun." Bliss nudged me with her elbow. "I heard you laughing. Do you know how long it's been since I heard you laugh?"

"I used to laugh all the time back when things were funny." A long time ago, I thought. Before real life set in. "Grown ups aren't supposed to have fun. Hasn't anyone given you the manual yet?"

"No. I never got the memo." She faced me, now truly concerned.

"I'm just exhausted. I haven't slept in a few days. I'll be fine," I muttered through my hand shield where I was doing my best not to have a mini-breakdown.

Bliss managed to squeeze tissue between my fingers. "Guess what, you deserve a good cry. Because that's the other thing I haven't seen you do in a long time. You've been marching around without missing a beat. You're a wife, a wonderful mother, a rocking business owner, and the best sister a girl could ask for. I'm constantly amazed at how you keep it together."

"Oh please." Instead of her pep talk making me feel better I welled up again. I wasn't keeping anything together. Continually wondering how much longer I could hold up the facade. If she only knew what was rolling around in this head of mine. That's when it hit me. She knew exactly what was going on in this wild haired noggin of mine.

I dropped the shame act and cut my eyes toward her. She blinked a few times as if to say, what?

"Don't play coy," I said defiantly. "You're already trying to set me up with another man when I'm not even sure I'm going to go through with it."

This was our mode of communication. I'd never said *it* out loud, or even left a hint, but Bliss knew.

"I think you're very sure, but you're scared. You don't have to be afraid. You're a very attractive woman, four kids and all. You don't have to be scared that you're going to spend the rest of your life alone. Now you know. Marco DeVon couldn't get enough of you."

"Thank you, doctor Busy body. I still love Jake," I said, finally feeling like a ton of bricks had been moved out of my way. I could talk about it finally. Guilty as charged. Wanting a divorce, or something, I wasn't quite sure what to call it. The feeling gnawed at me day and night. I couldn't identify the what, or why, the boiling anger I felt when I thought about Jake, us, and our marriage lately. It was like a mysterious illness. I had no diagnosis, only symptoms. Anger. Resentment. Stabbing pains of extreme fatigue from our entire long distance situation.

"You can still love someone and not want to be married to them. You know, if you love someone, set them free and all that jazz," Bliss offered.

"Again, priceless wisdom. Thank you."

We arrived at Chicago O'Hare and the driver hurried us out of the car, so I didn't have to acknowledge that she was right. That maybe Jake and I needed a do-over. If we were truly meant to be together, we'd find our way back. What was happening right then and there wasn't working and I couldn't pretend it was, not any longer.

Chapter nine

THE TAXI TURNED ON our street and I noticed a sad, abandoned looking car parked out of its element maybe half a block away. I craned my neck to keep staring as we passed. Our nearest neighbor was close to a quarter mile away. I panicked thinking about various scenarios that included burglars and rapists.

"Did you see that car?"

Bliss hunched her shoulders. "What car?"

I entered the house cautiously. The place felt cold and deserted as if the heat hadn't ran the entire time we'd been gone. It was early October when the mornings could turn frigidly cold. I marched nervously from room to room checking on my babies. The twins lay in their beds with their favorite stuffed bears neatly tucked beside them. I leaned over and kissed their foreheads. I missed their voices, smiles, and touch. Days, no matter how hard, always felt easier with their sweetness in the air.

Next, I found Christopher wrapped head to toe underneath his covers. I closed the door back quietly. Inside Mya's room, the nightlight danced in speckled stars on the ceiling. She still hated the dark as much as she pretended to be a tough girl.

As I was coming out of Mya's room, I saw a nightgown floating over bare feet like a ghost and nearly jumped out of my skin.

"You scared me," I whispered.

"You scared me first," Jezzy announced, holding a long wire hanger, her weapon of choice.

"Why is it so freakin' cold in here?" I led her away from the children's rooms.

Jezzy smirked. "This, you call cold?" Though she was an import of Panama, she'd lived in Buffalo, New York with her aunt before moving to Georgia. Her bare feet and exposed arms proved her core temperature was ramped a bit higher than my Southern California soul. I hadn't seen snow until I was in college, and even then a machine made it.

I punched the temperature to a reasonable 68 degrees. "My babies aren't polar bears, Jezzy." I faced her. "By the way, there's a car parked out front. Do you know anything about it?"

She gave me a mean glare. "It's four in the morning. Why would I know who's car is parked out front? I don't have guests," Jezzy said, annoyed with the accusation.

"I wasn't accusing you of...anyway, you're allowed to have guests. I was just wondering."

"Don't know. There's your answer."

"What's all the noise out here?" Bliss peeked out of her bedroom. She'd already changed into her pajamas and roped her hair into a bun on top of her head. "A girl needs her beauty rest."

Jezzy and I both stifled our giggle. Bliss had a face full of green paste with only her nostrils and lips exposed and her eyes blinking like a giant frog.

"Good night," Jezzy said, leaving first.

"We're fine," I told Bliss. "I asked her about the car down the street."

"Someone probably just ran out of gas. Go to bed. Try and get some sleep," Bliss ordered.

I finally made it to my bed and dived in, clothes still on. I was exhausted. Sleep should come easy, I thought.

When I popped up not more than an hour later I wanted to scream. Insomnia wasn't for the weak. You had to be tough to be able to function with only a couple of hours of rest each night.

My bout of sleeplessness started three months ago. I knew this because it was Christopher's birthday. Turning thirteen was sort of a rite into official teen territory and yet, neither Jake nor I had planned anything for him. Jake was in Los Angeles and I was elbows deep in mashing mangos and squishing avocados into hair goo.

Cake, candles, and cards, all forgotten giving Christopher a wide-open opportunity to take advantage of my guilt. He only had to ask once. "Mom, can I go out for pizza with Matt. His brother is going to drive us. I promise to be back by eleven." His pitch came completely straight faced even though he knew a car full of teenaged boys after dark was at the top of his father's forbidden list. Whether it be cops, gangs, or just plain stupidity, the odds were high trouble would find him. That's what a dad was for, to know and remember those days growing up and try to prevent the same pitfalls for his son. Endangered species, that's what Jake called young brown men and boys.

Seemed there was a new high profile story of a shooting every day. Being in the South only made Jake more uncomfortable with Christopher leaving the house past sundown. But Jake wasn't home to enforce the rules. I was left alone to do the heavy lifting. All the disciplinary action fell on my shoulders while Christopher and Mya slowly came to resent me. I wanted to be liked, to be the fun one that made them laugh and smile with my witty quips when I walked into a room instead of seeing their mood drop like I'd pulled the happy plug letting all the air out of the balloon.

I was an easy target that day. I let Christopher go with his friends. I gave a stern curfew of eleven and threats of what would happen to both of us if his dad found out. By the time eleven came around Christopher wasn't answering his phone. After a round of phone calls to Matt's parents who weren't nearly as concerned as I was, I began to pace the hallways, staring out the window every five minutes. My stomach was a big knot of regret and worry.

When Christopher came home it was past midnight and I was a frantic mess, yelling at the top of my lungs as if I wasn't simply grateful he was standing before me. I was all too thankful, my heart racing with 'dear God, thank you lord, and never again'.

I thought about it all the time, keeping the children safe. The paranoia was like a self-fulfilling prophecy. Now, I jumped at every noise, skipped a breath at every vibration. I thought about the car parked out front. The temperature debate with Jezzy had thrown me off, right along with Bliss and her avocado puree facemask, making me not as thorough. I checked on the kids, but I hadn't physically seen Christopher, only a jumble of blankets lumped together.

I got out of bed and beelined it down the hall thinking I missed something. I pressed my ear against Christopher's door before twisting the doorknob ever so slightly but this time it didn't turn. Locked bedroom doors were outlawed; another item in the Jake Parson-Do-As-I-Say-While-I'm-Gone manual.

I went back and got the key pin that fit into all the bedroom locks. This is what my life had come to. I was the warden of the prison called home. I waited for the click. The knob turned easily. I stuck my head in and peeked inside. The room smelled like a gym locker, stale laundry, sweaty socks, and the cheap cologne advertised to boys that would make them irresistible to girls. Except the commercials failed to mention the necessary shower before hand.

"Who's there?" The hoarse voice called from under the crumpled sheets and comforter.

"It's me," I whispered. "Did I wake you?"

Christopher sat up and flicked the light switch on next to him. He squinted from the light. "I was already awake."

"What's wrong? You can't sleep?" I sat on the edge of his bed. His eyes blinked catching what little light came through the blinds. I kissed him on the forehead. "I missed you."

"You were only gone one day. Technically, not even a whole day since you're here now and the sun hasn't come up yet."

I brushed a hand across his full head of soft hair. He and a few of his friends had decided that the Afro needed to make a come back. "You locked the door."

"Yeah," he said with his head down. "Sorry. I know we're not supposed to."

"Is something wrong?"

He hesitated before meeting my gaze and still only briefly. He shook his head, no.

I clicked off his light. Before I could rise for my exit Christopher reached out and hugged me.

"I'm glad you're back home, mom," he said. His narrow chest trembling with a second breath.

"Are you cold, sweetie? I can turn up the heat?" I held on until he let go first.

"No. I'm good," he said before scooting down into the covers craving warmth.

I headed out back to my bedroom. I checked the temperature on the thermostat. It was back to normal. I hoped he wasn't cold and shivering from a virus.

I climbed back into my bed and buried myself under layers of cover and was now shivering too. Fear, I thought. He's afraid of something. I knew the feeling all too well. I promised myself I'd get to the root of what was bothering him. I wouldn't wait until he volunteered to come to me.

Whatever was bothering him had to be dealt with head on.

Chapter ten

THE WOMAN ATTACKED Sirena, biting into her shoulder like a wild demon. Sirena fought, pulling the woman's hair and used the other hand to dig her thumbnail into her eyeball until she released her grip. Still it was the guards who finally saved her.

She rose from the pillow in a start, gasping for air. Her hair was wet from sweating and fighting in her dream.

For a few seconds Sirena believed none of it really happened. The last three years, just one big nightmare. She could've been in a trance state where her mind existed outside of reality. Those kinds of experiences were common she'd found after continuous therapy sessions. The sessions were in the woman's correctional facility, which meant she'd seen and lived the horrific memories that floated in her mind. Not just dreamt them.

Her eyes came into focus seeing the soft white curtains billowing across the room. The feathery comforter around her body was the best quality. The light airy hotel suite must've cost a grip. She sat in the center of the king-sized bed wondering if the vase with red roses on the glass table a few feet away were meant for her or part of the general decor.

Being naked used to bother her before. Now, she threw off the covers and swung her legs around to the plush carpet. She tiptoed to the roses and plucked the card.

Enjoy room service. I'll be back for lunch,

L

She of course would be the *lunch* he was referring too. Detective Lucas Heights had finally made his grand appearance, sneaking up behind her while she sat in front of Jay's house. She already had enough to be embarrassed and ashamed about to last a lifetime. Being caught spying on the Gingerbread house was a new kind of low.

She heard the key go into the lock. Sirena braced herself, checking the time. Was he back already? The door opened.

"Room service," the housekeeper called out.

"You ever heard of knocking? Get out," Sirena yelled. The door quickly closed. She got up and threw the dead bolt in place.

She had to get out of there before Lucas came back. Sirena knew her jailer would be looking for her. She hadn't slept in her bed. Minor offenses, regardless of their level of importance could end her probation. She would have to find her way back to Jay's house to get her car, then drive all the way back across town to check in.

The thought of it exhausted her. She sat back down on the edge of the bed and wondered as she often did how she landed in piles of mud, to put it politely.

After a fast shower, something she knew how to do, she threw on her clothes. Before she could make it out the door, Lucas was standing in front of her. One step forward, two back.

He nudged her back inside. "I told you it was lunch time." He flipped the bolt on the lock. He took ahold of her face and plunged his tongue into her mouth.

She wanted to stop him from shoving his hand down the front of her panties. She wished she could mean it when she said, "Stop please, I have to go."

"You have nothing to do except be with me. I had a talk with your house manager. He's happy to ignore your absence." He kissed her neck and breathed fire into her ear. "Now you're free to stay here as long as you like." He backed her up one step at a time to the edge of the bed. "A 'thank you' will suffice," he said before raising her sweater dress over her head.

He stared at her full breast and licked the center of her chest. "God, you smell good." He kicked her legs apart and shoved himself inside of her. With each thrust he made her forget where she was supposed to be going.

Sirena fought to stay silent until the joyful pain seared past her inhibitions.

Her car. The Gingerbread house. She couldn't remember what her goal had been before he'd stopped her from leaving. All she knew was his touch and heat consumed her and what was so wrong with that?

Chapter eleven

THE MYSTERY CAR WAS still out front. Two days parked in the same spot. When I passed I memorized the plate number long enough before I came to a stop to type it into my phone, a text to myself. I should at least report it in case it was stolen and left abandoned.

I was on my way to meet with Marco DeVon who'd made good on his word to keep business personal. He'd flown into Atlanta earlier in the day and had scheduled a lunch to meet with Bliss and I.

At the last minute, Bliss complained about a headache claiming she could barely hold her head up. There was nothing I could do except show up alone, even though every logical bone in my body told me it was a bad idea.

The restaurant where we were meeting was on the tenth floor. The elevator doors opened to a hostess wrapped in a tight black dress and dramatic red lips.

"I'm meeting Marco DeVon."

"Yes, this way."

I glided behind the hostess with self-confidence that quickly began to dwindle as I approached the table conveniently tucked in the far corner of the restaurant with a sky view that was more appropriate for a romantic date than a business meeting.

I wanted to feel nothing when I saw Marco DeVon. Instead, I felt an instant attraction that I hoped wasn't written all over my face. Marco was wearing a light grey suit that did something dazzling to the color of his eyes. He stood up to greet me with a soft handshake.

"You're on time. I like punctuality."

"After you flew all this way, it would be rude to keep you waiting." No need in divulging the truth, that I'd sat in the parking garage a few extra minutes. He leaned in with the handshake and kissed me ever so softly on the cheek.

I had to compose myself, repeating that I was paranoid and over reacting. This man was not interested in me; I certainly wasn't interested in him. It was a business lunch.

"Bliss couldn't make it." I wasted no time taking a sip of the water sitting in front of me.

"I took the liberty of ordering a few appetizers."

The waiter arrived with a bottle of red wine.

"What's Bruschetta without a nice Cabernet to wash it down?" Marco approved the bottle. The waiter took his time opening the cork.

"This is a nice place. So your condominium is in this building I presume."

"Twentieth floor. You want to take a tour?"

"No. Not today."

The waiter poured a small amount in my glass. I stirred it around for a quick second then sniffed and tasted. I knew I was being tested in more ways than one. "It's good. Very good."

Marco nodded, giving the waiter the okay to fill both glasses. "So tell me about how you started Two Sisters."

"Starting a business of your own never gets easier. I'd ventured out before, the first time with a flower shop and wedding planning service called In Bloom. I eventually sold it. It's still very profitable. The brides were excited about their future and fun to work with. It was the mother's of the brides who drove me coo-coo. I remember telling one mother who had veins coming out of her head while she snapped at me, 'take it easy, the odds are you'll get another shot at it. Who only get's married once?' I knew then I should probably get out of the wedding business."

At least I'd gotten a laugh out of him. He nodded slowly. "I don't usually hear that as a woman's perspective on marriage. Mostly it's the belief in happily ever after and death do you part."

"For a long time I believed that too," I said quietly. My mood suddenly dulled at the thought of losing Jake through natural causes or stupid mistakes, either one didn't seem right.

"I still don't see the leap. How did you find your way into the hair product business?"

"There's no bridge. No connection. I found something that interested me and I ran with it."

The waiter arrived and refilled my wine glass. Still no appetizers. I realized why I'd become a blabbermouth. I was nervous. I'd consumed the first pour without eating a single thing. I was beginning to wonder if he'd planned it that way.

"In other words, you have no real connection. It's just a business, a good idea and you ran with it." Marco DeVon leaned back as if his work was done.

"You're implying that I have no emotional ties, therefore why try to hold onto the business. Better to just sell to the highest bidder and move on to the next venture."

"You said it best."

"That's all you've got?" I shook my head. "You could've at least waited until we made it past the first course."

"I figured we could get the hard part out of the way." His perfect lips curled in a satisfied grin.

"Getting the hard part out of the way included you getting me half drunk as well?"

He hunched his shoulders. "I didn't know you were a such a light weight."

"There's difficult history behind Bliss and I, the business is our connection to each other. I don't think I'm ready to sell. I'm sorry you flew all the way out here. It's just not that easy."

"Your sister seems to think so." He reached into his case and pulled out a faxed copy of the contract. He flipped to the last page and showed me where Bliss had already signed. He kept his eyes on mine trying to gauge my next move.

"Why do you want *Two Sisters*? There are tons and tons of natural hair products out there. A new one pops up everyday."

"You have the most incredible lips," he replied instead of answering my question.

I told myself to get up. I demanded, *get up, walk away*. I willed my knees to pull back from the hold he had on them underneath the table.

"Do you want to leave?"

I nodded my head, yes. "That would be a good idea."

He didn't bother addressing my concerns. Had I drank too much? Was I sick? Did I want to kiss him as much as he wanted to kiss me? None of that seemed to matter. He slid a hundred dollar bill out of his wallet and laid it underneath the bottle of wine. The swiftness by which he gathered himself and made it look like there was an emergency somewhere was impressive.

He got up and politely pulled my chair out and took my hand, leading the way to the exit. He pushed the elevator button. He took ahold of my pinky and linked it around his. I pulled my hand away. There was a brief moment when I panicked and told myself to run. Take the stairs, because once I was locked away in those closed elevator doors alone with Marco DeVon, things were not going to go well.

My heart was racing, pounding out of my chest. "Marco."

The bell pinged signaling the arrival of the elevator. The doors opened and a woman with her dog stood in the center. My chest relaxed. Relief. We got on. He pushed the lobby floor and the woman put out her hand to keep the doors from closing.

"Oh, no, I'm not going down. Sorry." The woman slid past and got off the elevator leaving us alone.

He didn't wait for the doors to close. He pulled me close, inhaling me for a few moments kissing me lightly but deeply at the same time.

When we landed on the lobby floor, my feet wouldn't move. It was my chance to make a break for it and I just stood there facing him. He pushed his card key in and hit the number 20, illuminating the button. As we moved upward at rocket speed, I came to my senses. "I can't do this." I stepped off the elevator, alone.

He accepted the defeat and smiled softly with regret.

Meanwhile I was convinced it was all a dream. I told myself that none of what happened really happened. I had not just kissed another man on the wildest elevator ride of my life. But it was real. I still tasted his lips on mine. I reached my car and sat for a while before I could start moving. Even then I didn't get far. I sat at the stoplight processing every moment like a slow motion picture. Someone honking a car behind made me finally ease off the brake. I drove, not sure if I was going in the right direction. I was lost in more ways than one.

Chapter twelve

BLISS STIRRED HER concoction over a low heat with her eyes closed, inhaling the simmering brew. When she opened her eyes, I was standing in front of her. The spoon flipped up with the hot liquid just barely missing both of us.

"You know, if I didn't know better, I'd think you put a hex on me," I said.

Bliss tried to stop from laughing. The fit of giggles was already bubbling up her throat. "So you coming in from a lunch date sexually frazzled is my fault? Look at you. You're completely guilty."

"I'm guilty of nothing." I placed both hands on the counter top. "You're not going to make me feel like I'm imagining things. I know what I know. You are responsible. Let's face it, you're..."

"A witch," Bliss answered. She stirred the pot and made an eerie noise, mocking me, before rolling her eyes. "Guess that's better than being a bitch."

"You said it, not me. Besides, I'm not being a bitch. All I'm saying is take some responsibility. Own it. Make peace with it and then give me some kind of warning before you create one of your little spells. I have a life and I think I want to keep it just the way it is."

"Some people enjoy misery."

"I'm not one of those people. What I enjoy is a since of stability. Knowing what tomorrow has to bring instead of waking up in pure anxiety. Now, look at me." I put out my shaking hands. "I'm a wreck, thanks to you. Why did you sign that contract and not tell me? That's what threw me off track. I was completely blindsided."

"I did tell you."

"When? We haven't even talked about it since we came home from Chicago."

"I told you I thought it was a good deal." Bliss looked up innocently. Her hair was parted down the middle in two long braids. She focused back on her pot. "I want the money, my half. I'm sorry, but that's the way I feel."

"Well, I guess you can always come up with one of your spells and make me sign it too. For now, it's not going to happen."

"Rudeness," Bliss whispered. "I wish I had a spell to cure that." Bliss waited until I marched off to let out her amusement. She chuckled loudly, knowing it would get under my skin.

I did an about face. I stomped back in the kitchen holding my shoes because now my feet were throbbing right along with my head. "Stop it. That's not funny."

"It is funny. You have the audacity to think your attraction to another man is my fault. That's pretty darn funny if you ask me." She stirred the pot and couldn't stop grinning. She shook her head with pity.

"What?"

"My dear sister, you should know this by now. No one can make you do anything. Although it never hurts to make someone see their potential, give them a glimpse into their possibilities. There are no magic spells or hexes. Supernatural is a word used for what you don't understand. There's no sorcery or incantations. I really resent you saying that," Bliss finally admitted. "My feelings are hurt."

I came around to her side and put my arms around her. "I'm sorry. I was being rude. You're right. I needed someone to blame. I kissed him," I confessed, thankfully in a whisper.

"Hi Auntie Bliss. Hey mom." Mya came in yawning and stretching like a lion.

"Hey, what're you doing home?"

"The school called. I went and picked her up. She had a slight fever," Bliss answered for her.

I pressed my face to hers. "You are warm."

"Yeah, but I'm hungry." Mya plopped down on the barstool. "What're you making?"

"Something sweet like you." Bliss stopped stirring and put the top back on the pot. "You just gave me an idea for a new name. Sweet Poo."

Mya laughed. "That's not a good name. Sounds like poo-poo. No one wants to put poo in their hair, Auntie Bliss."

"We'll just see about that."

"We've got soup," I called out from the cupboard. "Chicken Noodle. Eureka."

"I'll take it," Mya said. "I'm not picky today."

"You have every right to be picky. Life is too short to settle," Bliss offered. She'd done something right in the Johnston household. Her niece appreciated her pieces of wisdom. It was like having Grandma Sarah there. Bliss liked to repeat her anecdotes that put the way things worked into perspective. Sarah Johnston passed away at the age of ninety-six. Her memory and spirit remained a bright guiding light.

It was our connection to Grandma Sarah that made us not want to give up on each other no matter how much we disagreed.

While I heated up the soup, Bliss pulled out the bowl and spoon. We were a team, always in sync. She was right. No one can make you do anything.

I swirled the noodles in the pot thinking about Marco's kiss. As much as I tried, I couldn't shut it out of my mind. I kissed him because I wanted it as much as he did.

Chapter thirteen

EVEN WITH THE HOT SHOWER steaming, Sirena's naked body shivered from the aftermath of Lucas. He was the wrong man, she told herself. No matter how she felt about him, he was the wrong one.

Even now after he was gone, the mere thought of his hands caressing up and down her thighs sent waves of pleasure all over her naked body. That and the conditioner she squirted in the palm of her hand. She hadn't left the shower. The pressure felt too good. A place of serenity. As long as Lucas kept paying for luxury hotels, how could she refuse him?

Her current dwelling barely had a good stream of water, let alone hot enough water to steam up the mirrors and glass. She rubbed the conditioner into her wet curls.

This was a record for her. Three years and counting without a single extension or weave. She'd kept it short on purpose, not just because she couldn't afford a salon visit or a good lace front. It was the joy of washing and rinsing, even more since discovering the Two Sister natural products. She read the bottle again. Lucas had taken her shopping and she bought a new bottle called GRACE. She was definitely the picture of grace. Accepting without reacting, that was what the bottle read.

She was doing the right thing. She hadn't tried to contact Christopher again. She hadn't stormed Venus and Jay's doorstep demanding the money they'd stolen from her. And she hadn't blackmailed Lucas into doing what she dreamt about in the dark recesses of her mind.

No. For once Sirena ignored the urges and let the clock tick without worrying about running out of time.

There was in fact, plenty of time. No rush. Everyone would get what they deserved. She was already reaping the rewards. Lucas made it possible for her to spend the nights with him. She didn't ask how, if he slipped an envelope in her PO's hands, put a gun to his head, or simply asked nicely, it wasn't her business.

For the first time, she wasn't concerned about the 'how' or 'why'. Somehow she knew everything would work out.

So now what? Did that make her some kind of love slave? As demeaning as it sounded, she didn't care about that either. If letting Lucas Heights have his way with her was what she had to do, so be it. Warmth she couldn't control swam through her body with the thought of him penetrating her. In all honesty, he wasn't the only one enjoying himself.

She turned off the shower water. As soon as she did, she heard the phone ringing in the suite where she'd been holed up for the last few days. Probably the hotel manager, concerned that the housekeeper couldn't get in and it was well past checkout.

She wrapped a towel around her and let wet footprints drip across the tile. "Hello."

"Good, you're still there. Get dressed, get your things, and come downstairs," Lucas ordered.

"Yes, sir."

"Ha-ha." He hung up.

She wasn't sure if the ha-ha meant the joke was on him or damn right he was in charge.

She dried off and slipped on the knit dress that made her feel as girly as her hair products. She pushed her feet into the Todd flats she'd purchased at the consignment store. She'd always worn high heels before. After three years of wearing nothing but cheap cloth shoes, her arch was nonexistent and flat shoes were the only thing comfortable. She stopped at the door and caught a full length of herself in the mirror. She was hardly the same Sirena Lassiter that once graced movie posters, sold out stadiums, and magazine covers. Her seductive one sided smile was gone, replaced with a full face from one too many bowls of rice, beans and tasteless gravy. Would it kill the state correctional system to offer a salad or carrot stick?

Outside, Lucas sat in his large undercover cop car. He looked the role, a sleek for hire contract killer. She wondered who his latest victim might be. Some poor wifey who wanted relief from her abusive husband and knew no other way but to stop him from hurting her. Or maybe someone who'd been a loyal employee for years only to be fired with no warning. The people who called Detective Lucas Heights wanted redemption, the kind that could only be delivered by a bullet to the temple.

She may no longer agree with the act of killing someone, but she understood the rage that led up to the decision to make the call.

"Did you miss me?" Lucas asked when she opened his car door.

"Always."

"I'm starting to believe you," he said slipping a hand around her neck and pulling her in for a kiss.

"Then you're more gullible than I thought," Sirena responded flippantly as possible. She didn't want him to know she felt the same way, that she craved his touch when he wasn't around, or missed the deepness of his voice in her ear. "I need to go pick up my car. What if they find out it's registered to me?"

"I had it towed. It's back at your place."

"I also have a job that I haven't been reporting in for. You going to fix that too?"

"As a matter of fact..." he nodded.

"Thank you," she said genuinely grateful. He seemed to always be one step ahead. She liked that about him. There were also things she didn't like, even hated. "Tell me something, do you ever regret what you do? Does it ever weigh on your conscience, lying to people setting them up?"

"I'm saving lives. Why would I regret that?"

"You lie to people and pretend to be someone you're not, the same way you got me thrown in prison."

His rough, harsh laugh filled the car. "So, you spent your life on stage, singing about love, hope, broken hearts, and renewal, and you're trying to pay some guy to kill somebody. Yeah, okay, so I'm the phony." He hit a drumbeat on the steering wheel to end his punch line. "So my answer is, no. I absolutely have no regrets for doing my job. If there weren't so many psychopaths in the world, I wouldn't have to pretend to be something I'm not. And by the way, I saved your life. If I hadn't intervened in your half-baked plan you would've been in prison for murder, you got off with attempted kidnapping. You're welcome."

"Why didn't you just tell me you were an undercover cop, if you cared about me, why didn't you just tell me the truth?"

He reached out and took her hand, bringing her palm to his lips. "You are a smart, sexy, beautiful woman who stole my heart. I was hoping you were smart enough to make the right decision. There's nothing else to say."

"In other words, I'm the stupid one." She snatched her hand away. "I couldn't make the right choice then, but I bet I can now. What do you want, Detective Heights, what exactly can I do for you?"

"Who said I wanted anything? Can't I just be happy to be in your presence?" His smile could light up a room and he knew it. Best to turn away. She kept her eyes trained out the window. *He wasn't the man she wanted*, she repeated to herself. He was a means to an end, nothing more, nothing less.

Sirena shook her head. Seemed they were going in circles, literally and figuratively. She was sure they'd passed the same corner for the third time. She'd asked the question a thousand times in her mind. Why her? Why had she been the chosen one? There had to be other more suitable women, the kind he could bring home to mother, not a psychopath, as he so kindly put it.

"Earth to Sirena. Hey, whatever is going on in that head of yours is probably wrong."

"Everyone wants something. You're using me. I want to know why," Sirena calmly stated.

"You know exactly what I want." He slid his hand up the center of her warm thighs.

She grabbed his wrist. "Don't. Just don't. If you can't be honest with me, we don't have anything else to talk about."

"Is that what we've been doing, talking, being honest with one another?"

"You know what, I rather spend the rest of my nights in that rat hole than be your toy. Pull over. Stop the car. I've had enough of this."

She fumbled with the lock. Each time she pulled it up; he automatically locked it from the other side. He didn't stop, nor slow down. He sped up and just like that they were on the highway headed north on the I-95. "All right. Calm down. I'll tell you what I want. Exactly what I want. Once I do, don't even think about walking away."

Sirena wasn't afraid. Whatever he wanted would only put him more in her debt. As the old song said, 'a fair exchange ain't no robbery.' She needed him more than ever if she was going to get what she was due.

Jay may have had her heart, but she wasn't going to let him get away with her money too.

She reached out and grabbed Lucas by the hand. "You can trust me. I'll do whatever you want me to." She leaned in and kissed him full and hard on the mouth. She meant it, whatever she had to do, she would do.

Chapter fourteen

JAKE CIRCLED FOR THE BLOCK for twenty minutes looking for a parking space and finally had to relent, handing over his precious baby to the valet who smelled like a cigarette factory and would surely leave that smell behind in his car.

Most of his annoyance came from another place, one he wanted to ignore. The part of himself he hated was when his inner control freak reared it's ugly head. If his wife just did what she was supposed to, he wouldn't have this problem. Would it kill her to call him back, report in, let him know his family, his children, and his castle were safe?

He had a valid reason for wanting her to stick to the schedule. He'd gotten a phone call from the record label again, this time telling him that Sirena Lassiter was threatening to sue if the money wasn't returned to her. He'd laughed it off until she assured him that Sirena wasn't making idle threats.

"She visited our offices," the woman with the nasal tone had said.

"How did she visit your office? She's in prison."

"Apparently, not anymore, sir."

Jake called the only person he knew who could give him a straight answer. The District Attorney's office apologized for not having told him that Sirena had been released early. There'd been a list of inmates who were released early due to overcrowding. Sirena Lassiter had proven herself rehabilitated.

Now, his every waking thought was of Sirena descending upon his life, his family.

He took a deep breath to calm down. The last thing he wanted was to appear agitated while meeting with his agent. Jake saw him at the table and told the Maitre'd he'd seat himself.

Harvey sat hunched over his Blackberry studying the screen with laser intensity.

"Wassup, man," Jake put out a hand betting Harvey wouldn't let go of his phone for a shake.

Harvey did the unthinkable and stood up for a hug along with the shake. "Jay, you're looking good." The dinner meeting may not have been as random as Harvey made it sound. The show of affection made Jake wonder if bad news was coming. The last thing he needed was more bad news.

Facing Harvey with all seriousness Jake simply asked, "What the fuck, man? Am I getting cut from the show, or what?"

"Cut? What? No. I guess you're not one for surprise birthday parties either."

"I don't like surprises of any kind. Just tell me what's going on."

Harvey leaned in and lowered his voice. "It's pilot season. I got a call from Bert Yancy. He wants you as the lead in his new spin-off crime drama. Those CSI's run for ten years. Never, in the history of one of his shows have they canceled. He usually pulls the plug himself. Yancy wants you. It's like a lifetime membership to a CSI Trust Fund, baby."

Jake shook his head in shock. "Wow."

"Just wow? I think you should go for it."

"But..."

"I knew you were going to feel guilty about this. Trust me, actors jump ship all the time. Wait, strike that, not all the time because the opportunity rarely happens. You can't pass this up. There's no such thing as loyalty in Hollywood. Make hay while the sun shines. There's no pension plan for the discarded actor."

The reality of what Harvey was saying made sense. Jake would be a fool clinging onto loyalty when he could be written out of the show with a stroke of the keyboard. He was a peripheral character, nothing more.

A woman walking towards their table locked eyes with Jake. Dark familiar eyes, he thought before realizing he didn't know her. He relaxed in his seat.

"I'm sorry to bother you," she said. "But I've got to take a picture with you." She didn't wait for Jake's approval. She stuck her face against his and held her camera phone an arm's distance away and snapped the picture. "You are one gorgeous man," she whispered before turning to walk away. Her backside was extraordinary. She turned around abruptly catching him staring and giving him a follow me nod.

Jake turned his eyes away and put his attention back where it was needed. "All right. I'm in. Let me talk to Josh before you put the word out. I owe him that, especially since he took a chance on me when no one else would."

Happiness spread over Harvey's face with a red burst of color to his cheeks. "I'll work out the details."

"Just don't open your mouth till I give you the word."

"Absolutely. I respect your integrity," Harvey said with a sincere grin. "Now let's eat. I'm starving."

"Me too," He said, not adding but definitely thinking, *in more ways than one.* A starving man was a dangerous man. It didn't help that women were constantly throwing themselves in his path.

"We should order a bottle of Dom to celebrate."

"No. None for me. I have something else to do tonight."

"Something, or someone?"

"Yoga. That's all."

"Yeah right? That's short for Yoga Instructor. Don't tell me, you're getting private lessons?"

Jake blinked innocence. Harvey opened his phone and held up the list of names and numbers. "Everybody's got a yoga instructor. Ladies who charge by the hour. Do you see a familiar name on there?"

Jake didn't have to scroll down too far before he saw Nahlia's name. He handed the phone back to Harvey but kept his silence.

"Hope you're getting your money's worth." Harvey smirked.

Chapter fifteen

TURNS OUT THE quick nap lasted into the late afternoon. Instead of being panicked and worried the world was spinning out of control without me at the helm, I was calm and euphoric. A miracle had taken over my mind and body giving me a full satisfying eight hours of sleep.

I should've felt guilty for that kiss. No. I felt the complete opposite. I was rested and clear headed. Had it been that simple all along? I'd forgotten how good it felt to be wanted. I leaned back on the down pillow and closed my eyes to remember his arms around me.

His soft breathing in my ear on the elevator, the warmth and strength of his heartbeat against my chest. His entire body pressed against mine. This memory would have to be my elixir. I'd use it every night if I had to. What was the harm in remembering? The damage was done.

I reached over and grabbed my telephone. Eleven missed calls from Jake. Seven missed calls from Marc DeVon. It was already weird.

The phone only rang once before the deep voice answered. "Well look what the cat dragged in."

"How original." I smiled into the phone and hoped he couldn't sense feline satisfaction.

"I was starting to take it personally when you didn't answer my calls."

"There's nothing personal to take. The kiss was definitely unexpected. I'm not upset, I just wanted to say, that's not who I am."

"I know that." He shuffled around on the other end of the line. "Can I ask you a question?"

"You get one, so make it good."

"Are you happy?"

"How original?" I slapped a hand to my forehead. "Well, here's an original answer, yes, I'm happy. I plan to stay that way."

"Good," he said, not shaken from his path in the least. "So dinner?"

"I can't."

"Why not? We still have business to take care of. The contract, remember, I need a decision." He stayed silent on the other end. His presence was undeniable. Almost as imposing as his lips near my ear the day before. There was no pretending he didn't have an instant effect on me.

"I decided, remember?"

"No. It's all a blur. Kind of like your decision."

"You're right. I have a lot to think about. I don't know if I'm ready to give up the one thing that's been keeping me together. Even if Bliss wants to sell, I'm not sure it's the best thing for me."

"Distractions. They work for a while but then the wall comes down."

"Would you stop with those open ended responses? You're making me doubt everything I say."

"I see."

"Fine, I may as well hang up if you're going to continue like this."

"There's nothing abstract about what I said. *I - see,* is a clear response."

I wished I had something sarcastic to say, something witty to pretend he wasn't getting to me. Instead. "What do you want from me?"

"Nothing you're not willing to give."

I clamped my eyes shut wishing he hadn't made it so easy. "I'm not willing to give my dignity. It's just the way I'm wired. I don't need another romantic setting with you to make a decision. I'll get back to you in a few days."

***

I wanted to bury the rift between Bliss and I. I knew she was still thinking about my rude accusations though I'd apologized a few times already. I knocked on her bedroom door.

I whispered, "Bliss, you up?"

I heard soft footsteps before she appeared. "I'm up. I was waiting for you."

I came in and sat on the edge of her bed. Her laptop was open to a list of all the ingredients for the Two Sisters products.

"I want to apologize for the mean things I said yesterday. I was mad, kind of being spiteful."

"You think?" Bliss squished her nose into my cheek. "I told you it's okay."

"I can't believe we're really selling this company we built. We haven't talked about it and I think we should."

Bliss reached out and touched my arm. "It was fun, but now its just work. I rather take the money and do something exciting, like travel. There's so many places I want to see, so many things I've never been able to do."

"Yeah, like where?"

She left that part blank. She didn't have a destination. "Grandma Sarah left me the property but I can't sell it. It's a home for the elderly and sick. All those people living there have no other place to go. If you hadn't taken me in, I don't know where I would be. You are the best thing that's ever happened to me," Bliss said before welling up. "I know you're hurt by my wanting to sell. It's the bond we have, but it's not the only bond. We're sisters. Now that we've found each other, we're never going to lose each other again." Her arms stretched wide before wrapping around my shoulders.

I squeezed her waist with a tight hug. "I get it. I'm glad we talked and came to an understanding about everything. I'm going to sign the contract. I'll have it delivered. I can't see Marco again."

Bliss smiled defiantly. "Well, at least you know you still have a pulse. You don't deserve to be stuck in your castle waiting for your ruler to visit whenever he sees fit."

"Don't say things like that. Jake and I are going to work things out. You'll see. What about you and Nigel? Any plans?"

"Nigel is sweet. If I were interested in having a relationship, it would definitely be him."

"Why aren't you interested?"

"I think you know. Way too much work. I rather spend the energy working on myself than someone else. Men are difficult creatures. Would you honestly marry Jake all over again if you knew what you know now?"

"Nobody's perfect, including myself. I've had my share of transgressions."

"If that's what you need to tell yourself," she said pleasantly enough but the words hit and stung before she recoiled.

Bliss had painted a bleak picture. It was a few months ago when she came to me about her vision. Most of it was already coming to fruition. The call, announcing Jake's new role that would keep him away even longer.

The woman was another part of the vision, someone Jake cared about deeply. Bliss couldn't see her face, only a snapshot of their bodies entangled. She didn't want to tell me that part, but I forced her. Now I was busy punishing him for something that hadn't really happened. If it had, there was no real proof.

I realized letting myself be attracted to Marco DeVon was part of that punishment.

"I'm going back to bed. It's the weekend and I still have some catching up to do. I think I may have found an answer to my sleep problem."

"I made a new tea," Bliss offered, "I bet that would help."

"The last time I drank your sleepy time tea I woke up more tired than I started. I had bad dreams that made me think I was running the whole time." Insomniacs will try anything at least once.

"This one is different. I promise. Very calming. If nothing else, it will stop your worrying about everything under the sun and moon."

She handed me the cup. I took the tea back to my room. I sipped the tea and ignored the bitter aftertaste.

I took another sip before I sank into the pillow and closed my eyes in the darkness. I wanted to forget about the ridiculous behavior, the lunacy of being in another man's arms.

Instead, it's all I could think about. I threw my eyes open, not wanting to see Marco, without his shirt, his strong wide chest flexing with the slightest movement. All too real. I fought to keep my lids open as they drifted downward for sleep. Each time my eyes closed I felt Marco DeVon's mouth against my ear, on my neck, his hands trailing up my thighs.

This wasn't happening. I flashed my eyes open again. I was losing the battle. My lids fluttered unable to resist.

This is what you're missing.

His tongue lapped gently at the tender skin around my nipples, teasing, driving me crazy. His strong weight pinned me down and wouldn't let me get away. His mouth encased every sensitive part of my body.

I'm going to take my time with you.

His mouth slowly gravitated to the tip of my tiny bulb of pleasure. "I can't hold it any longer. I'm ready to climax."

Wait for me.

"I can't. I can't wait." The vibration, the rhythm of his breath and tongue working in unison to sent waves rippling through my core and made my heart race, my toes curl. A wail of satisfaction left my vocal chords. I couldn't wait.

That was the last thing I remembered. It was hours before I awakened, exhausted. My legs were loose and weak as if I'd ran ten miles, or had the longest sex marathon of my life.

I looked over at the half empty cup of tea and knew who was responsible for this.

"Bliss!" I called out in the hallway as I fought to keep my balance, still dizzy after the tea induced orgasm. It was 5:30 in the morning.

Jezzy came out with her robe double lapped around her long frame. "What's going on? A fire? What the hell?"

"I had a nightmare. I'm sorry to wake you," I whispered, though I knew it was too late for apologies.

Christopher rushed out of his room with his narrow bare chest beating in panic. He held a fake sword in one hand and a shield in the other. "Mom? Are you okay?"

"I'm fine, sweetie. I'm sorry to wake you early on a Saturday morning. But guess what? We're going to California. We're going to see your dad."

"All of us?" Mya appeared too, gravitating under my wing.

"Yes. All of us," I said full of resolve. Bliss was now standing outside her door.

"I can't. I have a game tomorrow," Christopher announced.

"It's not going to kill you to miss one game," Mya said, stifling a yawn. "Don't you want to see Dad?"

"My last game of the season in case anyone cares, is tonight. Maybe he's the one that should be coming here." Christopher disappeared back into his room and shut the door.

Mya rubbed her still tired eyes. "I'll go with you to see Daddy, Mom."

"I think Christopher has a point. Maybe we should all go to his game." The hallway meeting was adjourned. "We'll see dad next weekend."

"You promise," Mya pleaded near tears. It was the most vulnerable I'd seen her in a long while.

"I promise." I kissed her on the forehead.

Bliss disappeared back into her room without a single word.

Jezzy shook her head with disdain from all the commotion. "I'll take care of the children. You need to go see your husband. It's written all over your face."

That's not what was on my face, but nodded. "Yes. You're right."

"You don't mind going to Christopher's game do you and taking the kids to see him play?"

"Yes. Can't wait," she said with exaggerated excitement. She took a few steps closer before whispering, "That boy wants his dad at the game. Doesn't matter how many of us pretty ladies are sitting in the stands." Her expression turned matter of fact before she spoke again. "It's time you put your feet down."

"Foot," I corrected her.

"In your case, it's feet. You need to stop floating in the clouds and put your man in check." Short and sweet. Jezzy said her peace before sashaying down the hall.

Single women's advice to married women was the worst kind of counsel. Except this time Jezzy's insight was a direct hit straight to my gut.

I had to lay it out for Jake and tell him how things were going to go from here on out. Dreaming about another man holding me through the night was not going to work out. If we were going to survive this distance between us, there were going to be new rules. I packed a small bag, kissed the babies and caught the first plane to Los Angeles.

Chapter sixteen

SIRENA HELD ONTO the railing looking over the cruise boat fighting the urge to hurl the heavy cocktail she'd consumed. The minute Lucas told her what he'd wanted her to do, she should've said no. Luring her with the promise of half a million dollars was unfair.

Even more unfair was his promise to return the favor. He would grant any wish she wanted. "Any wish?"

"Anything." He'd nodded sincerely before assuring her. "I know you've changed so I don't have to worry about what that wish will be. Whatever you want," he said sweetly.

She'd almost laughed in his face. She hadn't changed at all or she wouldn't have agreed to do him this favor. She wouldn't be on a giant yacht pretending to be someone she was not. However, today she was the lover of a wealthy businessman. Her alias, Dafina Arroyo, spoke softly and wanted nothing more than to be stroked and cuddled like an overfed cat. She didn't have much more details. Only that Lucas's plan didn't involve the police, FBI, or any other law enforcement which meant if things didn't turn out as he'd meticulously planned they were on their own.

She was on her own either way. Her stomach felt weak. She wasn't sure if it was the prospect of dying at sea, or just the motion of sailing at full speed on the ocean. No land to be seen from any direction. She gripped the rail and closed her eyes. Criminals could pray too. What Lucas was doing was dangerous. And here he'd accused her of being the psychopath.

"Here you are, my darling." The Nigerian accent came from behind her. Lucas, aka Nikko Nwomeh smiled holding two drinks in his hand. His white shirt and tan slacks gave him a breezy billionaire appeal. For a few seconds Sirena forgot they were only playing pretend.

He handed her the drink and kissed her softly on the lips.

"How much longer?" She whispered before taking a sip.

"As long as it takes, my darling." He moved a wisp of wind blown hair from her face. The wig, the tight dress, and the high heels were all making her sick. He moved close to her ear. "Remember the signal."

Sirena took his hand and followed him back to the deck where the rest of the private cruise party sat. The silver haired man with tan skin held a thick cigar between his fingers. Sirena sat across from him and crossed her legs seductively. One of the women who sat by the silver haired man's side gave her the evil bitch-don't-even-think-about-it eye, which only made Sirena smile.

Lucas leaned forward clasping his hands together "I guess we should get down to business."

"Not in front of the ladies. I don't want to hurt their delicate ears." The devilish older man winked at Sirena.

Lucas faced her holding his drink and cigar in the same hand. "My darling, do you mind going down below and letting the men talk."

"Not at all. I'm not feeling too well." Sirena pressed a hand to her forehead. "Maybe too much sun." She stood up but only long enough to fall back down. She fainted. Her body began to tremble. The other guests gasped in panic.

"She's having a seizure," Lucas announced in mock panic, coming to her aid. "I need her medicine." He kneeled at her side. "Darling, can you hear me?"

Sirena arched her back and rolled her eyes. She may have been over doing it. Pain from her head hitting the too hard deck made her cringe, and then there was what she'd heard the silver haired man say. "Go, quickly, do what you have to do," he growled. "Because if her ass dies she's going overboard. Last thing I need is a dead whore on my boat."

With that said, Sirena flailed her torso and legs to show she was still alive. *Hurry up, Lucas.* She heard footsteps coming and bucked at a slow and steady pace.

The silver haired man's voice sailed over her shaking body. "What's taking him so long? Why the hell did he bring this broken doll on my ship? Go find him?"

Sirena was getting tired, losing steam. She knew if she stayed still even a second too long, the silver haired man's goons would scoop her up and toss her like shark bait over the side of the yacht.

Time was moving in nano seconds. Soon she'd be struggling to keep the water from filling her lungs. No amount of money was worth this. Nor what she'd imagined as the biggest wish, revenge on Jay and Venus for stealing her son. She didn't care about the royalty checks. Nothing was more important than her making it off this ship.

She suppressed the wail when the needle went into her thigh. Vitamin C, Lucas said. A simple super dose of Vitamins. A calm coolness ran up her leg landing in her chest and slowly to her brain. Rainbow colors flashed in bright hues. She saw her childhood. Sirena was a good girl. She did what she was told and listened to her parents. Always so obedient. But then her mother left. She was only ten years old. She needed her mother.

"Babe. My darling, are you okay?" The Nigerian accent called out, "Darling, please wake up."

She grabbed his hand before he slapped her again. She coughed and fought her way to consciousness. "I need to get to a hospital." This was the last part of her Oscar winning role.

"We need to go ashore. I need to get her to a hospital," Lucas repeated as if the entire crew and their guests weren't witnessing their performance. "Now!" He shouted for good measure.

By the grace of God the boat switched gears and began turning around. She wouldn't be shark bait after all. She sipped the cup of water someone had brought her but maintained her desperate recovery. It wasn't all an act. Something in that shot made her see clearly. More clearly than she'd ever seen before. Life was short. It was time she took control of what was left of it.

Chapter seventeen

THE PLANE LANDED with a thud and I was on my long lost home turf, Los Angeles where I'd been born and raised. I didn't tell my parents I was coming. I had one mission, getting Jake half way across the country in time to see Christopher's last game. It was still early thankfully. The extra three hours crossing into the Pacific Time zone gave me a head start. The man behind the car rental desk took his sweet time helping the two customers ahead of me. I tried to be calm and pleasant when it was my turn.

"I'll take whatever you have available."

"Let's see," he said looking on the blue screen in front of him. He surveyed his inventory with a keen eye. The reflection illuminated his glasses.

"I'm not picky. If it starts and does at least the speed limit I'll be fine."

"How about a Dodge Dart? Good gas mileage on those. Oh wait, I got a Taurus. Love the new Taurus." He scratched his grey stubble. "How many miles do you plan to use?"

"Miles? I don't know. What difference does it make?"

"Well, you can have the package with unlimited miles or say you're only going to a local hotel and back, you can save a lot by using the under sixty-mile package."

Before he could go on. "You know, I'm running late. Anything you have is fine."

"Well, which one? Under sixty or unlimited?"

"Unlimited," I said standing on my last leg of patience. A mini lifetime passed before I got the contract and keys to the red Dodge parked out front like we were meant to be together all along. It was the smallest car I'd ever been in. Since becoming a mom, Vans and SUV's were my only choice of transportation. In this tiny box with four wheels I felt threatened by all the bigger cars towering over me.

Once I was on the 405 Freeway headed to the city of Santa Monica where Jake stayed I began to relax. Jake's place wasn't that far. He'd found a house to rent close to the water. When we first dated he lived in the same area. The beach cities brought about calmness. The ocean air cleared your mind. He never missed an opportunity to remind me how much he'd wanted to live here permanently.

I missed it too. There were good memories like our first night together. Him standing on the balcony staring out at the moonlit sea with no shirt on like a hero in a romance novel. We'd made love with the sound of the wind and shore in the background. As chaotic as our relationship started, it was also the happiest time. Meeting Jake was a Godsend. Just the sound of his voice on the other end of the phone made my toes curl. I wondered how I'd gotten so lucky. What had I done to deserve such an amazing man who loved me unconditionally? Those memories kept me grounded for a long time.

I parked on the street and looked up apprehensively at Jake's window. I felt like he was there peeking down at me. As much as I wanted to see him, I was nervous and scared about my impromptu visit.

Calling ahead would've derailed the plan. Jake was the most logical man I knew. Things had to make sense and follow a certain order. A plan of action was necessary for everything, from grocery shopping to traveling the globe. He followed his list or itinerary to the letter. Unpredictability led to expensive mistakes. Spending unnecessary money was high on his list of annoyances.

We'd had our problems with being in the red in the past and never wanted to see those lean days again. The price of my airline ticket with only one day notice would be an issue to be discussed, later. For now, I had one goal that I'd planned to follow to the letter.

I pushed the buzzer. I had the entry code and key but waited a few seconds out of courtesy. Not to mention I didn't want to get mistaken as a burglar. This was a surprise trip after all. I didn't want the story of the spouse being shot accidentally showing up unannounced on the evening news.

I let myself in. "Hello, babe, are you here? It's me," I called out taking in the bachelor minimalism. One tan colored leather wrap around couch. A glass table on Teak wood. Four black leather chairs seated around more glass. At least that one was round. I pictured all the places the twins would get hurt bumping and grabbing things.

But this place wasn't for the children, or me, I supposed. The floors and walls were white and spotless. If not for the large sliding glass window being open with the ocean breeze whipping the curtains around, there'd be no energy in the place at all.

I went to his bedroom. Just as I thought, his bed was the picture of perfection. Pillows stacked and fluffed like a hotel advertisement. The only thing missing were the chocolate and rose petals on the silky white comforter. I went to the bathroom and checked there. Not even a towel out of place.

He had a housekeeper, but she only came once a week. I wasn't a professional sleuth or anything but I knew the signs of an unused sink, faucet, and shower. I fought scale and water spots in my own home like a Ninja warrior. Here, there was nothing but polished chrome. Which begged the question, if he wasn't sleeping here, where was he laying his head at night?

It was time to end the surprise element of this plan. We didn't have time for cat and mouse. The last flight from Los Angeles that could get us to Christopher's game on time was a mere three hours away. I called his cell. The phone rolled to his voicemail. "Guess what, I'm here at your place. I wanted to surprise you, but, *surprise*, you're not here."

I'd hung up feeling lost and foolish. I wasn't sure if he filmed on Saturdays. After all our years together I should've known this wasn't going to work. Jake was always one step ahead. While I was still stuck planning snacks and lunches for a toddler pool day, he was taking over the world, discovering a new artist or planning his next move.

I collapsed on the couch. I kicked off my boots and put my feet up. I took a long needed deep breath and focused on the chandelier overhead.

Not just any chandelier, the real kind, flamboyant, girly with too many crystals twinkling, and calling for attention. This was not something Jake would've wanted in his space. And it certainly wasn't there when he'd moved in. That no-nonsense man of mine would've considered this elaborate hanging ornament a show of boastfulness. We all knew boastfulness was the work of the devil, right up there with idle hands and drinking out of someone else's glass.

I sat up and studied the intricate elephant in the room knowing with absolute certainty a woman had influenced his decision. A sales woman's influence? No. This particular woman spoke with a voice that could make Jake listen and pull out his Black card. Something that wasn't easy.

For the first time I was angry. I replayed what Bliss told me about her vision of Jake with another woman. I suppressed the bitterness and anxiety, swallowing it into silence. All those endless nights of not being able to sleep. Now I knew why.

No matter how much Bliss had told me about her vision, it was my own instinct I'd ignored. Jake was a good man. No matter who was in the room, from the assistant who brought him his Green tea Macchiato between takes, to the director who held his career in the palm of his or her hand, he made that person feel respected and special.

I'd trained myself over the years to accept Jake's success and generosity as a placebo to his other not so great attributes. I'd ignored my gut, my intuition, and also the facts.

The same way I wanted to turn a blind eye to knowing Jake had not slept here last night. I stood up and stretched then got to work. Underwear drawer, side tables, bed, cabinets, all given my special touch of snooping like a hound dog on a mission, or in other words, like a *bitch* searching for a bone.

An hour later I'd found nothing. There was no evidence. No panties between the leather couch cushions. No dropped earring left under the bed or chair. Not even a stray piece of paper with a phone number written down. All there was for me to see was the enormous light fixture hanging over my head, taunting me, whispering, *you'll never know.*

I tried Jake's cell again. The voicemail immediately picked up. I spoke softly with a big message. "Jake, call me. I'm still at your place, but I won't be for long."

I stared up at the twinkly sparkling prisms on the chandelier with glossy tears threatening to fall. The not knowing part was what drove me insane. That piece of missing puzzle left me incomplete and frazzled. I realized I would never have the satisfaction of knowing how many times Jake had not slept here, therefore would probably always feel like something was missing, from me, from us.

I left the condominium as good as I'd found it. I got back into my Red Dodge and drove to the one place where I'd sworn I wasn't going to go.

Chapter eighteen

JAKE WOKE UP IN THE middle of the floor staring up at the ceiling. He didn't know how he'd ended up flat on his back. Which meant only one thing, at some point during the night he'd lost control of his mind, and from the looks of things his body. He was laying in nothing but his silk black boxers. Josh had rented the hotel suite for the cast to celebrate the show's season finale. Empty champagne bottles and glasses littered the floor along side of his clothes.

"Hello? Anybody here?"

He wasn't expecting an answer. But one came. "I was wondering when you were going to wake up?" Nahlia kneeled to greet him with a kiss on the forehead.

"What happened?" Jake sat up still wobbly.

"Oh. That's nice. I don't think I've heard that response before." Nahlia handed him his pants, then his shirt.

Jake grabbed her wrist when she went to give him his shoes too. "Nahlia, seriously, what happened last night?"

"You really don't remember." A snide chuckle followed. "I guess I should've known." She shook her head. "I actually thought you were finally letting go, moving past your doubts."

He put a hand to his head and squeezed his eyes shut to block out the excessive light outside. The last thing he remembered was the camera flashing, smiling faces, and laughter. He'd been surprised to see Nahlia at the party. He hadn't invited her and she didn't work on the set, yet she'd been there mingling with the rest of the crew. She held up a glass and said, "Congratulations on your new show," over the crowd and music.

Josh was the only person he'd told about leaving for the new opportunity. The party turned into a celebration. "May you find success and joy on your new show," Josh said with a toast. "We're going to miss you. And if they kill you off, you know you can always beg for your role back as Jeremiah Blackmond," He joked, but the send off was still heartfelt.

The champagne was cold and tingly. The minute he took the first swallow he felt different. Someone drugged him. There was no doubt in his mind.

"Nahlia, did we sleep together?" The fear on his face was undeniable. He hated to ask. He was afraid, deftly afraid of the answer. Never ask a question you didn't already have the answer to. Somewhere in the recesses of his memory, he did have the answer.

"Did we have sex last night, you mean?" She pulled her wrap dress tighter to close the exposed part of her cleavage. She hunched her shoulders "I guess last night wasn't that memorable for me either. Sorry, I don't recall." Her dark hair flung over one shoulder. She stood and gathered herself before disappearing into the bathroom.

If he were a woman he'd go straight to the police station and report that he'd been drugged and sexually assaulted. But by who? Nahlia wouldn't have done this to him. She seemed hurt at the thought that he hadn't remembered a thing about last night. Hurt because she wanted whatever happened to have been real. Not from a narcotic haze.

He knocked on the bathroom door. "Nahlia, I'm sorry. Whatever happened, I wasn't in my right mind. Okay, that's all I'm saying. Someone put something in my drink."

She fumbled with the knob briefly before peeking out. "I think you should leave." The door closed just as quickly.

He couldn't remember where he'd parked. He checked his wallet to see if there was a valet card from the hotel. A grateful sigh left his lips.

Outside, he handed the parking stub over to the valet and stood nervously under the shade wondering if whoever played pharmacist with his drink had also done something to his car.

Porsche engines had a specific rhythm. He heard it swerve around the ramp. He resisted the urge to look until it was stopped and directly idled in front of him. He opened one eye at a time to see the light bouncing off the gleaming hood of the car. Still beautiful. Not a scratch on her. A small mercy compared to not knowing if his life was in jeopardy. The thought of being exposed to—no, if anything, he was more afraid of his wife than any STD known to man.

Not until Jake was in the car did he reach for his phone. His phone that wasn't in the cradle charging. His phone that wasn't in his front pocket. His phone that he never ever left behind, was gone. His only connection to the real world, the one that mattered, had slipped out and fallen under a couch or chair.

The car could stop on a dime, that's what the dealer told him. His foot slammed on the brake. He pushed the gear in reverse and then into Park. He tossed the keys back to the valet. "I'll be right back."

He rushed inside and went straight to the reception counter. "I just checked out, but I left my phone. Can somebody let me in?"

"Of course, sir. What room number?"

Searching the foggy haze of his mind, the room number didn't come into focus. "It was a suite, on the eighteenth floor." Jake kept the elevator in his line of sight. If Nahlia was leaving, he'd catch her, and ask if she knew the whereabouts of his precious line of communication.

The clerk tapped a few keys. "I can look it up. Your ID."

"Well, it wasn't in my name. Josh Bein, he paid for the suite. I mean, how many suites do you have? Huge. Facing North. Double door entry. If you could just send me up with somebody with one of those master keys." He slid the clerk a twenty.

The clerk pocketed the bill and typed a few more keys. "I think I know which room."

"Thank you," Jake whispered to mask the desperate tone in his voice. "If we could move pretty quick, I'd appreciate it."

There was some noise coming from the room when Jake and the suit wearing security guy stood in front of the door. "This one, you're sure?" He asked before knocking.

Jake nodded with confidence, though he wasn't sure at all. "Hey, I got an idea. You mind if I use your phone to call my number. If it rings, I know it's inside."

"What if it's on Vibrate?"

Of course it was on vibrate. Jake tossed his head back. "Right."

The security guy knocked one more time before he slid his magnetic key over the black box. Jake followed him inside. Music was coming from the bedroom. The suite already looked like someone from housekeeping had been inside from the stacked glasses on the bar and table. There was no sign of Nahlia.

"Go ahead, dial your number."

Jake dialed, waited for it to ring then began his search. "Hit it one more time," he told the guy. He listened, pushing furniture around, and lifting where necessary.

"All right, that's a wrap. Looks like it's not here."

"Call the housekeeper. Someone cleaned this room and must've taken it."

"Maybe one of your friends took it and their holding it for you." Security guy offered up his own advice. "Hey, do you have the Find My Phone app? I heard those work. You punch in your code and number and a tracking signal starts."

Jake couldn't say for sure if he'd enabled the feature remembering his thought process at the time. Privacy was a big issue. Allowing his every move to be recorded on a digital tracker was considered self-destruction for a married man, any man for that matter. "Yeah, I'll do that. Thanks for your help," Jake said, passing on the useful tip before handing back Security guy's phone.

"You know, you look familiar. I've seen you. Are you on TV, that show, what's the name of it, the one with the ex-Baywatch lady?"

"Yeah, I get that all the time. It's not me," Jake said before peeling out of there. Like he'd confess to who he really was. The day was on a downward spiral. He couldn't imagine it getting any worse. The last thing he needed was to be recognized as the actor who'd partied too hard and lost his phone and dignity all in the same night.

***

When the store tech loaded up his new phone with his back-up data he checked to make sure all his previous files were intact. All the music he'd written in his off-hours sitting around waiting for his cue. All of his contacts still stored. He left the store grateful to have the world at his fingertips again.

He saw the messages load up right away. He pressed the button and a video started playing. Grainy at first. Everything was filmed too close as if whoever was taking the shots was also holding the camera. The picture eventually focused on eyes, a face, and pulled back to entangled limbs. Only Jake recognized it wasn't just strangers, a man and a woman in a compromising position. It was he and Nahlia doing what they did well. He was bent over her lithe hips with his legs sprawled. He cringed, though the laughter around the two of them was filled with approval and encouragement.

Laughter? Who would think this was funny? It was a woman voice directly behind the phone. Whoever was holding his phone while filming he and Nahlia, were thoroughly entertained. "Go, baby," one amused woman yelled over the sound of panting and exhaling. "You know how to dig that dog. Uh, me next," the mystery woman howled over the video.

Jake shut it off before it played to the end. He'd obviously been the night's fodder doing his yoga positions wearing nothing but his boxers, half naked. He cringed and fought the dizziness that clouded his mind. Someone had to have drugged him. He was more convinced than ever.

He scrolled down to his sent messages out of pure instinct. Sure enough, the video had been sent to a multitude of people on his contact list. The first, and most important person on the list was his wife.

He closed his eyes and wished he could transport himself to another universe, another time zone, another life because this one was ruined.

Chapter nineteen

I HADN'T EXPECTED MY mother's hug to feel so good. I hugged her back and inhaled the familiar combo of coconut and lavender coming from her hair. She now wore it in a short cut that framed her face nicely. After her fight with cancer, she'd hidden her natural hair underneath wigs for a long time. I hadn't seen her in over a year and couldn't believe how healthy and vibrant she looked.

"Mom, you look beautiful." I squeezed her until she stopped hugging first.

"What brings you to LA? I could've been on a cruise. Don't you know better than to just show up on somebody's door? And, where are my grandbabies? You didn't leave them with that Ju-Ju woman, did you?"

"Mom." I shook my head. She'd refused to give Bliss a chance which caused the friction between us in the first place. She'd heard rumors about Bliss's mother practicing Voodoo and was convinced she'd put a spell on my father.

No way Henry Johnston would've cheated on Pauletta in his right mind. Not much different than me accusing Bliss of making me kiss Marco DeVon. The proverbial apple didn't fall far from the tree. We all wanted to blame someone else for the bad things in our lives.

I stifled my smile. "Jezzy is with the children," I said, refusing to go down that road. I lunged forward for another juicy hug before she stepped sideways.

"Okay, what happened? What's going on?" She demanded giving me the look of suspicion.

"Is dad home?"

"Your father, he's in charge of bible study on Wednesdays. I want to know what's brought you here. Jake have some fancy party you were invited to? I've been watching his show. He's the only reason I watch. Too much legal lingo. But I don't want his show getting canceled from lack of viewers."

"Good, mom. You not watching could make the difference."

"You're darn right. One person can always make the difference. You have to do your part. You can't watch it later on DVR, you have to do it in real time. That's what Oprah says. I watch all her shows too."

"Mom, I don't want to talk about Jake. I wanted to see you and just..." Before I knew it, I was in tears.

"Well now." She folded her arms around me. "Guess you need your mom after all."

She started toward the kitchen. "Come on. I have some chicken in the oven. You should be hungry after traveling."

I followed behind slowly, using my sleeve to mop up my cheeks. I looked at all the pictures on the wall from elementary school to my prom, in chronological order, in simple black wood frames. I stopped completely to look at the only family picture with all four of us. My older brother Timothy hadn't been home in almost five years. He worked in Kenya for a non-profit group teaching children.

"Wow, looks like you've been doing some remodeling around here." I sat at the kitchen table and checked my phone. Still no call from Jake. I wasn't angry so much as I was worried something may have happened to him. My mother caught me looking at my phone and the pained expression on my face.

"Your father is at church. Suddenly he's Mr. Faith. I tried to get him into church for thirty plus years and he didn't want to have anything to do with sitting in the pews. Now he's there volunteering Monday through Sunday."

"People change."

"Do they? Now that you know who your father really is, I don't have to tell you it's probably a woman."

For a second, I thought I was hearing myself talk. The apple didn't fall far from the tree, apparently was more than a cliché. It was truer than most people could guess. I'd inherited my suspicious gene. Jealousy, like a food allergy or brown eyes versus blue, was passed along and I had nothing to do with it. The possibility also made me sad because I didn't want to be doomed to suspicion hell, always thinking Jake was seeing someone else.

"Dad loves you."

"What's not to love?" she said with a dignified wave of her hand. "I'm still as beautiful as the day he met me. He's the problem. He just can't be satisfied."

"If you don't trust him, why do you stay with him?" I figured if I had her answer, I'd have mine too.

"We've been married for forty-three years. Why would I let all my hard work go to waste? Let him go take care of some other woman?"

"I don't want to live that way," I said out loud. I wanted to leave that very minute knowing she'd take it as judgment of her status when it was really a judgment of myself.

"You live your life the way you need to live it. Don't worry about mine. I've got everything under control. Trust me."

My stomach bounced around until landing in a firm knot. "I love Jake. I hate always wondering."

"You married a celebrity. He's always going to be admired. That's the life you chose. As long as he puts you first but if you're not happy..." She exhaled. "The last thing I should be doing is giving you advice. I'm sorry."

"Sorry for what?"

"For not leaving your father when I was younger and finding someone to love and really love me back so you could see what it looks like." She blinked away the tears pooling in her eyes. My mother reduced to tears was a rare sight. This may have been the second time in my life I'd ever seen her cry. As strong as she pretended to be, all she wanted was to believe that my dad loved her unconditionally. So much of her happiness was dependent on my father. I understood all too well.

"I love you, mom." I kissed her on the cheek and held on this time even when she'd stopped hugging first. I wished I knew how to make her happy, how to make her stop feeling the way that she did. If I had the answer for her, I'd have it for myself as well.

We said our good-byes at the door. I promised I'd come back and bring the kids. She promised she'd come to visit, though I knew as long as Bliss was there she probably wouldn't. But in that moment I realized the best thing I could do was stop waiting for other people. If I wanted something I had to go after it pure and simple, no one was going to knock on my door with a box of happiness, special delivery.

If Jake didn't want to be found, so be it. I started the car and backed out of the driveway of my childhood home, giving my mom a wave and an air kiss.

I took a deep breath and turned on the radio for the first time since renting the car. I pressed the buttons until I heard the tune that made me smile. Smiles were free, why shouldn't I use them as often as I wanted.

For the first time in a long time I had a Jerry Maguire moment, that scene when he's in the car driving down the highway singing at his highest pitch, *I'm free, free falling.*

Feeling like things were finally going my way, if for no other reason than because I said so.

Chapter twenty

WHEN THE PLANE LANDED I felt instant relief, glad to be home. How could I have believed it was a good idea to surprise Jake with a visit? I'd been down this road, showing up unexpectedly and finding more than I bargained for.

I pulled my bag from under the seat in front of me, and right away turned on my phone like the hundreds of others who didn't follow the rules of waiting until the plane was parked in the jetway.

The sound of beeps, bells, and ringtones filled the cabin before the plane was completely stopped. I had a message from Jake. I was relieved to see his name light up my screen. At least I could stop imagining the worse, like a car accident. So if he wasn't wrapped around a rail, where had he been? I stared and contemplated what he could possibly have to say.

What had I expected? Like my mother said, he was a celebrity living in California like a bachelor with unlimited freedom on his hands. What made him any different from all the others? He wasn't a saint, that much I knew.

I didn't bother opening the message. I wanted Jake to suffer from my silence. It was my only weapon of power for the time being.

Before I could put the phone back in my purse it buzzed and shook again like the message was urgent. I finally pressed the button. The mail went straight into video mode. The darkness on the screen opened up to a clear shot of two people. I couldn't make out the faces at first. When the view focused I let out a yelp like a puppy who'd been hit or stepped on.

I turned it off unable to watch anymore. It was clear enough what was happening. The passengers started moving. I stood up, lightheaded. I forced myself to calm down but it didn't stop the center of my chest from aching. *Oh God, I'm having a heart attack.*

This was my final lesson. I'd been with Jake through the fire and we'd come out okay, even better than we'd started. But this time, I wasn't sure I was going to make it.

I folded myself up and waited for the screaming in my head to turn into a whisper. *You married a celebrity. You chose this life.*

There was a moment, however brief that I tried to talk myself out of what I was about to do. The next thing I knew I was dialing his number.

"Are you still in town?" I asked, believing I had a wistful air in my tone. I didn't want to sound like I was on a mission of spite and revenge.

"Yes. Still enjoying your lovely habitat. I planned to leave in the morning." Marco DeVon said sleepily. "What do I owe this honor? Did you have a change of heart?"

"As a matter of fact, I did," I coyly responded. "I was wondering if you were available to meet, tonight."

Marco choked back his shock. He now understood my full intention. "Where are you?"

"Not far." My voice turned seductive. "Should I bring anything?" This was me making a booty call. This was me deciding if Jake wanted to play, I'd show him how it was done.

***

Marco opened the door before I could knock. His fervor sent a shiver of uneasiness down my back. He reached out and pulled me inside, greeting me with a passionate hug. Once the door closed he wasted no time sliding my purse off of my shoulder and slipping his hands around my face. "Hi," he said casually, but the kiss was chaos mixed with promises of a new beginning.

I pulled back to set the record straight. Kissing was for lovers. He obviously was on the lover's path. I, however, was on a completely different road. One of melee and deception. I was out to fight, destroy, and deconstruct everything I once was.

"Are you okay?" He realigned my face with his and parted my lips gently with another kiss, the kind that dropped pretense and wet panties all at the same time. I tried to pull away, just to give myself a chance to rethink what was happening. What was I doing?

But he held me tight, inhaling my reservations and doubt, making them disappear. "I thought you'd never get here."

That made two of us. I never thought I'd be this woman, this kind of woman.

I thought about how many times Jake had lied to me, made me believe I was blowing things out of proportion. "Make love to me," I said in a low whisper.

This time there was no apprehension. Marco DeVon knew how to take an order.

Two hands scooped me up, lifting me off the ground. He moved us effortlessly to the bedroom. I landed on the bed. Within moments I was free of my jeans. He fingered the edge of my panties with admiration. The printed T-shirt with a globe of peace on the front came off next. The bra too, left behind. His eyes flashed greed but he maintained patience by leaving me in my underwear.

He lifted my ankle to his lips. His chest rippled with each movement. "You're so beautiful," he whispered into my skin. His hand massaged the length of my calf, lightly trailing my inner thigh and stopping just short of where I needed him to be.

The few seconds that passed with him intensely staring into my eyes made me realize this was going to be far more than a passing ship in the night. He meant business pulling me forward establishing his domain. The moment he pressed his weight against my body I wanted to cry out with grateful glee. *Someone wants me. You see, even if it's not you.*

As if he could read my mind, Marco grabbed my face and made me focus on his eyes. "Do you see me?" He slid his hand down the center of my breast until he traveled the distance to my core. His fingers tasted the wetness before diving inside. I wanted more than his fingers.

"I see you," I said to appease him.

"Will you regret this?"

"What?"

"Tomorrow, are you going to wish this never happened?" This question came all the while his face was pressed against my inner thigh. I could hardly breathe let alone answer any questions.

He rose up and slipped my bra off my shoulders and kissed me there too. "I don't want you to regret this. If you're going to hate me, or wish you never met me, I'll stop right now." The intensity in his eyes spoke for him. He planned to do damage, leave a footprint, and simply making love wasn't enough of a description.

"You're asking me that now?" The thought of walking out, leaving him, was too much to bear. I climbed on top of him pinning his arms at his side. "Do you have protection?"

"Of course."

"Then I'll have no regrets. I didn't come here to talk." I planted my mouth on his. I wanted sex. I didn't want the conversation that went with it. I loosened his tie and unbuttoned his shirt. It was my turn to do the seducing. I worked my way down to his belt and zipper moving with urgency.

"What did you come for?" His strong arms moved underneath lifting my hips. He teased my pelvis with an erection ready to burst out of his pants.

I couldn't lie to him. "My husband cheated on me."

Marco dropped his arms in disappointed fashion. "Nothing like a good revenge fuck, huh?"

"Exactly."

He gripped my shoulders. "Wrong. I waited for you, to call. But this isn't what I was waiting for. You're better than this."

"Am I?"

"I should at least be glad I'm the first person you called." He stood in front of me with his broad chest exposed, strong and still vulnerable. "I was the first person you called, right?"

"Yes." This wasn't what the doctor ordered. I didn't need a lecture.

"You don't want to do this. You should go, because if you stay, I can't guarantee I'm going to do the right thing." He leaned forward and took ahold of my chin. "I care about you. I think you're smart and beautiful, and worth waiting for."

I shook my head, for him to stop. What he was saying was too personal. I wasn't looking to talk about my feelings or share my hurt and loneliness. It was none of his business.

"We're going for a walk." He tossed my T-shirt, where it landed on my face. I took my time getting dressed.

"Let's go," he ordered slipping on his shoes near the door. The only thing missing was a doggy leash. He kept a firm grip on my elbow as if I'd planned to make a run for it.

The dark sky filled with clouds hid the stars. The air was tempered with moistness. A storm was coming. I walked with my eyes forward, determined not to look in his direction. Embarrassment and exhaustion filled in the silence.

"Do you think I go after married women as a common practice? Because I don't," he said before I could answer. "I'll tell you the truth, I fell for you the minute I laid eyes on you. Probably before I even walked into the room. I felt ridiculous. I knew who you were. Almost everything about you, Mrs. Jay P. But I ignored my logic and flew out here anyway. I had every intention of that first kiss. I really didn't care what happened after that. You're fun, sexy, and beautiful. The real kind of beautiful, naturally glowing."

I began to wonder who this mysterious person was he was talking about. I wasn't sexy or fun. *Naturally glowing?*

I focused back on what he was saying.

"I started telling myself maybe their marriage is in name only. Celebrities don't like for things to get out. So maybe, just maybe, there's a chance, if I'm patient. I even gave it a time frame. Hell, I even wondered if you could squeeze out another kid or two."

"I can answer that, ah no."

He smiled. He stopped walking and looked me in the eye. "You don't have to compromise yourself." He brought my hands to his lips. Before I could look away he pulled me closer. "If he doesn't care about you, or he makes you feel less than you are, then you have to make a choice. You deserve better," he said before kissing me lightly on the forehead.

I closed my eyes and let the tear easily slide down my cheek. I was no longer ashamed or embarrassed. I was understood.

"I just wanted to be held," I confessed.

"I can do that." He wrapped his arms around me. "But here's the deal, the next time you come to me, come because you want to be with me. Not out of spite, or revenge, do you understand?"

"There's not going to be a next time." I swallowed the lump in my throat and tried not to let his words fill my heart.

"If you say so."

"I say so," I said with conviction. I didn't want to love another man. No matter how bad Jake treated me, no matter who he made illicit videos with, I didn't want to admit I'd wasted all those years.

Chapter twenty-one

"WHERE HAVE YOU BEEN?" Jake's voice traveled through the dark living room where he sat contemplative and hurt. He pulled the chain of the lamp snapping the light on.

"I wanted to surprise you." My purse suddenly weighed a hundred pounds. The strap fell off my shoulder and landed with a thud. My phone slid to the floor and coincidentally lit up with a silent call coming from Marco. It landed a few feet from Jake.

I reached for the phone but he was quicker than me.

"You couldn't answer your phone?" He held it up like ransom. "I've been calling you nonstop. Is this about the video?" He must've come home on the next flight, desperate to explain.

"What video?"

He looked like he'd swallowed a canary. Feathers choking him, a beak scratching his throat. "I thought you saw the video."

It took everything I had to keep my mouth from quivering. He was directly in my face. Leaning close as if he were looking for clues. "You didn't see the video?"

"No."

When I wouldn't look at him he put his finger under my chin and presented the earlier question. "Then where were you?"

"I was trying to make my way back home. I guess I took a wrong turn." My eyes flashed with something he didn't want to see. He took a step back.

"Christopher is missing. No one's seen him. Do you know where he is at two o'clock in the morning?"

I held out my hand. "Can I have my phone?" I said before we moved on. "I'll call his friends and see if they know where he is."

"What is it that they would know, that you, his mother wouldn't know? Why would they know more than you?"

I stood baffled, silent with no answer guilty of whatever his choosing. His ability to turn the tables on me was unprecedented. Though it was he who'd made a sex tape and hadn't slept in his bed for God knows how many days.

I held my breath steady. "Let me just make a couple of calls, I'll find out where Christopher is."

He finally placed my phone in my hand. I saw the tiny message across the screen revealing a voicemail left from Marco.

"Hey, you didn't tell me where you were," Jake said. "How did I get here before you?"

"I was trying to get home. My flight was canceled. I had to take another one that left me in Houston for three hours." I hunched my shoulders for effect. Lying was never my skill set. My mother always told me I'd never be a good politician, actor, or gambler because my face would give me away. I turned away. "I have calls to make." I moved further away. Maybe with a little distance he wouldn't be able to hear my heart beating past my chest, or see that my legs were trembling. I could barely stand.

"So this is what goes on around here. Chris is gone all night and you have no idea where."

I faced him. "Now that you're home, I'm sure we'll all come to our good senses." That would teach anyone who thought I was incapable of a poker face. I raised the stakes and moved even closer, slipping my arms around his waist. "I'm glad you're home. We'll find Christopher and then we'll spend some time together."

I didn't know what else to say. There was nothing for us to talk about except the children. Anything beyond that would lead to a place I wasn't prepared to go. I could feel his suspicious glare follow me until I was out of sight. I wanted Christopher to be safe but I was grateful for the distraction.

Bliss was coming out of her bedroom when I rounded the corner. "You're home," she stated with an uneasy look past me. "Did you see Jake? He's home."

"Yes. And Christopher is missing. Do you know where he went?"

Bliss shook her head, unwilling to say anything out loud. Whatever information she may have wanted to offer, she wasn't willing to do it with Jake within hearing distance.

I pulled Bliss close. "This isn't good. Where could Christopher be? He went to his game, right?"

Jezzy came from the darkened hallway, answering before we could see her clearly. "I took the twins to his game. We sat in the bleachers and cheered him on. His team won. He said he was going for pizza with this team. I told him, be home by twelve."

"But his curfew is eleven, Jezzy," I blurted.

"His team won," Jezzy repeated, enough said.

"Well he's not back yet. Jake's furious."

"Mr. Jay is here." Jezzy didn't like lawlessness. She needed structure in her life and at this point we were bandits and thieves running amuck. She seemed relieved to have Jake home while Bliss and I felt like two teens caught smoking.

"Can you think of anyone Chris might've left with after the game?"

Jezzy shook her head. "It's probably that girl, the one who's been treating him like gum on her shoe. Ratchet girl. She's got control issues. She's a cheerleader. I wanted to throw something at her while she down on the field, but I have to lead by example. I didn't want the twins seeing their Jezzy acting a fool."

I had a new piece of the puzzle that could help. I didn't have Milan's number but I knew who would have it. I dialed his friend Romeo who obviously was determined to live up to his name by romancing every girl he saw, including his friend's mother.

"Hey Mrs. Parson," he sang answering on the first ring as if he was routinely up this late. "I knew you'd call one day," he said jokingly, but not really. His flirtatious smile traveled through the phone line.

"Hi Romeo. I'm looking for Christopher, have you seen him?"

"Um, yeah. Last night, after the game."

"Where exactly? And who was he with?"

"Um, a lot of people. It was the season ending game and we won, you know."

"Right. Yes. So, was one of those people Milan?"

Romeo's usual glib personality turned stone cold. Giving up information to a parent was the highest order of treason.

"Romeo, if you have her number, and I'm sure you do, can I have it, please?"

"Um, yeah. Hold on." A few tapping sounds later, he read off the number. "But I don't think he'd be with her. They broke up," he added.

"Who do you think he might be with?" I asked growing irritated at the slow rate of forthcoming information.

"I don't know. I saw him get into a car but I didn't see who was driving."

"What kind of car?"

"Blue. I think. Yeah, maybe dark blue. Could've been black, but more like dark, dark blue."

"Okay. Romeo, do you remember what kind of car, not just the color?"

"One of those big cop looking cars," he said. "My grandma drives one. Big hoopty."

Before I could ask another question, my phone was pulled from my ear. Jake took over the interrogation. "So you didn't see who was driving?" The change to a man's angry tone must've alarmed Romeo. Jake shoved the phone back to me. "He hung up. So three adults here, and nobody knows where my son is."

Bliss and Jezzy felt the sting of his chastisement, something I was use to but it was new to them.

"Mr. Jay, my job is to take care of Henry and Lauren. But I love all of these children like my own. That's what I do. I do my job without any time off because I love all four of your babies like my own." She cut her eyes toward me. "I'm sure Mr. Christopher is fine. He's a boy. Teenagers have their problems. But he'll be fine."

The pep talk seemed to work. Jake reined in his attitude and took a breath. "Thank you, Jezzy. I know you work hard. I appreciate all the time you spend here."

Jezzy was right. Christopher was a teenaged boy with problems of his own starting with a father who wasn't paying him any attention, and a mother who was swamped in her self made drama.

"I have to lay down," I said already moving unsteadily down the hall. Jake was on my heels.

Inside our bedroom, I kicked off my shoes and sat on the edge of the bed.

He kneeled in front of me and placed both hands on my jean covered thighs. "Are you all right?"

"I'm sorry," I said, genuinely feeling guilty. "If I hadn't been gone, Christopher wouldn't have been able to sneak off."

"You have nothing to be sorry about. Like Jezzy said, this is what boys do. I'm the one who should apologize." He unexpectedly switched to compassion, a big difference from his accusatory tone from a few minutes earlier.

"I'm just thinking how much he wanted us at his game. I let him down. I've been preoccupied lately."

"I understand. You can talk to me. I would've flipped out too if I saw that video. You have every right to be angry."

I tried to appear unfazed. So there it was, the setup. His way of segueing back to his infraction. He wanted to get it over with and out of the way.

"I told you, I never saw the video that you're talking about. Do you want to show it to me now?" I asked, testing him. I opened my nervous, shaking palm, knowing exactly what he was going to do.

"It's not important." He pressed the delete button sending the video message to oblivion. "Someone thought it was funny to snatch my phone and film me doing yoga. I swear, I think someone dropped something in my drink," he said half joking. "But it's okay. I'm just glad you didn't see it. I wouldn't want you jumping to wild conclusions."

"Yeah. I'm glad I didn't see it too. Did it get sent to Christopher?"

"I don't know. I didn't check where it went exactly. The only person I cared about was you." His eyes pleaded sincerity.

"Wow, must've been pretty serious."

"No. Really, it was nothing." He stood up, case closed. Now we could focus on finding Christopher. I was content to change the subject too. He couldn't know how hurt and angry I was about the video without me telling him everything. I'd end up telling Jake about the lengths I'd gone to out of vindictiveness. He'd then know where I'd spent the past few hours. In another man's arms.

My stomach was filling with disgust. I thought I was going to be sick. I fled to the bathroom, closing the door. My hands felt numb and my mouth was dry. What had Jake and I become?

I stuck my face under the faucet. I ran water into my hands and drank for my parched throat.

"Are you all right?" Jake knocked lightly on the door.

"I'm fine." The mirror reflection staring back at me was pitiful. Circles rested under my red eyes and a scowl I couldn't seem to erase. I wanted to stop the emotional bleeding. A soft towel muffled my last bout of pity for myself. I went back out to face my husband. "Let's go find our son."

Chapter twenty-two

WE'D TALKED TO ALL of his friends and exhausted every lead. No one knew anything. No one had seen anything except Christopher getting into a big blue car. We had no choice but to call the police and report him as missing even though we didn't want to believe it was true.

Jake and I greeted the detective at the door. He was a tall, imposing man who made direct eye contact and dared you to look away. "I'm Detective Brewer. So your son has been missing since yesterday and he's thirteen years old." He sat calmly on the couch as if it were an everyday occurrence.

Another black teen missing in Atlanta was not a priority. There was also the problem of Jake's reputation. Jay P, the hip hop star turned actor had been accused and arrested for the murder of his accountant. It was a lifetime ago. We'd moved to Atlanta to get away from the spotlight of rumors in Tinsel town and wanted to get a fresh start. Who knew the Atlanta set was shining just as brightly. Seemed we were invited to a party every weekend.

Eventually everyone learned those gatherings were expensive. No one could afford to host a big catered party and act like all was right in the world. Still, we were an elite club of who's who. Or who used to be. Celebrities, entertainers, and athletes in our own exclusive club.

None of that mattered now. Jake and I were average people who'd lost a child. There was no extra protection from the universe or the local police department. They didn't send out their most promising, career driven sleuth. They sent whoever was available to take the case.

"I'm going to eliminate a kidnapping scenario since no one has contacted you. I'd like to check his room. Does he have a computer? Does he have a cell phone so we can check his calls?" Detective Brewer inquired.

"Yes. We've called him but it only goes to voicemail like it's turned off or something. I've contacted his friends and no one knows where he is. Someone else has to be involved. He's not the type that would run away," I offered to get past the niceties. We needed action not an inquisition.

"Mr. Parson, do you have any issues with anyone who might have wanted to settle a score, revenge, that type of thing?"

If there were ever a wrong question. Jake stood up. "What kind of question is that? I'm not in the mob. I don't sell drugs. I'm a musician and an actor," Jake said with amazing calmness. "Would you ask Brad Pitt if he had a score to settle? Now that we've gotten that out of the way, you want to see Christopher's room."

***

Day three. It was as if Christopher had been zapped by an alien ship and vanished into thin air.

I heard the doorbell ring and marched from the kitchen. Jake had already opened the door. Detective Brewer, who'd fast become our new best friend stood with another police officer, this time a woman. From their stoic expressions I knew it wasn't good news.

"Come in," Jake offered, escorting them to the living room. We all sat down on the couch and chairs, except for Jake who could barely sit still. He spent all of his time pacing or standing.

"This may be our only lead," Detective Brewer began. "Christopher's biological mother was released from prison a couple of months ago. We found out from his phone records and texts that he's had some pretty intense exchanges."

Jake didn't look surprised. Not as shocked as me. "What do you mean? She's supposed to be in prison for the next thirty years. At the minimum twenty." I held out a shaking hand to take the transcript.

"I circled the ones between he and his mother."

"I'm his mother," I said before I could   stop   myself. This was no time for pettiness. Jake came and stood next to me to read what he could before I turned the page. Pages. I was speed reading a continuous dialog of endless bullying.

"I don't understand. How could she have gotten his number?" Jake asked, which was the least of the important questions.

How did she get out? Didn't the parole board know she was a danger to society? A danger to me? Jake wrapped his arm around my shoulder, feeling the rumbling where I was about to implode.

"One of his earlier texts asks that she not come around anymore. Meaning she must've seen him face to face. After her initial contact, he may have given her his number as a way to keep her from visiting him in person."

I couldn't believe what I was reading. She was cruel and saying the most horrible things to Christopher, calling him a traitor and a little bitch. "The name calling," I shook my head and covered my mouth. "He wouldn't go with her, not voluntarily."

The lady officer finally spoke up, though softly. "This is pretty common. Making the kid feel like he did something wrong and needing him to make amends. There're no more texts after the fifteenth, the day he went missing. She would've at least sent him another few texts and maybe assumed he didn't want to talk to her. Instead, there're absolutely no more attempts to contact him. Meaning she no longer needed to text. She had him."

Detective Brewer chimed in. "We're sure she's responsible for taking him. The communication stops dead cold." The use of the word 'dead' sent a chill of silence through the room. "I'm sorry," he said with a flag of his hand. "All I'm saying is this is the best thing we could've found out. We know she has him. Now we just need to find her. We already have an FBI agent assigned to the case since it looks like she's left the state."

"Left the state? How do you know?" Jake asked.

"We tracked the phone she was using. The last call signal was picked up in South Carolina."

"If you have her number, can't you track her there? That's where she has Christopher," I added. "We can go get him."

"The signal stopped. At some point, she must've realized it wasn't too smart to carry the same phone around. Like I said, now we have the back up of the FBI. Her leaving the state was the best thing that could've happened. The FBI has the resources to find your son."

Jake tightened his grip around my trembling body to hold me steady. At some point Bliss had entered and came on the other side of me. I was sandwiched between the two of them as if they knew I was going to make a break for it. "How long is that going to take?" My raised voice stopped Detective Brewer before he got out the door.

"We'll keep you informed of any progress," The lady officer said with the same stoic expression. They let themselves out.

"How could she have been released and no one warned us?"

"I don't know," Jake answered into the air above my head. His heart was thumping hard. He was comforting me but he was also reeling from the news. "This is the worst possible scenario," he said. "I kept wishing, hoping, he was somewhere pissed at me and ran off to teach me a lesson. That's what I kept hoping. But this..." his voice fell into a whisper. "I swear if she hurts him..."

"She won't. She won't hurt him," I tried to say convincingly. Knowing what kind of crazy we were dealing with made my confidence feel like a complete lie. Especially after reading those texts it was clear Sirena was insane and capable of just about anything.

"She never wanted Chris. Now all of a sudden she's dying to be his mother." The more he spoke, the quicker his heart beat until the rasping sound began from his inhale and exhale. His asthma, which he'd had under full control, was making its first appearance in years.

"Honey, calm down. Breathe slowly." I led him to the couch. "Sit." I rushed off to the kitchen and found one of his inhalers. I hoped it wasn't expired. It'd been so long since he had to use one. I dialed the disk for a fresh load of inhalant and put it to his mouth. He inhaled and waited before releasing the medicine from his lungs. We both thought the exact same thing but Jake said it first. "I hope he doesn't need his medicine."

Christopher was afflicted with the same condition as Jake. Allergic to the same things, right along with having the same temperament. Calm and logical up to the point where he was likely to take someone out with one blow.

"That's something we should tell Detective Brewer, about his asthma and allergies. They can alert the hospitals. That way if he had an attack, someone might recognize him."

Jake nodded his head up and down but I could tell his mind was elsewhere, thinking of ways to find Sirena and destroy her. All this time we thought we were rid of her once and for all when she'd gone to prison. She was the least of our problems. We had our own issues for once that didn't include her meddling.

Maybe that's what was wrong with Jake and I. We had no one to focus on but ourselves. A dollop of drama and tragedy now we're back in each other's arms. I was almost ashamed of making the connection, linking this calamity to our reunion of heart and mind.

I couldn't stop wondering if this meant we would be whole again. One union. When Christopher came back, this punishment for our self-indulgences would end and things would be different.

Chapter twenty-three

HE WISHED THINGS COULD GO BACK to the way they were. The sun peeked through the clouds giving Jake a glimpse of what he'd left behind in sunny Los Angeles. He missed breezy warm afternoons while he shifted through traffic in his convertible. Life seemed perfect just a few days ago. Now he could hardly stand to wake up in the morning.

He secured his helmet and revved the engine of his Ducati before backing up. A delivery truck blocked the driveway. He stopped just inches before contact. He took off his helmet, put the bike in place and gave it a minute before he got off and headed for the van.

Patience wasn't a friend of Jake's, not lately. Every waking second seemed wasted on things that weren't getting him any closer to finding his son. Nothing moved fast enough. The wheels grinding in his head screeched loud with 'what ifs'. The anger was directed at himself.

He asked himself why he hadn't warned Venus the minute he found out Sirena was on the loose. A warning to Venus, to Christopher, all of them, would've kept everyone on high alert.

But he had his reasons for not telling anyone. Sirena had found out about him cashing her royalty checks. The money, the checks, he'd cashed and put into accounts, half for Sirena, and half for Christopher, which he deserved after what she'd put him through.

She was released on probation with an agreement that she wouldn't contact his family.

"Really? So you took her word for it, did you?"

The District Attorney wasn't daunted by Jake's sarcasm. "Mr. Parson, that wasn't my doing. The Probation Board believes rehabilitation is the goal. If she presented herself as a model citizen she most likely wouldn't serve the entire 25 years, you knew that."

What he knew for sure was that a crazy woman was free to inflict her wrath.

She was supposed to spend the next thirty years in prison and suddenly she's out, walking the streets as if the whole kidnapping and attempted murder thing was a fluke, an inconvenient accident amongst friends.

He wanted to tell Venus. His first thought was to call and blurt out the injustice of it all. Then something clicked.

Telling her the truth, that Sirena was out of prison, would cause a cataclysmic reaction. Suddenly every noise in the house would be attributed to Sirena. Every person who made eye contact for two seconds too long would be one of Sirena's converts. Every phone call made by an unidentified person became a message sent by Sirena. If the clouds aligned and sent a hailstorm, that too would be Sirena.

He knew how this worked. There was only one viable solution. *Come home.* The request, albeit subliminal, would be one he couldn't refuse. The call to protect his family would be loud and clear. He had no intentions of throwing away his momentum to sit around waiting for Sirena's imaginary attack.

If he'd done the right thing—

Jake knocked on the delivery van window where the guy was oblivious he was blocking his way out.

The window went down. The delivery guy stuck his hand out. "Hey there, I'm George, you must be Jay P." The emblem on his shirt read, Fast Express. "I make all the deliveries and pick-ups here. I know your family pretty well." George extended his hand for a friendly shake.

"I'm kind of in a hurry." Jake wasn't in the mood to exchange pleasantries.

"Sorry. I'll move," George said, taking back his hand now limp from embarrassment.

"You do that." Jake eyed him suspiciously until he put the van in reverse and started moving.

Ironically it was Jake now seeing every person as a potential threat. The delivery guy, 'George' who was blocking his car could've been under Sirena's spell. She had that ability to enthrall anyone who came into her grasp. She could make them believe her lies. A good liar was a good manipulator. He ought to know.

Bliss came out carrying a large box. "Hey, what happened? Where'd he go?"

"Guess he was in a hurry," Jake said, not bothering to explain he'd scared him off. "If you don't mind, Bliss, could you not make friends with every Tom, Dick, and delivery guy, that comes around the corner."

Her usual big inquisitive lashes narrowed. "Please don't tell me what to do. I'm not part of your admiration society."

"You're living in my house, then you're part of my society. My society has rules."

He watched her mouth turn into a straight line. He got back on his bike and waited for her to go back inside. "Did you say something?"

Bliss stayed quiet but her expression was a big fat F-you.

"I thought so," he said, egging her on even more. Miss Higher Spirit had nothing to say. "Lock the door when you go back inside," he said, punching the engine. Right now he wasn't concerned about hurting anyone's feelings. His son was missing. All the talk about Bliss being able to see things and communicate with spirits...why couldn't she see his son was in danger?

He hit the gas pedal and left smoke when he peeled out not caring how she felt one way or the other. If you weren't helping, you were hindering. Therefore, you were useless. Jake hit the speed he felt most comfortable, fast.

Chapter twenty-four

The water in the pool caressed her body like silk. The sunshine overhead felt like a warm welcoming blanket. Sirena smiled with genuine emotion for the first time in years.

The backstroke was her only technique. She'd never learned how to swim, not officially. She taught herself how to float on her back. Survival of the fittest. Head up, feet out, arms gliding by her side. Panic and you sink. Flap and you drown. Sink or swim. There was never a truer analogy for life.

Surviving was what she was good at. After almost being thrown over the side of a hundred foot yacht to be eaten by sharks she was savoring life. Living each moment as if it were her last. She didn't care that Lucas hadn't paid her the money he'd promised for help in scheming those crooks. She had something better than money; loyalty.

Every day felt brighter and full of possibility. She swam to the edge until she was close enough to stand up without drowning. "Hey there, enjoying yourself?"

Christopher nodded, but he was obviously sullen and feeling guilty for not telling anyone where he was or who he was with. He knew the price to be paid if he did.

"Are you going to get in? The water's warm."

"I don't know how to swim," he said in between looking up from the new electronic tablet she'd bought him. Gullible. All she had to do was load it up with the latest games that his father refused to buy, and he was putty in her hands.

Jake and Venus didn't want him being distracted from his schoolwork.

Who needed school when you had millions? Lucas may not have written her a check but she trusted him to take care of her and Christopher. They were going to be rich. She could be one of those useless housewives who's biggest worry was which kind of dog food to buy for her poodle.

"Well, you know what, Christopher? We're going to get a house with a pool. You'll be able to swim whenever you want." Sirena pooled up a stream of water from her mouth like a dolphin. She rolled over, hoping the boy hadn't noticed she'd almost drown.

"I have a pool at my house," Christopher snapped.

"That's not your house. It will never be your house. They don't care about you. They only care about *her* children. I don't know how many times I have to keep telling you this."

Sirena pulled herself out of the water and grabbed a towel to wrap around her dripping body. She sat next to Christopher. "When are you going to grow up?" She caught herself before she went too far with the verbal lashing. She was his mother now. She had to act like it.

Gone were the days when he thought she was his sister, the older irritating sister. By the time she'd confessed she'd given birth to him, he was already ten years old. Becoming a teen mother wasn't part of her plan. Not Sirena Lassiter. She'd been destined to become a superstar.

A decade later, there was no warning when the light began to dim. First she blamed it on bad marketing, then bad representation.

The invitations stopped coming in the mail. Her manager swore it was cyclical. You're only as good as your current hit. No hit, no attention.

Once the opportunities dried up she realized what was important; family. Jay had taught her that family was the only thing that could sustain you through the highs and lows.

Unfortunately, by the time she'd accepted the advice, Jay had moved on, and was married to someone else. But the one thing he didn't have was a son, at least not one he was aware of.

Sirena was sure once he found out the truth he would see her through different eyes. He would look at her the way he looked at Venus, nurturing, loving, and respectful.

Sirena closed her eyes not wanting to relive the emotions she felt about Jay. New day. New plan. New attitude. If she couldn't have Jay, she could at least have Christopher. "You know what, let's do something fun. When's the last time you went to Disneyland?"

Christopher grimaced. "I've never been, and I don't want to go. That's stupid. You just said I needed to grow up, and now you want to take me to Disneyland. How about you just take me home."

"For now, this is home," Sirena said apologetically. She wasn't sure how she was going to convince Christopher that she knew best. Thank goodness perseverance was one of her strong suits.

"Is there a problem over here." Lucas stood over her blocking the sun. A small smile lingered on his lips. His eyes sparkled from one too many Scotch and sodas. His masculine shoulders came closer, leaning forward before meeting Sirena's lips. "Why do I hear you two all the way from over there?" Lucas slid into one of the patio chairs before sipping his drink. He was officially retired from his job as an undercover cop, a reward to himself for carrying out the risky, almost deadly, heist.

While Sirena was lying on the yacht deck faking a seizure, Lucas had been down below accessing the wealthy criminal's computer, transferring an unholy amount of money into an overseas account. Sirena didn't know the true amount, but she figured if Lucas was happy, she was happy. Men were not generous creatures by nature. Nothing unsettled them more than giving away their hard earned money.

For him to spring hundreds a night on this extravagant hotel and taking her and Christopher shopping like it was Christmas, he had to be loaded to the gills. But she also knew there was a price to pay, which was what she was trying to teach her son. Nothing was free, especially not devotion or love. Those things came with constant payment. If those payments stopped, so did the love and loyalty.

"We're fine. Just having a little mother and son discussion."

Lucas reached over and took Sirena's hand. "I'd like to have a discussion with you, right now." He brought her hand to his moist soft lips. "It won't take long."

"Please," Sirena whispered, sending a nod toward Christopher. She'd asked him not to come at her like that. Not in front of the boy. Surely she was making some headway.

"He's a big boy. I'm sure he won't fall in."

"I have a better idea. Why don't you two hang out while I grab a shower?" Sirena rose up not waiting for an agreement from either man. Lucas treating her like a common tramp took away merit points. She'd asked him nicely, explaining that she didn't want to leave Christopher alone. It was too soon. If that meant she and Lucas weren't going to have any adult time, so be it.

Lucas slid a hand up her thigh as she passed. "Whatever you say," he spoke warmly but his eyes radiated impatience and annoyance.

This was a perfect example of constantly paying. As long as she continued to lay down with Lucas he would take care of her and keep her secrets safe. If, and when, she stopped playing love games he'd undoubtedly find a way to make her suffer. "Christopher, think about what you'd like to do, you know to celebrate." Sirena gave his head a soft rub. His only response was slurping the last of his Pepsi. She turned back around to watch them before she entered their suite with a private entrance. They'd driven four hours straight from Atlanta. The further away the better. She didn't want to take a chance on him walking out the door and making his way back to the Gingerbread house.

At some point she'd expected the search to begin. Until then she'd enjoy her vacation, order up some room service and pretend she wasn't a felon on the run.

She jumped into the shower and doused herself with the shampoo and conditioner. She loved the new scents. With each different one she tried she was convinced whoever had created the lovely concoctions were angels sent from heaven.

Normally she'd stay in for as long as she could. She didn't want to leave Christopher with Lucas alone for too long. They'd only just met. It was the first time she'd ever introduced Christopher to anyone she was romantically involved with. Although, she wasn't sure if that's what you would call it.

Romance was hardly what she and Lucas shared. She thought once she and he exchanged favors they would part ways. After they'd made their escape and were safely hidden from the guys on the boat, they spent the entire night ferociously making love like two animals who needed to feed off of each other to survive. He made it clear he wasn't letting her go so easily.

No matter how good he made her feel she could never say she loved him. And she was absolutely sure he'd never say it to her. There was only one man who she knew absolutely had loved her, and that was her father.

When she thought about how he'd died, how she'd been responsible she only wished that she could turn back the clock. Take back the night he'd died, and not be the selfish daughter who only thought of herself. There were so many regrets. Just once she wanted to be a better person. Maybe now, with Christopher she'd get her chance.

She wrapped the towel around her head and peeked out the window to the pool. Lucas lay there with his mouth open and slack, asleep. The chair next to his was empty. There was no sign of Christopher. He was gone. She scanned the pool area before rushing outside. *No!*

"Where is he?" She kicked Lucas and shook him. "He's gone. You were supposed to be watching him?"

He opened his eyes one at a time squinting from the bright sun. "What do you mean, he's gone?"

"You know exactly what I mean?" Sirena only had a towel wrapped around her and could only get so far without every step exposing her naked body. Yelling Christopher's name only made the few other resort patrons eye her suspiciously. She hurried back inside to get dressed. Christopher couldn't have gotten far.

Chapter twenty-five

DAY FIVE OF CHRISTOPHER being gone and it felt like a year had passed. Waiting for something to happen every minute of the day was the worst kind of torture.

Jake stood over me holding a tray. "I brought you something to eat." He'd been distant for the last few days.

Seeing him standing there, humble and sad made me want to stop being angry. Who exactly was I mad at anyway? Me, that's who, rushing off to find Jake in Los Angeles when I should've been home. Then running into the arms of another man for solace. I became bitter each time I replayed my actions. More blame, more punishment, for heading straight to Marco's place instead of coming home. More anger for not trusting my gut when I'd seen the woman who looked like Sirena in the grocery store.

It was her. No doubt. But I'd ignored the fear that washed over me that day. I talked myself out of believing what I'd seen.

I pulled myself up on my elbows. I hadn't gotten out of bed all day. My entire body ached.

"You have to eat, babe."

I surveyed the plate of eggs, toast, and fruit. Food was the last thing I wanted.

Jake had gone on a couple of news shows. A missing child, regardless of his or her age was a crisis. Not one call came in with any leads. Not even the fake kind from cruel people who enjoyed watching other people suffer. The FBI still hadn't found where Sirena was hiding. It was as if no one cared. No one.

"Thank you." I forced a piece of toast before picking up the cup of coffee to help wash down the dry bread. I'd sworn off caffeine months ago but how was Jake to know. Caffeine was not an insomniac's friend. Nor was sugar, which I required to drink the dark brew.

He sat on the edge of the bed. "I was thinking I'd go to his school again and talk to some of his friends. Maybe Christopher told someone about what was going on. Maybe he's contacted them and begged them not to tell. It only takes one, one kid to say he knows something, or saw something."

"Ahuh." There was a lump in my throat I was sure was never going to go away.

"What? You don't think I should?" Jake slid a hand over my shoulder. He added a gentle massage that made me bristle.

"No. Absolutely. I think you should," I said, hoping he left right away. Anything at all was better than giving up. We were never, ever, allowed to give up. I read this online, or heard it from one of the many sites where other parents who'd suffered from a missing child shared their stories. I'd run out of ideas.

Jake squeezed my shoulder again before leaving me with my breakfast and coffee. I shoved the tray off, to the side, and grabbed my phone that was buzzing.

I didn't recognize the number or the area code. Any other time I would've pressed ignore. Not any more. Unknown numbers brought a moment of hope. It could be Christopher or someone who had information.

"Hello," I answered with a full breath.

"How're you holding up?"

"Hi," I said quietly, afraid if I said his name out loud the vibration would break the dam holding all of my fears and regrets.

"I've been thinking about you. I just wanted you to know that. After I'd heard about your son, I figured you needed to devote all your energy with your family."

"I appreciate that."

"I wish there was something I could do to help."

"I wish there was too. There's nothing anyone can do except wait and pray." I wanted to hang up. I was going to start crying at any second and it would only make him care more, dig deeper with concern. In turn, I would reveal how much I wished I'd never met him. Because now of course, I was being punished. Karma. God. The Universal Order. Yet, it wasn't his fault.

"Thank you for calling." The brisk change in my tone seemed to tell him what I could not. I didn't want to be rude. I wanted to appreciate his compassion and not see it as more proof that the past is never the past. Instead, the past was always a precursor of what was to come.

"Okay, then," he said.

"Okay, then." I hung up and checked to make sure I was still alone and then I let the harsh sob leave my throat. I'd lost a child before.

Jake and I had lost our baby son. I'd carried him to term. The same way I felt then was how I felt now, no difference, absolutely none. Everyone wanted me to get over it, move on, stop mourning, including Jake. I wondered if he'd feel the same way now.

I wondered if he would encourage me to let it go. *Things happen for a reason,* and so on. It was my anger talking. Maybe too soon. Too soon to think the worst has happened. Too soon to anticipate the stages of grief, unbearable grief. The sadness he'd feel too would be unbearable.

"Mom, it's me." Mya stood at the entrance holding a piece of paper. "I have to get this signed." She tipped in cautiously.

"The school trip," I said, proud that I remembered. I read the details that I ordinarily would've ignored, when, where, and how. A bus trip. I held the pen over the signature line. "Maybe you should sit this one out," I said.

"What do you mean?"

"I mean, maybe, you could skip the field trip. I'm not comfortable with you going somewhere without..." My words trailed slowly. "It would be best, for now, if we all stayed close to home."

Mya shook her head. "I have to go. It's part of a class project. Just sign it, mom," she said sounding more like the adult in this conversation.

"I can't." I handed the pen and permission slip back to her.

"It's going to be okay, mommy. Christopher is coming back. He's going to be okay." She hugged me before leaving with her pen and paper in hand.

I figured she would find Jake and have him sign it. There was nothing I could offer in the way of convincing her. Mother's know best. Not even I believed that anymore.

Bliss must've been waiting outside the bedroom door. As soon as Mya left she came in. She wore a bright patterned scarf twisted around her hair. She didn't say anything at first. She moved the tray before curling up on the bed next to me.

"How're you holding up?"

"Barely."

"Nigel asked about you. He says Marco is beside himself. He's worried about you."

"I never should have gone over there. All because I was hurt from Jake's scandalous sex tape."

"It wasn't sex. It was yoga," Bliss sarcastically responded.

"I don't care. I stopped caring along time ago."

"If you didn't care you wouldn't have tried to find retribution in Marco's bed," Bliss said gingerly. "It's okay. When all this is sorted out, you can make a decision, a real decision."

I wasn't sure which decision she was talking about. There were so many. "Sorry I haven't been very helpful these last few days."

"I enlisted Jezzy. She's fast, a little too fast. She's been filling the bottles half way. Suddenly we have 50% more inventory. Now I see how those companies start stretching their bottom line by skimping on the product. One ounce, two ounces, next thing you know you've got more at half the cost."

"We can't send out half filled bottles." I really didn't care but I let out a conciliatory chuckle. "Although, Jezzy is a smart one. We can learn a few things from her."

"Did I just hear my name?" Jezzy popped her head in. She saw room on the bed and took it as an invitation. "What I do?"

"Nothing. We're grateful for your help."

"But not your advice," Bliss added.

"Advice? What'd I say?"

"Your grand suggestion for Venus to go find her man. What she found was a slap in the face?" Bliss announced with a critical tone. "And here we are."

Jezzy narrowed her eyes. "Oh no, I don't think you want to go there with me."

I was sitting in the middle of them. I put my hands up for a time out. "Guys, please."

"No. What's she accusing me of? She's trying to say it's my fault Christopher is gone?"

"It's no one's fault."

Bliss peeked her head up. "All I'm saying is, next time someone offers advice, take it lightly. Very lightly."

"You're one to talk. Did I send her out to be turned out by another man?"

Those were fighting words. Bliss stood up. "Have you been ease dropping?"

"I don't need to ease drop," Jezzy said standing up on the other side of the bed. "You two and your bickering make it hard not to hear everything. You better be glad it's only me hearing ya two talk."

"I take full responsibility for my actions. We're all done with the blame game."

"Your actions going to get you killed. Since when a woman take revenge running into the arms of another man? What happened to an old fashioned hot bleach treatment? You throw his clothes in the tub, pour a bottle of bleach, run some water and done." Jezzy smacked her hands together.

"Yeah, that'll teach him," Bliss said from underneath the pillow she'd conveniently pulled over her head.

"Anyway, your man is just being a man. There's a different standard for us women."

"A double standard," Bliss mumbled.

"Enough. Are we done with this?"

"Fine with me," Jezzy said on her exit.

Bliss revealed herself. "Is she gone?"

"Yes, she's gone." I took ahold of Bliss's hand. "You'd tell me if you felt something, if you saw something, a vision, wouldn't you? No matter what it was?"

For a second, I thought I saw a twinge of guilt. "I would tell you, yes. I haven't felt anything. I've tried. Trust me, I've tried to read Christopher and came up with absolutely nothing. Hopefully, it means he's not in any distress. That's what I didn't want to tell you. You might've interpreted it as a bad sign. But I think it's good sign."

She was right. That's exactly what I was thinking. No distress, no signals, might mean the worst.

"Come here." Bliss reached out and hugged me. "It's going to be okay."

"Everyone keeps saying that but nobody knows. I've already lost one son. I couldn't survive the loss of Christopher. I just couldn't."

Chapter twenty-six

SIRENA PUSHED THE REMOTE OFF. She sat on the center of the bed with her knees pulled to her chest. She wasn't sure what she was feeling. Frustration. Seeing the look in Jay's eyes while he sat on television pleading for his son to come back. How dare he?

How dare he look into the camera as if this mess was created out of thin air. Didn't he understand everything that happened was because of him? The entire situation was all on his shoulders. He wasn't innocent like he pretended to be.

She'd taken Christopher merely as a way of making him understand he wasn't in control. No one mattered when it came to getting what he wanted. She wanted him to understand he didn't make all the rules.

He would take out anyone or anything in his path. They weren't all that much different. They both believed in doing whatever was necessary to achieve their goals. Didn't he know this was coming? Did he really need to act like such a victim?

She pushed the remote off on the television when she heard Lucas come in from searching for Christopher. His face told her everything she didn't want to know. No sign of him.

"Sorry," he said, not truly sorry.

"Whatever."

"Look, I think we should get out of here. If someone finds him and he talks, we're sitting ducks."

Sirena closed her eyes. "I'm not leaving here. He might've just taken a walk, a break. When he comes back, we need to be here."

"Cee-Cee, baby," he said, using the pet name he knew to soften her edges. "Christopher doesn't want to be here. He made that clear. Let's just get on a plane to that warm tropical island we talked about. You don't want to go back to prison, do you?" He put a firm hand on her wrist. "If he talks, we're both going to be in trouble."

"Let go of me." Sirena demanded.

Lucas stood between her and the door. She refused to spend another second in the same room with him. He hadn't stopped pleading his case. "I told you he was going to be a problem. Why are you so damn stubborn? Let's just leave, get out of here before he has the FBI at our door."

"How about I just leave?" Sirena said plotting the best way to get around him.

"It's for the best. Can't you see that? You don't need to go backwards, in the past. Not when you have me."

It was happening all over again. Trying to persuade her to forfeit her plans, her desires in exchange for him. Sirena rubbed her hands through her hair, squeezing her eyes shut. She couldn't stop the rage. She was infuriated with him.

"You let him go. You probably gave him money and told him to leave."

His eyes darted away then back to her. "What do you want me to do? He's gone."

"How far could he have gotten? He's a thirteen-year old boy on foot. You probably didn't even go past the parking lot." She'd let him talk her into staying in the hotel while he searched. He probably did nothing but sit in the car listening to music while Christopher got further away.

"I looked, he's nowhere to be found."

"I don't believe you." She tried to move around him. He put his arms out and grabbed her, as she knew he would. She swung around and stomped on his foot then pushed her elbow into his chest. His grip released while he cradled his sore ribs.

"Where are you going, huh?" He wasn't giving up so easily. He renewed his grip this time around her neck before she could make a clean break. He dragged her back inside.

They struggled until Sirena realized she was never going to win. He was bigger and much stronger.

He straddled her on the floor and put his knees on her arms making it impossible to do more than grunt.

"I hate you," she hissed.

Unfazed, he leaned in close to her face. "Different side of the same coin. If you hate me, that means you loved me."

"No. I hate you. I really do," She seethed. She tried to lift her legs to kick him only to strike air. "Get off me."

"Are you going to be nice?"

She wanted to spit in his face but realized it would only land back on her. He rested on top of her like he had all the time in the world. Her heart was racing, knowing that Christopher was out there, somewhere. What if some freaky perv found him? He was a smart boy but he was still just a boy. "I'll be nice. Please, get off of me. I can't breathe."

For a brief second he believed her. A mischievous grin crept on his lips and she knew he'd dismissed the idea of letting her up.

"I promise, I'll do whatever you say. Please, just get off me." Sirena felt the moisture drip down the side of her face. Her own tears. She'd given up on crying a lifetime ago. Shedding tears meant regret, a wasted emotion. Nothing could be gained by mourning past decisions.

He slid a finger across her face. "Oh, baby, don't cry. You've got to trust me. I only have the best intentions for you. Chris is going to be okay. I gave him enough money to get home. A taxi is taking him straight to the bus station. He's not going to tell anyone where he's been, who he's been with. We can walk out of here and get on a plane, fly anywhere you want to go and be free of this nonsense."

Sirena willed the tears to stop flowing, clouding her judgment, hindering her ability to speak. She nodded, yes, her eyes pleading for mercy.

"That's my girl," Lucas said feeling proud of himself for breaking her down. Her weakness became his prize. He kissed her gently at first. He slid a hand down her center, landing in his favorite spot, cupping her warm moistness before slipping his fingers inside. "Yeah, that's my girl."

He'd staked his claim from the first time they'd met. Had she known...she closed her eyes knowing it wouldn't have made a difference. He'd never planned to let her go. She'd never been owned by anyone, subjected to subservience. Not even locked away behind bars had she felt so imprisoned.

He was going to take whatever he wanted from her till death do they part. Sirena thought about the gun he wore strapped around his ankle. He must've thought about it too. The same time she fantasized about grabbing it and pulling the trigger in his smug face, he snatched it out of her reach. He slid it a safe distance away on the floor before focusing on his mission.

"Now we can be alone. You were going to get bored of that kid, just admit it."

The plastic ties he carried in his back pocket came out. He looped them around her wrists and pulled them nice and snug. His tongue plunged into her mouth sucking what air she had left from the weight of him on top of her.

He unzipped his pants, thrusting his thick erection inside of her and waited for her to respond. "There it is. You see, you can't even help yourself."

She would never forgive him for this. Never.

Chapter twenty-seven

IF IT WERE UP TO BLISS, she'd simply hand Jake over on a silver platter. *Take him and leave everyone else alone.*

That's where her brilliant plan had come from, if they broke up, Sirena would be free to have Jake and leave Venus alone. Bliss saw it as a simple sacrifice. A perfect plan. Genius if she'd said so herself.

Grandmother Sarah didn't agree. Their conversations were less frequent now but still as rich and whole as when she'd grown up on her knee. "You should always have more questions than answers. The day you think you know everything is the day you die." Grandma Sarah disagreed with Jake being cast out and sent into the arms of the enemy. What would Venus do without her soul mate?

Find another. Preferably one who didn't have a stalker-killing-maniac attached like a plastic security tag that was supposed to beep with a warning when you left the store but somehow made it out the door with you anyway attached to the hem, impossible to wear and enjoy.

There were plenty of men out there. Unattached, free of baggage.

Bliss had been fair about doing thorough research. Finding out what the connection was between Venus and Jake was important. Seeing what made Jake tick, getting into his mind to see what he cared about most, and understanding what Venus had loved about him was part of the research. She'd tried many times channeling his motivations and desires only to come against a solid picture perfect image that kept her out like a wall.

His strong will and grounding made it almost impossible to see beyond the images put up like a security screen. A happy childhood with a single mother who wanted nothing but the best for him. A loving wife who would stand up for him in the toughest times.

He only wanted people to see what he allowed them to see. He was the young sexy bad boy next door who happened to be a successful businessman, father, and husband. Bliss knew he was hiding something but could never get to the core.

Then the breakthrough happened. She saw the small house in the harsh neighborhood where he'd grown up. He and his brother eating sandwiches with nothing between the bread but butter or mayonnaise. The day he came home and flicked the light switch and nothing happened. The electricity bill hadn't been paid and it was cold. Those days when he watched his mother go through one boyfriend or another and vowing he'd be a better man.

His first time with an older woman who happened to be his eighth grade teacher. He couldn't tell anyone. There was no one to tell. Bliss understood how these things shaped a human soul. He'd been let down, betrayed, and refused to give up control again. Control. Order. Logic.

Then why can't you control Sirena Lassiter? Bliss asked in her subliminal state. Once she'd gotten through his barrier, she had so many questions.

"I've tried," he responded. "Trust me, I've tried."

That wasn't the right answer. Bliss had gathered enough information to make an impartial decision. "Jake must go," she'd reported back to Grandma Sarah. It was the only way she could keep Venus safe.

So focused on protecting Venus, she hadn't seen Christopher as a target. He was off limits. "Do you hear me? Off limits," Bliss hissed into the empty room. That part Bliss would take responsibility for.

The energy swirling around her head made the room hum. She'd wanted to make someone pay. Revenge wouldn't bring Christopher back. Her nephew was the innocent victim stuck in the middle of a battle he didn't start.

Now Bliss sat cross legged on the soft center of the bed with her palms open and relaxed on her knees. She closed her eyes and drew in the air around her. Deep breaths. Within minutes her mind was soaring overhead. She left the building, flew through the blue sky above the clouds and floated beyond reach.

Where are you, Christopher? Auntie Bliss is coming to find you, baby. Hold on.

Chapter twenty-eight

"DETECTIVE BREWER, IF THERE'S any news, please call."
I left the same listless message every day.

There was nothing else to do but wait and be patient.
Jake and I had gone on a local morning news channel and
pleaded calmly for anyone to come forward who might
know something. We'd used the radio and Internet to
reach out for anonymous tips. I believed Detective Brewer
when he said the FBI would be able to find Christopher.
Prayer had become my only hope.

I prayed that Christopher was coming back, unharmed.
From the day he came to live with us good things
happened. Henry and Lauren were my miracle babies. I'd
given up on having another child. After the stillborn birth
of our son from complications I was told I probably
couldn't have another child.

I'd given up on the idea of giving Mya a baby brother or sister and welcomed Christopher into our life with open arms. I didn't care if he was the offspring of the She Devil herself. I didn't care that he was a smart aleck with way too many opinions about the way I did things and spouted facts like a pretentious Ivy League professor instead of the kid he was supposed to be. He was Jake's child, that made him mine too.

His Big Pop, as Christopher called him, had taken care of him while Sirena toured the country pretending he didn't exist. Not until Christopher lost his granddad to a mysterious fire, did Sirena step up and claim him.

Everyone believed Christopher was her little brother, including me, until I saw the boy trailing along with Sirena. He was Jake's mini-me, his spitting image. They looked exactly alike. Even more bizarre was seeing him in the hospital suffering a severe allergic reaction to milk after Sirena had force fed the boy ice cream.

Jake was allergic to milk and he had asthma. I still cringed from the picture of Christopher lying in that hospital bed. No one could say it was exact scientific proof. But I knew in my heart there was something I had to ask Jake.

I went home and asked Jake if it was true, if Christopher was his son. He said absolutely not. Sirena had aborted their child. I'd sat down shaking, not sure why I felt blindsided when I was the one who'd presented the question in the first place.

Everything I'd wanted not to be true was unfolding like a nightmarish fairytale. All those times I'd pushed and hinted about the possibility of he and Sirena having an affair and countered with, *don't be silly*, were now more than a notion. There couldn't have been a child to abort if they'd never had a relationship.

Had they fallen in love? Was it more than a one-time hookup? Had they been together again since we'd been married? Besides the other omissions there was now a child.

"How could you *not* know there was a child, Jake?"

"I just didn't know. I still don't know. You're telling me I have a son because you saw her kid brother with the same allergies as I have. I think I'd know if I had a son," he exclaimed.

"You told me nothing happened between you two."

"It was a long time ago and I didn't want you to start freaking out like you're doing now."

"So what happened? I want to know everything."

"She said she didn't want to be anybody's mother. Her career was more important and the last thing she wanted was to ruin it by having a baby. We fought, we argued, but in the end she made up her mind to have an abortion. She didn't care how I felt about it and I couldn't stop her. So we stopped talking. I couldn't forgive her for that."

I pushed my finger into his chest, still angry about his lies. "Her little brother Christopher, have you ever seen him?"

"Yeah, I've seen him."

I wanted to slap his face I was so angry. "Then how could you not know? He looks just like you, Jake?"

Jake wasted no time confronting Sirena. Seems I'd played right into her hands. She'd planned to play the son card on her own, just not that day.

I hated to admit it, but I regretted the Pandora's box I'd opened. Jake eventually turned his full attention to Christopher. His son. He worked full speed making up for lost time. Their relationship took a front seat while Mya and I were relegated to the back.

Sirena thought, hoped, and prayed that Jake's relationship with Christopher would lead to their reconciliation. When that didn't happen, she took a different route.

Reliving what Sirena did to me made me experience the exact same adrenaline and fear all over again. My vision blurred and my mouth felt dry.

The urgent knock and ringing of the doorbell sent my heart racing. I placed a shaky kiss on Henry and Lauren's cheeks before disappearing from their playroom. Jezzy gave me a concerned smile. I knew she was taking extra care to be nice even though what she really thought of me was hanging over both our heads.

"I have to get the door," I said, moving hurriedly. It may have been Detective Brewer. I treaded fast, but carefully down the stairs holding the banister.

It was George holding his electronic note pad. "Says you have a pick-up today." He averted eye contact. We hadn't been on chummy terms since the stunt I'd pulled calling him out about his marital status.

I hadn't thought about Two Sisters in a ridiculously long amount of time. I wasn't sure what was going on with our hair product business. I turned to look around to see if Bliss had boxes ready to go out. "Can you hold on for a second?"

"I'm on a tight schedule," George said. He was antsy and hurried.

"You know, I really didn't mean to offend you. I'm sorry. I just wanted you to know that."

He shifted but only slightly. "Yeah, okay. Like I said, I'm on a schedule. If you don't have anything ready, you're going to have to schedule another pick-up."

"George, would you like to come in?" I held the door open.

He peered around the corner. "No, thank you. Can you please get the boxes?"

"Give me a minute. I'll be right back." I left, hightailing it upstairs to find Bliss. I knocked on her door before letting myself in her room. "Hey...George is here," I said to an empty room. Bliss was nowhere to be seen. I checked her bathroom. "Bliss?" I walked the distance of the hallway to Lauren and Henry's playroom where I'd only been a few minutes ago. "Have you seen Bliss?"

Jezzy shook her head. "Not since yesterday."

"Do you know if we have a shipment to go out?"

"I don't know if there's shipments to go out because that's not my job to know," Jezzy announced. She went back to watching Lauren and Henry draw pictures at their craft table.

"Right." I nodded. She had a point. Bliss had to be somewhere in the house. I marched around from room to room, until I realized more than a minute had passed. I landed at the bottom of the stairs with a thud and rushed to return to the door. George was gone, replaced by a man holding a huge bouquet of flowers.

"Special delivery," the familiar voice said, poking his head from around the arrangement.

"Vince." I threw my arms around his body builder neck. He grinned against my cheek. "I'm so sorry for what you're going through. You know I would've been here sooner if I hadn't been on tour with the missus." He stepped inside. He handed me the huge vase with gorgeous yellow and pink lilies.

"Thank you, they're beautiful."

"I wish I could take full credit. I saw the order for Venus Parson and I decided to make a personal delivery."

I opened the card attached. "Thinking of you and your family. M. D." Marco had sent them. I wasn't sure how I was supposed to feel. Being grateful seemed wrong. Yet I felt a well of appreciation spring into a heartfelt smile. I balled the card in my palm and shoved it into my jean pocket. There was the question of selling Two Sisters. I still hadn't signed the contract. I couldn't see how I was going to avoid talking to him much longer.

"How're you doing, kiddo?" Vince asked.

"I'm okay. This has been hard on all of us. Do you have time to stay?" I led Vince to the living room. We sat down.

I talked and he listened. Sirena being involved with Christopher's disappearance didn't surprise Vince. He'd experienced her wrath first hand. "And people say my wife is bad," he added, talking about his other half, Trevelle Doval, the fallen Christian evangelist who'd rejuvenated her career as an opinionated analyst on talk shows everywhere. She was the epitome of bad girl turned good. But that wasn't the case for Sirena. She was a bad seed and as long as she was watered, her tangled branches of destruction would keep growing and reaching out to destroy whomever was in her grasp.

"Christopher is a strong kid. He's going to figure out a way to come home. Next thing you know he's going to be on your doorstep."

I closed my eyes and said another silent prayer. "Thank you. I needed to hear that."

"Where's Jake?"

"I'm not sure. We've kind of hit a bad patch."

"When something like this happens and it's going to test the relationship. As Trevelle would say, stay prayed up. Things will come out in the wash. You two will be okay." He got up and took a few slow steps to the door.

I pushed my face into his chest and inhaled the scent of fresh cut flowers. "Thank you for coming."

"I wish I could do more," Vince offered, patting me on the back. His voice went low when he squeezed me for the final hug. "I know people who can help, just say the word."

He once lived a life where 'concrete graves' and phrases like 'swimming with the fishes' was more than a line out of a mob movie.

"No. I'd never ask that of you. I'll stick with prayer, faith, and hope. I've got all three."

He winked. "Just checking. I'm there for you, kiddo." The wind kicked up as Vince was leaving. Thick clouds moved quickly closing out the sun and sky. A thunderous clap came out of nowhere and a few seconds later heavy rain pummeled the cobblestone walkway.

"Wow, that was sudden. I better get a move on." Vince pulled his collar up around his ears and darted out in the rain.

Another thunderous roar lasted longer than the first one. I felt the tap on my shoulder and jumped. I turned around to see Bliss standing, blinking. Her face and hair were moist even though her clothes were completely dry. I figured she'd been outside, the reason I couldn't find her but it didn't explain why the other half of her was dry.

"You scared me."

She still didn't speak. She turned her stoic gaze to the ground.

"Bliss, what's wrong?"

"Christopher." She shook her head as if she couldn't say anymore.

I grabbed her arms. "What did you see?"

"He's not with Sirena."

"How do you know?" Panic rushed to my cheeks. Thinking of the worse, my stomach filled with dread.

Nervous heat swirled around my face and body. I did my best not to be sick. "Bliss, talk to me."

"Christopher's not with her. That's all I know." Bliss had to sit down before she fell from dizziness. She wiped her face with both hands. "He's not with Sirena, he's really lost."

I sat next to Bliss and wrapped an arm around her shaking shoulders. "Don't say that. He's not lost. Sirena has him. She has to. Unless she did something to him." The nausea threatened to overtake my stomach again. I pressed on the bubble of fear and tried to calm myself. "He probably got away from her, that's all."

I was trying to convince her she was wrong, and me too. I couldn't stomach the thought. Ironically, knowing he was with Sirena at least gave me hope. He was with someone he knew. He was alive. Knowing this kept me from curling up in a ball and going insane. Even as crazy and unstable as she was, the devil you know is better than the one you don't.

Chapter twenty-nine

JAKE SHOWED UP and immediately sensed something was wrong. "What's going on?" He put his helmet down and moved in front of us.

Bliss dropped her head again. She didn't want to be the one to tell Jake what she envisioned, poor Christopher lost in the abyss. Besides, the probability of him believing her was slim to none. Wasn't he the one who said it was all a farce? No one could see the future. People couldn't read minds or move objects with sheer force of will. Dreams didn't mean anything except you'd eaten too much sugar or chocolate before bedtime.

"We were just wondering how much longer until the FBI finds Chris." I was getting good at lying to Jake. He was the one person I'd prided myself on being honest with. He knew my past, forwards and back. He knew my passion for all things awkward and against the grain. Following the pact was an abominable sin as far as I was concerned. Yet, we'd always been in sync. No matter what kind of wrench was thrown in our gear we always found our rhythm. Until now.

In this time and space I could feel the mechanics of our well built engine tearing down. Jake shifted his anxious energy from me to Bliss.

"I had a bad dream," Bliss confessed. "That's all."

"Your dreams are kind of like seeing the future, right?"

"No. She doesn't see the future. That's silly." I sputtered at the ridiculousness of it. Suddenly her dreams held importance.

"Bliss, what did you see?" Jake asked bending down to her knees where she sat shivering.

She looked past him. "Nothing. I wish I had, but I didn't see anything."

Jake cut a dagger stare at me. "So what...now I'm the enemy? We all want to find Christopher." He raised his hands to show he was giving up. "You know what, if you're going to play the two against one game, I'm through. I'm sick of this...this weapon, this secret weapon you two are supposed to share and I'm the bad guy." His voice tightened with anger. "Every time I walk into the room, there's this look you two exchange. So what is it? This is how you want to play it?"

"You want to know," I said following his lead to honesty. It was time. I swallowed back my constant need to please and opened up the person who'd been scared, hiding underneath.

"Yeah, I want to know."

"Ever since you packed up and left here you've treated me, and everyone else in this house like the help. I am your wife. I am the mother of your children. I am the glue that keeps this shit together. Every day it's like the Flintstone whistle blows at three o'clock in the afternoon and you want your full report. Is everyone following my rules? Is my statue still being polished? I am the king, you know? Is everyone still under my rule?" I mimicked in the 16th Century bourgeois voice. "Do you ever ask me how I'm doing? No. Do you care whether I'm dying inside? No."

My voice kept rising.

"Then you come home and we're supposed to salute you every time you walk into the room. You know what, I'm sick of it. Yes. Your orders are being followed. No one leaves the house after ten. Homework is being done. Sorry, no, occasionally dinner isn't on the table. All right, more than occasionally. Hardly ever. I'm a little busy." I took a long deep breath. "There is your full report. I'm done. I'm out of the fucking reporting business. You want to know what you're children are doing? You get here and see for yourself. When this is all over, so are we."

For a second, Jake was speechless. He'd never seen me like this, hostile, hurt, and willing to tell him how much. For a second he clearly wanted to say, I'm sorry. But then his face turned into an incredulous sneer.

"I provide you with everything. But I'm guilty for wanting you to do your part?"

"My part?" I spat. "What have I been doing for the last ten years?"

"Good question," he snapped.

I lunged in his direction. Bliss held me back.

Jake held up a hand. "Just breathe for a minute."

"Is that what your yoga teacher taught you, to just fuckin' breathe?" I felt the onslaught of tears steaming down my cheeks.

"You said you didn't see the video."

"Well I lied, I saw every detail, every second." I didn't want to appear weak when I was trying to say what I had to say. Lately tears were my emotional expression of everything. Even a price ringing up wrong at the grocery store to me into a down pour.

"You don't have a shred of respect for me. You think you can run around and do whatever you want because you're the man of the house." I made loose air quotes. "Hey, no problem, make a sex tape with the yoga instructor, please, be my guest. Any other surprises I should accept and ignore because you are above recrimination? Well guess what, you're not the only one," I announced with vengeance. "Two can play that game."

Jake's attention turned laser sharp. His chest rose high, and close enough to my face, where I didn't dare say another word. The tension was heavy and palpable.

"So what, you call yourself doing a little payback? Is that where you were at two o'clock in the morning?" He leaned in even closer. "What game, exactly, are we talking about?"

I had no way out of the corner I'd backed myself into. *Two can play—sex tapes with their yoga teacher.*

"Enough," Bliss shouted with her head down and her hands over her ears like a child witnessing her parent's fighting one too many times. "Just stop it!"

Her outburst took us by surprise. Both of us looked at her like she was the one who'd flipped out. Though I was too grateful for her speaking out at just the right moment. Once again she'd saved me.

* * *

"That's it, you two. Time out." Bliss knew she had to do something. Any other time she would've been happy to see her sister standing up for herself instead of constantly suffering the down trodden housewife syndrome. But now was not the time for airing out all the dirty laundry.

"You're both losing it here." Bliss announced. "Jake," she said, snapping his attention in her direction. "I had a dream about Christopher." She wanted to tell him the truth, but more importantly distract him from the bone he'd sunk his teeth into and refused to let go of.

Two can play that game. If there was one thing Bliss knew for sure was that a man never forgot or forgave. Women were the ones who let go of their pride and ego for the sake of love and family.

Jake was a strong man, but a man nonetheless. In that regard all men were the same. Egos could bring down a family or an entire nation. Her grandmother always used different animal species to explain the minds of men. Grandma Sarah would sit in front of the TV and watch National Geographic for hours at a time. Men made the nests but women were left to take care of it. Just like birds.

Even before her grandmother had told her as a young girl, she'd noticed the habits of birds outside her bedroom window. Starting at the first sign of frost she watched what seemed like the same little bird gathering twigs, feathers, and whatever it could fit into it's tiny mouth to build a home. It was always the male bird who did the building since the female was probably too engorged with eggs. The male bird never came to the nest once the mommy-bird laid her eggs. Never checked on the eggs or even dropped off a worm or two after they were born.

"Men can leave, but the mother has always got to stay and take care of her babies." Grandma Sarah only knew what she knew. Most of it was true and made perfect sense, men left and mothers stayed behind. The nest wasn't always to the highest standards, but it was home and as long as it was safe with food and shelter, the daddy-bird did his job. But the mother's job never ended.

Bliss assumed there was no room for the daddy-bird anyway. She made these assumptions to justify her own father not being around, never calling, never writing. He sent money. He provided for the nest. Beyond that, what was he good for?

She stood now with her sister and wanted her to understand too, the ways of men. They were only human.

Afraid and insecure deep down inside just like the rest of us.

"What did you see, Bliss?" He asked stepping back and finally breathing. "Please, just tell me."

"He's not with Sirena. He's gone. I'm scared because now I don't know where he could be." The doorbell rang before Jake could respond to what he'd just heard. At the same time their phones began to ring like a cataclysmic event.

"I'll get the door," Bliss offered since they were both fumbling for their phones. She too heard ringing. Not from a phone, a different kind of ringing in her ears. The cool whistling sound swirled over her head and made her dangerously dizzy before she reached the door.

Bliss grabbed the brass handles for stability. "Who is it?" she asked cautiously.

"Me," the voice said through the heavy wooden door.

It took a second before Bliss understood who 'me' was. She put her face to the peephole and was sure she was seeing things. Her visions were a curse as well as a gift. "Christopher?"

"It's me," he said again, pushing his forehead closer like a distorted circus mirror. His large brown eyes were tired and glossy.

When she opened the door, he pushed his narrow body against hers, falling into her arms. "It's me, auntie," he whispered in a hoarse sob.

Chapter thirty

JAKE WRAPPED HIS ARMS around his son and held on tight. He fought the urge to cry, though they would've been tears of gratitude. He told himself to breathe slowly. He wanted to be still enough to listen to Christopher's heart, to hear what his son could not say, or was too afraid to say.

It was Christopher who finally pulled away. "Dad, I'm all right."

Jake gripped his face and gave him a hard penetrating examination before he accepted his plea. He turned to the officer with a handshake. "Thank you for bringing my son home."

"It's my pleasure, sir. I used to listen to *Juicy Lips Fat Hips* back in the day," the young officer volunteered before catching himself. He turned on his professional tone quickly. "Your son appears to be fine but in these cases we always recommend a visit to the hospital or if you have a physician, that'd be best." He handed Jake a card. "My name is Officer Vargas. If I can do anything for you, don't hesitate to call."

Jake was glad the focus was back on Christopher. He felt awkward appreciating someone's recognition at a time like this. "That's a good idea. Thank you."

"I don't need to go to the doctor. I just want to take a shower and lie down." Christopher said, turning to Venus who hadn't been able to speak beyond crying tears of joy. Her hand remained on Christopher's back as if he'd disappear again. "Mom, it's okay. I'm okay."

"You're home." Venus finally spoke. She took in a long jagged breath.

"Come on, sweetie. Let's get you upstairs," Bliss offered with a light nudge. There was too much emotion being heaped on the boy. She delicately guided him out of Venus's reach. He needed some space. He didn't need to know his parents were fighting only seconds before he arrived.

At the door, Jake asked Officer Vargas, "Was she arrested?"

The officer looked perplexed. "Your son was alone. He got off a bus at the downtown station and went to the information booth and asked someone to call the police. Smart boy. I arrived and planned to drive him straight to the police station but he kept saying he just wanted to go home."

"Thank you, again."

"You're welcome." He looked at his note pad as if he'd thought about asking for Jake's autograph but talked himself out of it. "Good luck with everything," Officer Vargas said before heading down the cobble path.

Jake went back to the living room. Once the officer left the silence was a telling sign. Venus sat on the couch. Jake remained standing. He hadn't been able to relax while Christopher was gone. Sitting down never seemed like an option. Even with Christopher's return, he felt nothing but frustration. No hugs were shared between he and Venus, and barely a glance in either of their direction.

He wanted to say he was glad it was over and that they could now focus on more important things. He wished he could say he was sorry for the heated exchange. He wanted to apologize, starting with blaming her for Christopher's disappearance but the words were caught in his throat. All he could think of was her victorious announcement, *two can play...* and wondering what she meant by it. Bliss had said this wasn't the time. He knew that too, and yet he couldn't let it go.

"Thank God," Venus spoke first. "How do you think he got away?" Her voice was weary and dry. She blotted the last of her tears.

Jake folded his arms under one another and finally sat down next to her. He attempted to lift an arm and put it around her tired shoulders but his brain and body seemed to be in disagreement. He willed his hand to hold hers, and still nothing happened. "I'm just grateful he's here."

"You have to ask him what happened, every detail. Sirena probably threatened him into not telling us anything but you have to ask him. We have to find her." Venus rubbed her arms as if she were freezing. "She can't get away with this."

If there were ever a cue to extend a hug this was it. Jake's arms remained folded into himself. He stood up again. His mouth was dry and he could feel his chest tightening. "I think we should let Detective Brewer ask the questions."

She nodded in agreement. "Yes, of course. Detective Brewer will find out what happened. Where is he? He should be here by now. We don't want Sirena getting away. I want her under the jail."

In all honesty Jake wasn't surprised by her response. If he weren't so afraid of the truth coming out, he'd be anxious to hear every detail as well. He didn't want to chance it.

The first thing Christopher might tell is why Sirena had taken him. She'd done all of this out of spite. If only he'd listened to the record label and forfeited the money instead of saying he didn't know what they were talking about.

"We'll get through this," he said, more as a declaration to himself. "Let's just be grateful Christopher is home safe. Let him rest. He's been through a lot."

He leaned down and planted a kiss on her forehead. He couldn't stand another minute in the house. "I need some air." He walked past the flowers in the hallway and couldn't think of the last time he'd sent her something like that. Birthdays and Christmas he bought the requisite jewelry and card but there was never much thought into it. She was right about everything. He couldn't remember the last time he simply called to talk about her day, or what was on her mind.

They would move past this. They always survived no matter the drama. They were probably the last remaining married couple to survive a reality show. Everyone knew it was a fatal curse, and yet they'd remained in tact as a family. Surely, this time they'd make it through too.

With Christopher back he felt like he'd been given a clean slate. Now that he understood and was willing to change, he could fix the damage.

But first there was the matter of his unsolved mystery. He still didn't know what really happened that night with Nahlia. He wasn't sure if what was on the video was all there was to the story. He couldn't very well begin wooing his wife back without knowing what he was up against. He'd have to tell Venus the truth, whatever it was. It was time he faced his demons head-on, all of them.

Chapter thirty-one

THE FIRST CALL HE MADE was to Anna Nahlia. He knew she wasn't going to answer, which was why he was ready with his rehearsed message.

"Hello," her voice picked up on the first ring, startling him.

"Anna Nahlia, it's Jay." He stuttered from hearing the unexpected real live person on the other end.

"Who?" She said with a light nonchalance.

"Jay," he said, knowing she wasn't going to make it easy for him. "I need to ask you something about that night, the last time we saw each other."

She didn't respond. He pictured her sitting in the center of her studio, crossed legs, meditation mode, staring at the ocean mural on her wall.

"Anna," he blurted, getting her attention.

"I'm busy. What is so urgent, Mr. Parson?"

"The video, did you see it? It looks like we were in some real compromising positions. I'm not sure how much happened before or after. I apologize for anything that may have hurt you, but I need to know—" He swallowed the question not knowing how to ask without sounding pathetic. "Did we at least use a condom?"

She sputtered with laughter adding to his humiliation. "No," she answered with a devious chuckle on the end. "No condom. Au naturale," she sang out.

His mind raced with the worst possible scenario. Before he could ask his next question she interjected, "Because we didn't have sex. Okay? Happy? It was just us doing some of our best yoga moves." She laughed. "Demonstrations are good for business. I already have a new customer. So if you'll excuse me." She wanted their conversation to be over.

If he were there, he would've hugged her with joy. He did the next best thing and kissed the phone. "Thank you."

She hung up leaving him with silence. Her way of saying, lose my number. He understood. He was used to it by now. Somewhere in the world like clockwork, a woman came to hate him. Expectations not met, dreams dashed. This time was no different.

He and Anna Nahlia were officially history. He'd miss her but that was what DVD's were for. He was sure he saw a program called Dinner and Yoga, sort of like dinner and a movie, except it was yoga in between commercial breaks instead of cooking.

Hopefully his next order of business would go as smoothly as this one had. He left the message. "Detective Brewer, this is Jake Parson. Christopher arrived on our doorstep about an hour ago. I wanted you to know, he's fine. I also wanted you to know we don't want to pursue any charges against Sirena Lassiter. I'd appreciate it if we could let this situation die down. My son has been through enough. He doesn't want to talk about what happened, and I want to respect his wishes." Jake hung up, finally being able to take a deep breath.

Besides, Sirena was probably far, far away, afraid of being caught and sent back to prison. In all honesty, unless Christopher was willing to speak on it, there was no real proof she'd done anything wrong.

Having his son back was having a second chance. He wasn't sure how to proceed. Second chances were rare. He didn't want to mess it up by harboring hate and spite. For whatever reason, Sirena came to her senses and let Christopher go. What more could he ask of the angels watching over him? His son was safe at home.

He hopped on his motorcycle and snapped his helmet in place. He prepped the engine with a light tap of the pedal before taking off, riding free with the wind at his back.

* * *

When he got home, he was still floating high on optimism. He walked into the house and felt the tension immediately. He marched upstairs and knew before he opened their bedroom door, the tide had changed that quickly.

"Detective Brewer said you didn't think it was a good idea to talk to Christopher," she said, not wasting any time. "Why would you say that?"

He tossed his jacket on the chair and sat down. He wasn't going to drag out the conversation they needed to have. It was going to be short and sweet. "Christopher's been through enough. I want him to be comfortable. He doesn't need this right now."

Venus may as well have slapped him on his cheek from the daggers she drew from her eyes. "Jake, if you don't do something about this woman, she's only going to come back, again, and again. She tried to kill me. She kidnapped our son. What else do you need to happen?"

"Babe, listen to me."

"I'm done listening to you. I thought I made that clear." She snatched her purse off the bureau where it rested conveniently for take off.

"Where're you going?"

"Anywhere you're not," she said, hitting the door with such force he thought it was going to fall of the hinges.

"Wait a minute. Stop being irrational. Can we talk about this?" He followed her down the stairs.

"Irrational? Are you kidding me right now?" She shoved past him. Once she was gone, he thought of all the right things to say, but still nothing would've been good enough.

Chapter thirty-two

SHE'D PARKED A COUPLE of blocks away, and walked the distance to stand under the nightshade of trees across the street. She watched the house, studying every detail. There was still no light coming from Christopher's room.

The Gingerbread house wasn't the usual cheery love nest. She could almost feel the dreariness coming from the walls. That's what they deserved. Except now, she thought, by now they should've been celebrating and cheering for Christopher's return.

What if he never made it back? She couldn't live with herself if something happened to him.

She could feel the turmoil in the air. Whether they were sad, hurt, or defeated, was irrelevant. The fact that they weren't jumping with joy meant Christopher hadn't made it back safely. Her heart skipped a beat believing he was lost, or abducted by someone dangerous. Someone who didn't have his best interest in mind. Sex trafficking boys was just as prevalent as stealing girls, but no one ever talked about it.

Sirena stood frozen, afraid to blink, afraid she'd miss the light going on and off in his room. How would she find out if Christopher was inside? She'd been inside the house many times before, invited and not so invited. She knew how to get inside without anyone seeing her. No security system. Jay thought the private community gate was his security. What a laugh. Those guys waved her in each time without so much as a question. Anyone could get through here. *Anyone.*

She felt the tingly hairs rise on the back of her neck. She should've killed Lucas when she had the chance. He'd be right behind her, knowing exactly where she was headed, once he broke free.

Waiting for him to fall asleep and using his convenient wrist ties she was able to make a fast exit. Thinking about torturing or doing harm was the last thing on her mind. She took his keys and went straight to the bus station. She couldn't ask anyone directly if they'd seen Christopher without incriminating herself.

She got on the highway and made the trip in record time. Now she was starving and needed to pee something awful. She moved back, further into the dark grove of trees and prayed nothing jumped out and bit her. She pulled down her jeans.

In her wildest dreams she never pictured herself taking a piss in the open air surrounded by things that could bite her on the ass. Although it was safer and cleaner than many of the bathrooms she'd been in lately. She had to tell her body to relax. She was nearly through when she heard voices coming from the Gingerbread house. Just when she was getting started she had to stop midstream.

Sirena couldn't resist. She peeked her head out.

Voices. Jay's voice to be specific. The words weren't clear but Sirena knew the distinct tone having heard it often enough when they'd argued; how he tried to play it down after saying what he had to say by laughing a little at the end. It was his way of being diplomatic, though there was nothing ever compromising about how he lived his life. Jay wanted what he wanted and the hell with everybody else.

This time it was Venus getting an earful. She responded in a brief, shrill, "Go to hell." Followed by the car door slamming, engine starting, and her profile heading down the street.

What had the perfect couple been fighting about?

Sirena moved with desperate speed adjusting her clothes and nearly falling. She made it to the clearing where her car was parked. Out of breath, she jumped in, started her car and skidded out in time to catch the back of Venus's taillights making the right turn out of the neighborhood. Thank goodness Venus drove like a snail. Sirena was able to catch up and easily follow her without looking like a mad woman.

Where was lil Miss Muffet going this late in the evening anyway, alone? Maybe a trip to the grocery store to get some curds and whey. Her life was about as interesting as a child's nursery rhyme. Sirena never could understand her allure for someone like Jay. Boring housewife material. She stayed securely predictable by doing nothing.

Yet on this very night, Sirena couldn't stop herself from trailing behind the constantly pressed brake lights ahead, wondering what had caused the fight and her storming out of the house.

There was also the fascination of watching someone who didn't know they were being watched. The feeling of stumbling upon an opportunity to expose Miss Goodie-two-shoes raised her dedication two fold. Normally, being stuck behind someone driving this slowly would've sent Sirena over the edge like a caged rat. Instead she hung back a few car lengths.

At the stoplight she had no choice but to be directly behind Venus. The dark reflection against the windshield would keep them from seeing each other.

Sirena got a glimpse inside when Venus dropped the sun visor and opened the lighted mirror. Checking her face, wiping her eyes. Tears, of course. Weakness.

Now a green light. Venus still hadn't let off the brake. Sirena felt like honking like a normal driver would. But there was nothing normal about their situation. She waited, swallowing her impatience in one large gulp. Good things came to those who waited. Sirena rolled her eyes, *as if* she'd ever believed such bullshit. You had to go after what you wanted in this world. Patience was for suckers.

Shortly before the light turned yellow, Venus let her foot off the brake and inched forward slowly. So slow, Sirena found herself running the red light as she followed behind. The last thing she needed was to get stopped for a traffic violation. Running a red light and having to produce her driver's license would present a problem.

She was driving a car that didn't belong to her. She was also carrying Lucas's gun. She'd taken it with no purpose in mind. She had never even fired a weapon before. Lucas had been furious when she shut the door behind her. He was just waking up when he realized his wrists had been linked to the decorative iron bedpost.

"Sirena! Cee-Cee," he'd yelled, as if it would trigger some kind of emotional response. "Don't leave me, baby." She realized she had to leave him behind. There was no remorse. They were finished. He had no right to decide who she could be, who she could love.

Right now, all she cared about was what was in front of her, immediately in front of her. There was no future and yesterday was unattainable.

She followed Venus into the new high rise area on the east side of sprawling Uptown. The area was full of gorgeous shiny new buildings with glass and chrome everywhere. Restaurants were bustling with nightlife. Unless Venus had gotten a job as a hostess or a chef, she had no business being in this area this late at night.

Sirena parked her car a few feet away from Venus and watched her go inside. There was nothing she could do except wait. She couldn't take a chance on following her into the building with all the bright lighting. She stayed a safe distance away staring inside the lobby.

The elevator doors opened and a man appeared with strong open arms. Right before Sirena's eyes she saw the man pull Venus in for a loving hug, then a gentle kiss on the cheek. The embrace lingered long enough to make it obvious this was no relative. Friend...lover...another man?

Yes! Venus was with another man. Sirena grabbed a hold of the smooth stucco wall to maintain her balance. She was holding on, praying she didn't falling into the lush landscaping where she was hiding. She could hardly feel her feet or the ground underneath her, either from the shock or the cold. She had to be seeing things. She blinked and took several deep breaths. When she opened her eyes again the lovers were gone. The elevator doors closed. The well lit lobby was empty.

Sirena couldn't move, stunned into paralysis. It was like being given a brand new car and no keys. Having this information and not being able to shout it from the highest mountain was a perfectly cruel irony.

Here Jay thought he'd found the woman who would always be loyal and have his back, and she was having an affair.

Sirena had been devastated when Jay told her outright that he'd never leave Venus. He loved his wife, loved everything about being married with children. If that was the case, why had they spent that night together in New York? She remembered like it was yesterday instead of three years ago. Him lying in bed beside her, relaxed and heading down memory lane. A storm had shut down the city and forced them in the same room since no others were available. His kiss. His hands. Finally, she'd thought, he was going to be hers.

Sirena was beside herself with excitement having him all to herself. But then a light switch went on in his head. "I can't do this," he'd said.

Even though he already had, the minute she'd put her tongue around his erection, the deed was done. "You can never stop loving someone you truly loved. It's impossible, Jay."

"Then maybe what we had wasn't really love," he'd said with those impossibly sad sexy eyes.

"How long are you going to be mad at me? The past is the past let it go." How much longer was he going to punish her? Sirena had atoned for all the dirt she'd committed in their past. Sleeping with his roommate—just one time. The abortion—that never really happened. At some point he had to forgive her and remember the good times.

"What's the point of rehashing all of this when all we want is to be together?"

Instead of seeing the point, he grabbed her by the arm and said, "Listen to me, I love my wife. I will never walk away from her, ever." The intensity radiating off his smooth brown skin told her he meant what he said. It was so like Jay to take everything so seriously. His marriage had turned into the Holy Grail and he was the Black Jesus ready to die on the cross as a sacrifice.

Sirena shook off the painful memory and was suddenly laughing hysterically picturing Jay's face of devotion. She couldn't contain the sporadic chortles. "Fool, you could've had me."

She couldn't help but feel vindicated. And Christopher too, hadn't believed her when she'd tried to tell him that Venus was a phony and never really cared about him or his father. Now she had proof. She saw the real Venus live and in action carrying on with another man while Christopher was lost somewhere. *She never cared*, Sirena almost screamed, but held her tongue.

Once inside the car where she was safe, she did scream. "You fucking bitch."

She wasn't sure what to do, or how to go about telling Jay. He needed to know, deserved to know. Venus wasn't a saint.

All this time Jay had made her feel like she wasn't worthy of his love. Look who had the last laugh now.

Chapter thirty-three

"YOU'VE BEEN HERE THIS WHOLE TIME?" I finally asked after he gave me enough room to breathe.

"I should've left but I had some other business," Marco said, hoping he sounded believable.

I smiled in an apathetic way to let him know I understood. He was waiting to hear from me and wanted to be close when my call came. The bigger question was how did he know I would eventually make the call. I was embarrassed realizing how vulnerable and transparent I must've been.

"Thank you for the flowers. With everything going on, I probably forgot to say it." I sat down on the spacious leather couch. I nodded in the direction of his open laptop and a cup of coffee sitting on the table. "At least you've been keeping busy."

"As long as I've got my computer, I can work anywhere. I probably could've gone two months easy without anyone even noticing I was MIA as long as Nigel covered for me." He brought me a glass of water before sitting with me on the couch. "So where was your son? Did he ever say?"

"Christopher hasn't talked about it, at least not to me. Jake says he doesn't think it's a good idea for him to be questioned by the police. He thinks he'll be traumatized because they have a way of making a victim feel like the criminal and he never wants Christopher to feel that way. But without a statement, it's going to be impossible to prove Sirena Lassiter is responsible. Jake knows that woman needs to go back to jail for what she did, but it feels like he's protecting her, yet again."

I concluded my rant, realizing I was talking to another man about my marriage like some pitiful soap opera character.

"It's okay. I'm just listening. I have no judgment." Marco pushed up his hand in a Scouts Honor. His blue dress shirt sleeves were rolled just below his elbow, showing off the strength lines in his forearms. "I promise I won't send out a tweet that says breaking news, married woman unhappy."

"I guess that really wouldn't be news," I exhaled knowing he was right. Every marriage had problems. I was being overly dramatic running to his door again.

"I'd expected all of our problems would go away once Christopher came back, but it seems like the nightmare is never going to end."

"I'm here to listen," he repeated. "I'm not offering advice or pretending to feel all broken up about it, since I'm just glad you're here. So feel free to vent away."

I wanted to take him up on his offer but knew I'd already overstepped a fine line. In all my years I never believed this person would be *me*. My marriage was indestructible. I'd planned to be with one person for the rest of my life. I hated dating when I dated. I hated living with someone without the vows of marriage. I hated breaking up and starting over. The last thing I wanted to be, was single. The thought of divorce scared me.

"I love my husband, I really do. We started out so great. It's like going from being a cashmere sweater at Bloomingdales to being a cashmere sweater at Walmart where it keeps getting marked down, and still no one wants it. Like that sweater, you know you're valuable, but no one see's your worth. Everything is taken for granted."

I stopped to peek at him to see just how far my babbling had gone. What kind of horrible impression was I making?

Marco's caring eyes hadn't wavered, still directly taking in every detail of my face with concern.

"But I never wanted to be my parents who stayed stuck together like glue regardless of the circumstances just because they were afraid of being alone. I was introduced to Bliss just a couple of years ago. Bliss is my sister from another mother, an affair my dad had. Finding out so far into my adulthood threw a huge splat of paint on my perfect childhood memories. Everything I believed went right out the window.

"My mother was miserable. My father was sad. Now I think I understand why. It might've been because my mother gave him an ultimatum to choose between her or Bliss. Days were filled with either arguing or silence. They loved each other out of loyalty and stayed together for their children. The glass house of lies shattered in tiny pieces. Now I see the falsehood, all the pretense, all the unhappiness I pretended not to see growing up.

"Now that they're older, they have a more genuine appreciation for each other, especially on my mother's part. That could've been an adjustment in her appreciation for life in general after her bout with cancer. She's a survivor." My subject shift was fast like a photo album flipping pages. My mother; happy, sad, then happy again. Then sad.

"These days I'm considered fraternizing with the enemy. My worst offense was letting Bliss live under my roof, which showed a direct lack of loyalty to Pauletta Johnston. Under her law, there was nothing worse than disloyalty."

Marco smiled and wrapped an arm around my shoulders. "I think we've learned there's a worse offense, being a cashmere sweater at Walmart, marked down no less. Really? Who does that?"

Now I was smiling too. I felt a hundred times better than when I walked through his door. Telling your private business, revealing family secrets, to a stranger you hoped you'd never see again was a special kind of release. Someone sitting on a plane, or train, were perfect candidates for this kind of mind purge. I wasn't sure if Marco would forget about me, and everything I'd said like a stranger on a plane. Either way, I trusted him to keep my secrets.

A beeping sound started like a timer. "Times up. Maybe for me too. I should go," I told him.

"Oh, no you don't." Marco got up and went to the kitchen.

"Wait, I know you're not baking cookies." The delicious smell wafted into the living room.

"Guilty." He turned and bowed in honor with an oven mitt held up as a symbol of his allegiance to the art of baking. "Everyone needs a hobby."

"I like this hobby. I thought I was imagining the smell living through my past. I haven't smelled fresh out of the oven cookies in years." I took in the sight of him pulling out the perfect golden brown batch from the oven.

He inhaled the aroma before placing them down to cool. "You're in for a treat. These are the triple threat, dark chocolate, milk chocolate, and walnuts. A couple of these and a glass of warm milk and all your worries will be gone."

"I'm afraid of you," I said genuinely shaking in my boots. A man who knew his way around a kitchen, cooking, baking, and looking good while doing it, was indeed a triple threat.

"Are you really afraid of me?" He asked, posing the question with a serious glint in his eye.

"No. Not really. I wouldn't be here if I was."

"Hmm, I liked the idea of you being afraid."

"Why? Why would you want me to be afraid of you, Mr. DeVon?" I got up and followed him into the kitchen. I guessed where the plates were and pulled down two saucers.

"Dangerous is sexy, haven't you heard? If you're comfortable, and it appears you are, then I'm a side-note, an after thought." Marco reached around my waist, nice and slow, grabbing the spatula, lingering near my shoulder.

I made sure not to move, not even the slightest budge, determined not to make contact. He turned his attention back to the pan. He slid the first decadent cookie off the sheet and onto the red square plate. "That means we're just friends and I have no chance of being your lover." He leaned close to me. "If I don't make you nervous, then I may as well throw in the towel. I'm forever going to be relegated to your sounding board, confidant, and well...you know what happens to friends."

"What happens to friends?"

"You take advantage of friends. You ask of them what you wouldn't ask of anyone else. You expect them to give when you have no plans to reciprocate. Friends expect honesty but are angry when you tell the truth. Friends take each other for granted and then one day they decide to move on and get new friends."

"Wow, sucks to be your friend."

Marco faced me, "I think it's too late. We've come to that point already." He moved in front of me with a tray that carried the cookies and two tall glasses of milk. "Follow me."

Where the trail ended was in the bedroom. I'd been here before. The mood was incredibly poetic this time. "Ahh, do you always light candles in your bedroom when you're home alone?"

"Why not? Don't you?"

I wasn't sure if he was being sarcastic. But he had a point. From now on, I told myself, I deserved some candlelight. Why not?

"Sit," he ordered.

I slipped my boots off and climbed on top of the duvet. He slid the tray in front of me. I took a bite of the cookie and had to close my eyes to hide the lust. "Oh-oh. You call this a hobby? These are absolutely the most divine thing I've put in my mouth. These cookies are the best I've ever tasted."

"Thank you. You should taste my oatmeal raisin." The flickering light captured a wicked smile. "So eat your cookies, drink your milk, and then you have a choice to make. Do you remember when I told you the next time you came to me what the situation would be?"

Smacking the chocolate between my lips. "This is a little different. I mean, I was in a dire situation." I chomped on another mouthful of decadent melted chocolate and wondered how many calories I was consuming and decided I didn't care.

He tilted his head. "You called, I answered, I told you I was here and you came. See how that works?"

I sipped the milk while I kept my eyes down. I dared not look in his direction. Door number two. The blue pill. The red pill. Of course this wasn't a game or the movie Matrix. This was real life. What I chose would alter everything, shifting the universe as I knew it.

All my talk of being better than the masses. Jake and I being the one couple out of ten who could survive anything, yet right before me was a man who could change my mind. Blow up my entire world. The energy running between us was like playing with matches near flammable gas. If I went down that road there would be no going back. I didn't want to guess, or think about the devastation, the damage left behind this kind of explosion.

"I thought we were going with the whole friend thing," I said out loud but keeping my eyes on the cookie knowing the clock was ticking.

He didn't offer a reprieve. He sat calmly sipping his milk.

"Well then, I think I should leave." I stood in the silhouette of my own shadow. My resolve filled the space putting a stop to the mind play. Though I wasn't sure what would've happened if he tried to stop me. His response was silence. I stuck my feet into my-rebel-without-a-cause boots. Motorcycle boots, short with buckles at the ankle and distraught leather. I bought them to take springtime rides with Jake on the back of his Ducati. He only took me out riding once, but I liked the boots. I wore them in the Summer time too. The Georgia weather didn't make sense. One day it was sunny, the next day rainy. These boots were impervious to the mood of Mother Nature and somehow made me feel invincible. Exactly what I needed to have the strength to walk away from Marco.

I found my purse on the counter, sitting next to the few cookies left on the plate. Shame on me. Selfish. All I could think about was taking the rest home. For me to sit up in this man's house thinking about no one but myself and wondering if he had plastic baggies to transport the cookies safely was plain old selfish. Foil wrap would do.

"So, what do you think, same time tomorrow night?" Marco said leaning on the wall behind me while I searched his kitchen drawers for something to put my cookies in. He went to a cabinet and pulled out a box of plastic baggies. He slid the cookies inside and handed me the bag.

I held it against my chest, the only thing between him and me. It wasn't enough. He slipped his hands under my hair and pulled me close, kissing me lightly on the lips.

"We'll figure something out." He obviously wasn't giving up on me and I wasn't sure why.

I stumbled out of his clutches and moved unsteadily to the elevator. In the ten years Jake and I were together, I'd never felt this way about another man. Well there was that one incident with Dr. Clint Fairchild a long, long time ago, but that was more of an old connection. We'd been in a relationship for four years and had a bad break up. When I took a job at his hospital as a public Relations director we sort of had chemistry but nothing ever happened.

I suddenly detected a slight pattern here. Did it mean I'd fallen for every man I worked with in some capacity? Jake had even accused me of that very thing when he'd found out Clint and I were on a business trip together. "No, it does not mean I fall for every guy I work with." I told myself aloud while exiting the building.

I'd worked with Vince and never had feelings for him. And there were many others. So I was in the clear. This thing with Marco was just a thing. The kind where you're sad and lonely and need someone to make you feel beautiful and important because your husband treats you like...you're not, beautiful and important.

I squared my shoulders and took a deep breath. I began to think of all the things I loved about Jake from the first time we met. His strength, physically, and mentally. The way he dedicated himself to whatever it was he deemed important. Dedication was important.

That's when it hit me, Marco reminded me of Jake when we'd first fallen in love. Attraction so familiar I could taste it.

Everything was going to be all right. I could fix this. I couldn't see Marco anymore, ever. I would go home and mend fences with Jake and that would be the end of it. I would find the way back to the beginning and everything was going to be okay.

Chapter thirty-four

"HEY, BUDDY, YOU ALL RIGHT?" Jake stuck his head in Christopher's room. It was late and he should've been asleep. The light coming from under the door gave him away. "You want to join me for a late night refrigerator raid?"

"I doubt if there's anything in there to raid." Christopher lay on the blue and white striped bed holding the computer game with both hands. Seemed he only let go of the gadget to shower. Or not. Since Jake wasn't joining him in the bathroom he wasn't sure. It could've been waterproof.

He figured it was a guilt gift from Venus to make up for the things they hadn't done right. Ordinarily, Jake would've already rectified the situation. But if it made him feel better, Jake wasn't going to forbid him from playing it.

"I'm sorry I missed your game." Jake sat on the corner edge of the bed. He wasn't sure how to start, where to start. "Can you put that down for a minute?"

Christopher took his sweet time finishing the loop with a resounding explosion and crash before setting the game on his stomach. He kept his leisure position not bothering to sit up.

"Chris, tell me what happened. It won't go any further than this room, I promise."

"Why? What difference does it make? You always tell me that the past is the past. What happened can't be changed. We live with our mistakes and deal with the consequences." Christopher picked up his game again. The violent shooting noise replaced their silence.

Jake took the lightweight gadget out of his hands. "I'll give it back in a minute." Venus wanted him to get answers so that's what he was going to do. Who knew what Sirena was capable of next time? It took him a minute to see what Venus was trying to tell him. He needed a solution that would once and for all grant them freedom from Sirena and her insanity. If Christopher would talk about what happened then they would have their proof to send Sirena back to jail where she belonged and maybe there'd be peace in his house. First he had to make sure whatever Christopher had to say didn't incriminate him as well.

It was hard enough that Sirena was Christopher's biological mother. It wasn't easy for any child to point a finger at a parent, no matter what they'd done to them. He didn't want to put Christopher in that position as the bad guy but there was no other choice.

"I promise, what you tell me doesn't leave this room, unless you want it to." Seeing his son this miserable weighed on his heart. He'd silenced him long enough. He felt guilty about it. He was tired of constantly feeling responsible for every else's sadness or happiness. The weight of the world left him weary. He measured success by waking up each morning fully prepared to carry that weight without complaint.

He was blessed to have a career he loved and a family that was healthy and now safe. Jake could move on based on that alone. If it were up to him, he wouldn't bother mentioning Sirena's name again in his lifetime.

"I don't want to talk about it," Christopher said loud and clear.

"You didn't make a mistake, son. You didn't do anything wrong." Jake swallowed the lump in his throat to continue. "You are not responsible for what someone else has done to you. You're not an adult Christopher. You're still a child. I know you don't think of yourself that way, but you are. And when someone manipulates a child, or talks them into doing something, it's important not to let them do it again to anyone else."

"Does Sirena have another child?" Christopher achingly clinched his jaw. "Because it would be a relief if she could focus on him or her instead of me. I'm tired of being in the middle of this."

Jake saw the real pain in his son's face and understood what had to be done. Protecting Christopher was all that mattered. "I'm not going to let anything else happen to you. You understand? You're safe now," Jake said with full certainty.

Christopher dropped his guard and threw his arms around him, shaking with every breath. How long had he been afraid? He wondered how he'd missed the signs. The answer was simple.

He missed the signs because he wasn't there. He'd thought his timed calls, ten-minute pep talks, and three-minute advice sessions were enough of a connection from two thousand miles away. It wasn't enough, not by a long shot.

"I'm here." Jake held his son tight, grateful beyond measure to have the opportunity to make things right. He hadn't been there when Christopher was a baby, or a small child. He hadn't seen his transformation from awkward toddler to his first day at school. Missing those milestones made him only more determined to never miss another.

They finally released their embrace. Jake handed him back the game. Christopher reluctantly took it back and pressed the power button to turn it off. "I think I had enough for tonight." He slid it into the side table drawer.

Again, Jake was proud of his son. Small graces, that's all one could depend on, and Christopher was proof. He hugged him again for good measure. Whatever happened, he wanted his son to remember this moment.

Chapter thirty-five

There wasn't much else to do but tell him what she'd seen. She could show Jake how little Venus cared about him. He had no idea. Then Jay would know what she did all those years ago was out of love, a small act of violence for the greater good.

Now she had proof. Although she really had nothing but her word. She was betting that Venus wouldn't be able to lie straight to Jake's face.

His woman was traipsing around town with another man. The scene in the lobby made Sirena cringe. A white man at that. A sexy good-looking white man—whatever. Jay would die. Simply die. She didn't want him to die. She wanted him to put Venus on the curb and shut the door so he could live the life he was meant to have.

JayP and Cee-Cee, they were an unbeatable team when they were together. No one could deny their chemistry and passion.

She was taking an unbelievable risk by confronting Jay with his sham of a marriage. He'd believe her, that's all that mattered. She hoped to get there and state her case before Venus arrived. She waved and smiled at the security guard as the gate rose.

She drove around the circular entry and up the slight hill to reach the Gingerbread house.

She trotted to the back entrance. She pressed her face against the glass to make sure the coast was clear. The kitchen was the hub. If anyone was up this late, that's where they'd be. She reached above the door where the hide-a-key was stashed; though she'd noticed countless times the door was never locked in the first place.

Her nervous hand landed on the doorknob, shaking. What if he still hated her after she told him what she'd witnessed? Killing the messenger was truly more than a cliché. The deliverer of bad news was always the one beheaded.

Before she could overcome her fear with a click of the handle, light rushed her face. She ducked down not seeing who'd come into the kitchen. She panted, taking in oxygen too quickly and still not enough. *Calm down*, she told herself. If someone saw her, there'd be more noise than the banging around someone was doing.

Taking a chance, she lifted herself high enough to peek inside. Jay stood with his back to her, facing the stove.

Tea. Really? He was heating the water, standing waiting for it to boil. He was right there. She wouldn't have to breach too far into enemy territory. All she had to do was...

"Hey, you're home." Jay turned his attention away from the stove.

Sirena followed his line of vision to Venus who'd just walked in. She set her purse down on the kitchen table before rushing into Jay's arms.

Are you serious?

They stayed locked in each other's arms. Words Sirena couldn't hear were exchanged.

Regrets.

I'm sorry.

I just left my boyfriend, but I'm here now.

Sirena saw more light coming from another window a few feet away and moved over, hoping she could hear better. Luck had shined upon her. The window was cracked open just enough to hear what was coming next.

"Sirena needs to be punished for this. You're right. I was wrong. I'm sorry for not listening to you."

"You don't have to apologize. I know you're only thinking about what's best for Christopher."

Jay shook his head. "What's best for Christopher is not letting her run loose. That woman has absolutely no right to be out of prison after what she did. None of us are safe."

Hearing their reconciliation by making Sirena the bad guy made her want to go inside and blast them with the truth. And was it also her fault Venus was seeing another man? Last she checked, she hadn't forced that man's pelvis against Venus's hips.

"First thing tomorrow morning, I'm going to take Christopher to see Detective Brewer," Jay conceded, having made up his mind.

"I'll go with you. Christopher needs all the support we can give him."

"That's not necessary. I think it's better if I take him myself."

"No, really. I want to go."

Sirena had heard enough. Her pulse raced trying to get up the nerve to do something. Her hand was gripped on the hard smoothness of the gun in her purse now. How hard could it be? Stand up, she told herself. *Stand up for yourself.*

"Jake, there's something else," Venus said gently as if preparing for a confession.

She lifted her head slightly to see them. Jay took her by the hand and pulled her toward him. "Let me say something first." He led her to the table. They sat down still gripping each other for dear life. "Everything you said was true. I'd been so wrapped up in myself, my career, that I hadn't been paying attention. You are my everything. I promise not to take you for granted anymore. I promise to take every available chance to come home, even if I can't stay but a night or two, I will be here."

Venus smiled, taking his face with a firm grasp. "You don't have to. I've decided we're going to move to LA. I'm going to sell the business. Bliss has already signed. Now all I have to do is sign. There's no reason for me to stay here—without you."

Jay leaned forward and kissed her, then a hug as if he believed her every word. "Oh baby, that's even better. I love you. God, I love you."

Sirena kneeled down, sinking lower with each breath. She was sure she was going to be sick. Her stomach tightened with sharp pain. An anxiety attack, pure and simple. She slowed her breathing and talked herself out of walking in there and demolishing the whole family. She tried to focus on what she really wanted. *Jay.*

The light spilling outside suddenly went dark. The two of them had left the kitchen headed to their cozy bed. Right then, all Sirena wanted was to lay her head down as well. She was tired, so exhausted. She couldn't remember the last time she'd slept. Sure, she'd closed her eyes for minutes at a time, only to open them after imagining nightmarish scenarios. Being chased, caught, and thrown back in jail, exactly what was going to happen...unless.

She pulled herself together enough to stand. Her stomach still hurt with pangs of betrayal. Not of hers, but of Jay's. She couldn't believe she still felt sorry for him after all she'd heard.

She knew what to do. This time there'd be no failure. Her life depended on it.

Chapter thirty-six

THE DAY CHRISTOPHER WAS BORN his eyes opened with intelligence and wonder. She'd made the decision to give him up for adoption long before he arrived. "Someone will take good care of you," she'd whispered the lie with a kiss. There was no family bursting with joy waiting in the wings. She didn't know where he would end up. His only destination was the brooding nurse standing over her ready to take him from her arms.

Sirena had a hit record and a fresh contract for two more albums. A baby wasn't part of the deal. Her eighteenth birthday was three days away and she had no one to call.

"All right, time for me to take him," the impatient nurse announced having seen this type of thing enough to know a few extra minutes meant nothing. Another unwed teen giving birth was nothing special, even if she had a hit record.

"Wait. No. I can't." Sirena pushed back the tears. "I have to call my father."

"Look, the social worker is waiting. I have to get this little guy prepped and ready to go." Her solid thick hands reached for the baby, only to be pinched. She snatched her hand back with a yowl. "Have you lost your mind?"

"I said I wasn't ready. Okay, so back off." Sirena did what she swore she'd never do, and that was call her father and ask for help. Their relationship was non-existent. She hadn't spoken to him since she was sixteen after she'd received her first recording contract. It hadn't mattered that he'd facilitated her desire to be a singer, driving her to various auditions, paying for gas and motels. The entire time was spent with him telling her she was wasting her time, just like her mother who'd abandoned them believing she too would be famous someday.

When success finally happened, she was redeemed. Celebrating with her dad would've been the right and noble thing to do. Instead she felt nothing but resentment. Having to overcome his negativity along with the grueling nature of the entertainment business made her a callous and bitter woman before she was old enough to legally drive. Wrath was all she could muster for James Lassiter. Filing for emancipation was first on her list. She ignored his calls protesting, knowing it was killing him. Good, she thought, let him die a tiny bit each day the way she had from his berating.

She was doing just fine without her father. She may have been a tormented soul on the inside, but no one knew. To the world she was a budding super star. She had a pilot being shopped to the Disney Channel. She was dating JayP, the most wanted man in the hip-hop industry and, he was all hers, right along with anything else she desired. Free designer clothes, shopping, traveling, the world was hers to redefine as she pleased, until that morning she woke up to swollen sore breasts and the urge to run to the bathroom every five minutes. She didn't need a home pregnancy test to know a baby was growing inside of her.

A glimmer of joy touched her in her dreams. She and JayP were going to have a baby. Being a real family swam through her nightly fantasy instead of her usual visions of stardom and fame. Of course she wasn't 100% sure it belonged to Jay, but he wouldn't doubt her, or care. He loved her.

She rehearsed telling him, "Baby, we're going to have a baby," and seeing the smile rising on his proud Papa face. She waited for him to get back from a short tour so she could tell him in person.

He'd been working so hard. She gave him a day or two to rest before meeting him at the studio where he was already creating his next great hit. Mornings weren't her favorite time of the day especially with the threat of feeling sick but she couldn't wait any longer, arriving with a bag full of donut holes, his favorite, and a soy latte, also his favorite.

Greeted by the security guard with a welcoming smile, she walked in without the usual check-in process. She was family.

Maybe if the guard had known Jay was in the middle of getting a lap dance in the center of the recording booth, he probably would've called ahead. Instead, Jay peered through the glass walls to see her hurt and shocked expression.

"Wait a minute, Cee-Cee," Jay called after her once she'd already tossed his donuts and latte into the trash and fled the building.

"Lorie was just playing around in there. Nothing was going on," he called after her.

Sirena spun around on her heels. "I came here to tell you I'm pregnant. I don't know what the hell I was thinking. I'd be a fool to give up my life for a man, a baby."

Jay grabbed her and held her close. "Cee-Cee, there's only you. You know that."

"Yeah, glad to know." The rage in her chest made it hard to breathe. Before she knew it, she was throwing up the orange juice she'd sipped and the toast she'd only nibbled on.

Jay wasn't fazed by the mess. "Morning sickness. I heard it doesn't last long." He stroked a soothing hand over her forehead.

"You're damn right it's not going to last long. I'm getting rid of it."

"No. Please. Don't do that. You can't. I told you nothing's going on. Cee-Cee, shit, don't play like that."

"I'm not playing. I don't have time for games."

Jay let out a chastising laugh. "So how is this any different then me, walking in on you giving my homeboy a massage? I walk in on you two in the middle of the floor in my fucking apartment. I believed you when you said nothing ever happened between you and Tommy. You can't extend the same trust to me?"

Sirena narrowed her eyes, wanting to tell him that was his problem. He was far too trusting. "I'm not having this baby. It's my decision, my life. Now you should probably get back in the studio. That bitch might lose her sexy and have to start her lap dance all over again."

"Is the baby even mine, Cee Cee?"

"If that's what you need to believe to sleep at night." She flipped her middle finger and walked away knowing he wouldn't chase her. He'd never leave his artist in the studio. Time was money. How many times had she tried to take a break in the studio with a flirtatious kissing session only to be shunned? "Let's keep it professional in the studio, Cee Cee." Except on this day with three other guys looking on, it was okay to have his libido stroked like he was in a private strip club.

With every step she took, she hated him more. He hadn't bothered calling. Not even a message. Just like that, he'd washed his hands of her.

She had hoped he'd come to his senses and at least try to fight for her. Couldn't he see she was just angry and

was only making idle threats? The answer was obviously no.

Ambivalence led her to waiting until it was too late to end the pregnancy. She didn't really have the nerve to go through with it, afraid somehow she'd be punished by a higher power. Her baby boy was born. She knew he belonged to Jay the minute the nurse placed him in her arms. She was glad she didn't have the abortion. Grateful to see those tiny perfect feet and hands, those bright angel eyes.

Adoption seemed like the fair solution, until that little boy seemed to look right through her as if he knew her all too well.

She picked up the phone in her hospital room and dialed her father's number. James Lassiter had one more chance to do right by her. The arrangement was simple. She'd sign a closed adoption agreement. Her father would raise Christopher until she was ready to take him back.

It wasn't her fault that it took ten years before she and Jay found each other again. By then her father refused to give Christopher up. He was his father, plain and simple and Sirena was his big sister.

There was nothing worse than people ruining your plans. People took great joy in stepping in her way. Her entire life felt like a pinball game. She was the ball ping, pinging against those silly interfering fools. She was so tired of it all. She'd decided, no more. That was why she'd drugged her father to sneak Christopher away without a fight. It wasn't her fault he'd fallen asleep with a lit cigar. She felt the heat of the flames, watching the house burn.

***

Sirena awakened in her car with a start. She was grateful the fire was a dream and not the Gingerbread house up in flames.

She got out and stretched, inhaling the dewy morning air. If she wanted to see it happen she'd have to walk the block to get in position. She pulled her sweatshirt hoodie up over her head and first went into the grove of trees to do what had become her new living arrangement. Eventually she'd have to go back to her dump of a place and pay homage to the house warden.

But first she wanted to see Venus's face when she saw the note left on her car window. "Unless you want your husband to know about your affair, I'd stop him from going to the police." She'd signed with an S and added her lover's address for clarity.

Short and sweet. She knew without a doubt it would work. Venus wouldn't dare jeopardize her relationship with Jay, not even to put her back in jail. She also knew it would be Venus's car they'd drive in the morning. They planned to take Christopher to the police station to give a statement. They couldn't very well pile onto the motorcycle. All she could count on was that Venus was a good little girl and who would let her husband drive. The note was tucked into the window jam on the passenger side, folded, with the words, "my sweet", written on the front. Her heart would race with paranoia, not knowing if it was from her lover boy. That very second, Venus would realize she'd been caught and now someone knew she wasn't perfect. That's what Sirena had slept in the car all night to see.

Like clockwork, the clan filed out of the house. Christopher led the way. In so many ways he was just like Jay, headstrong, opinionated, and honest. In so many ways he was also like herself when she was young, eager to grow up, smarter than everyone gave her credit for. Even if her plan didn't work, she trusted Christopher's instincts. He'd know he was being manipulated for their gain. If someone got in the way this time, she was prepared to end it all. It was time.

Chapter thirty-seven

JAKE PUSHED THE BUTTON to roll down the window. "Babe, what's wrong?" He stared out at his wife who seemed frozen. He posed the question instead of saying what he really wanted to say. *Get in the car. Let's do this thing before Christopher changes his mind.*

Her mouth moved but nothing came out. It was possible she was ticked off that he hadn't opened the door for her. Occasionally she came across the sole gentleman in the world who still opened the car door for his wife or girlfriend. She would look on with envy and suddenly demand the same act of chivalry. "Why can't you open the door for me?" The thought never lasted long.

Jake leaned over and snapped the latch of the Range Rover, pushing the heavy door open. It was the best he could do. "Babe, let's go."

"I...I think I forgot my phone. I'll be right back." She scurried away leaving the car door open with the annoying bell going off as if the red warning light on the dash wasn't enough.

This was supposed to be the answer to all his problems. Making things right by taking Christopher to the police station to sign an affidavit that Sirena was responsible for his disappearance. There would be peace in his household, he told himself. He could almost taste the victory. Then why did it feel like a whole other pot of mess was brewing?

He was confident he could convince Venus to stay out of the room while the detective went through the questioning. That way she wouldn't hear anything as to Sirena's motivations.

Besides, he only assumed Sirena had taken Christopher as payback for the royalties he refused to give her. The real answer was that she was unstable.

After waiting impatiently, Jake popped off his seatbelt. "I'll be right back." Jake said to Christopher leaving him in the car with the heat flowing. The fall morning was cold and damp but by noon it'd be seventy degrees.

Inside the house, he found Venus and Bliss standing in the foyer. "What's going on?"

Venus spun around, startled. "Nothing." She took a deep breath. "Got my phone."

The two of them with their heads together meant there was something amiss. "Am I mistaken, or did we cover this already. Whatever's going on, you need to let me in on it."

"Nothing's going on," Venus replied sharply.

He eyed Bliss who wished to be anywhere but there, in the same space with him. "Did you see something? What'd I do now?" It came out rude and sarcastic though he hadn't meant it to sound that way.

"Everything is not about you all the time." Bliss beamed. At least he had her attention.

"I didn't say everything was about me. All I was saying was just once, it'd be nice to hear what's on your mind without begging." Jake kept his distance. He still wasn't sure what he'd walked into.

Bliss held something in her hand that slowly dissolved into a ball. A small piece of paper. A note.

"Where's Christopher?" Venus asked panicked.

"I left him in the car. He's ready. I'm ready. Now you're stalling. What's going on?"

Venus didn't answer, a horrified expression froze on her face.

"I'll tell you what's going on." The voice along with a brisk rush of cool air came from behind him.

He turned around knowing who would be standing there. What he hadn't expected to see was a gun pointed in his direction sending chills up his spine raising the fine hairs on his neck.

He instinctually moved forward to block anything from happening to Venus or Bliss. "Cee Cee, put the gun down." Sirena looked different. She'd aged from the last time he'd seen her and yet she appeared younger. He didn't know how to explain it. Some kind of vulnerability about her

making him feel sadness for this woman holding a gun in his face.

"Did she tell you?" She'd asked the question as if they'd been in a conversation for the past hour.

"Tell me what, Cee Cee? Please, put the gun down and we can talk about whatever you want to talk about." Jake took a desperate step closer.

"Don't. I heard everything you said about me. You think you have everything figured out."

"Cee Cee, my babies are in this house. If that gun goes off accidentally, anyone could get hurt. You don't want that. Put the gun down. I promise, nothing's going to happen to you." For a second he thought she was going to lower her arm. Instead she turned her attention past him where Venus was standing behind him clutching onto Bliss.

Sirena's eyes watered with sadness and something else, exhaustion. "You seriously weren't going to tell him. Wow, the girl knows how to keep a secret."

Venus searched for something to say. Fear weighed her down. Her anger was just as heavy. There was nothing she could say. Good, Jake thought. Words exchanged between the two wouldn't end well. "Cee Cee." He snapped to get her attention.

"She's a liar," Sirena blurted. "You don't know who she really is. That's your problem, Jay. You've always trusted the wrong people. You always choose wrong."

"I'm ready to make the right choice. Okay. Now I'm ready," Jake exclaimed. It was about time he put his acting to some real use. "You're right. I've made some bad decisions. I know that now. Give me another chance. Okay. But this waving a gun around, this thing has got to stop." He dropped his head and covered his face. He absolutely wanted to cry. Real tears, no bullshit. He was scared. How many times had he seen this coming? There was a saying for this, believe it and it will come. Good or bad, that was the way the universe worked.

No matter how he tried to restructure the course of fate this very scenario had played on repeat in his mind; a woman who'd put her trust, hope, and prayer, all on him, had decided she'd rather end his life than let either of them move on.

He'd made the decision to settle down with one woman. Stability was what he'd wanted. He fell in love with Venus. She quieted the noise in his head. She was nothing like Sirena or those other women who bled trouble, emotional terrorist, rigged to go off if their demands weren't met. He'd done his best to make this day not happen; yet here they were.

"Cee Cee, listen to me. We're going to get through this. Okay? I promise, everything is going to be okay. Venus and I...have been having trouble. We've been trying to keep things under wraps because of the kids. But I think it's time."

"Do you know why?" Sirena pushed past the blurry vision and leveled the question right along with the gun. Several minutes had passed and she still had amazing control of the heavy caliber gun, holding it upright and steady. "Did she tell you why?"

Jake leaned in with confusion. "Doesn't matter why? We're going our separate ways. So she's not going to interfere with us being together. Okay? You and me can be together. Tell me you understand."

A tear sprang. "All I've ever wanted was for you to let me in." Her words garbled into a string of mush. "Youneverletmein."

"Cee Cee, listen to me. We're done with the past. It's all about the future. Me, you, and Chris."

This struck a nerve and her face brightened. Her eyes awakened. "All I've ever wanted was a chance. A second chance. We could be a family. I didn't really care about the money. I didn't care that you were taking my share of the record money. I just wanted to be a part of your life, and Christopher's life."

"No!" Christopher joined the party slamming the front door behind him. He'd gotten tired of waiting in the car and came to see what was taking so long. "I'm not going anywhere with her, ever. She's crazy."

Sirena flinched with his declaration. A thirteen-year old's hurtful analysis felt like a harsh stab. She kept the gun poised on her target while turning slowly to Christopher. "You're a child. You don't make the decisions." She blotted the tears from her eyes with her sleeve.

"I thought I was a young man. That's what you kept telling me. Now I don't know anything. Yeah right. I know

I'm not going anywhere with you. I don't want to be anywhere near you."

"Chris, that's enough," Jake ordered.

"Dad, you said we had to stop her from hurting anyone else."

Jake could see Sirena's expression turn to hurt. Any empathy they'd shared was gone. All the work he'd put into convincing her they had a future together was destroyed in one fail swoop.

"I knew you were lying," she hissed at Jake.

"Son, over here." Jake opened his arms and waved Christopher to come toward him.

"Get your ass over there like your daddy says." Sirena shooed Christopher with a wave of her gun.

Christopher gladly slid behind Jake, grateful to be on the other side where he thought he was safe, obviously unaware that a bullet could easily penetrate through the average body. Jake wasn't made of steel contrary to what his son believed. Jake was scared too and fought hard not to let his voice shake. But he wouldn't give up. Not yet.

"Cee Cee, lets talk about this, just you and me. We can go wherever you want to go. Anywhere, you name it."

"Your wife is cheating on you," Sirena announced pausing long enough to squeeze in a forced chuckle before continuing. "Isn't that funny? I followed her. I saw her and her lover, together last night."

"Look what I found." A loud scream followed by the slam of something heavy hitting the ground. Jezzy stood in shock where she'd dropped the box she was holding.

Liquid pooled immediately at her feet. "Oh my God! I'm sorry." She turned running with flailing hands.

Why hadn't Jake thought of that? Why hadn't they all just scattered and run at the first sight of the gun instead of standing there having this absurd conversation? Right then, waiting for her next move, they could've all split in four directions while Jake tackled her for the gun. Instead, he remained contemplating what was real and what was unreal and wondering how he'd gotten everyone in this situation.

As if she'd read his mind her mouth dropped, astonishment replaced her bleak expression. "You've got to be kidding." Sirena continued, though it wasn't directed at him. She closed her eyes and inhaled the scent that immediately filled the room. "Is that what I think it is?"

Sirena inched toward the box and kicked the top flap. "Two Sisters. I love that stuff." Seconds passed before she came to a revelation. "You're Two Sisters?"

Venus nodded her head up and down still afraid to speak.

"I love Two Sisters. I haven't been able to find it lately. You really have to work on your distribution."

"It's good enough to eat," Bliss spoke for the first time. She kneeled down next to the box and picked up a bottle and handed it toward Sirena. "On the house. Here take two."

"For me? You shouldn't have."

Bliss brushed her hand before the slippery bottles made it past Sirena's grasp, which wasn't a good idea when she needed to keep the gun stable. Jake saw the opportunity and did his best to time the fumble.

Sirena juggled a bit. He had one chance. Making his move, he leaped forward and knocked her arm in the air taking ahold of the gun.

She wasn't giving up without a fight. He grabbed her wrists and pushed it back, hoping she'd have sense enough to drop it before a bone popped.

"Let it go," he warned.

The only thing he heard was the blast. The damn thing went off.

He heard Venus scream, "Oh my God! Call 911!"

"Dad!" Christopher was yelling. "You shot him."

Sirena clamped her teeth into his skin. He howled in pain before doing what he hadn't wanted to do. His elbow rose and swung into her face sending her backward against the wall. The gun flew up and Jake dived underneath it with both hands ready for the landing, praying it didn't go off again.

He snatched it, inches from smacking the ground.

Sirena had flown backwards, hitting the wall. She sat dazed, unable to do more than moan. Each time she tried to get up she fell down again.

"Call the police." Jake pulled out the chamber and emptied the bullets into his palm.

"I called," Bliss said holding the phone. "They're on the way. The ambulance too." Her eyes landed on the blood pooling down his face and around the collar of his sweater. Only then did he notice the stinging sensation at his temple. He'd been grazed. A hair closer and there would've been a hole in his head.

Chapter thirty-eight

VENUS RAN AND CAME BACK with a towel. "Dear God," she pleaded while pressing the fabric against the side of his head. Whatever damage the bullet made, he was glad he couldn't see it.

"It's okay, babe. I'm okay."

Within minutes there was a soft knock at the front door followed by a man's voice. "Police." He knocked again. "Hello, anybody in there?"

"That was fast." Venus rushed to get the door, stepping over Sirena's sprawled legs. Jake got up a bit slower, following behind.

"Babe, let me get it." He stepped in front of Venus, opening the door to a man standing in a brown leather jacket and jeans. He hardly looked like he was answering a 911 call. Jake assumed he was an undercover type. There was no urgency in his demeanor.

Jake looked past him expecting to see a couple of uniformed officers with guns drawn. An armed woman had attacked his family. Didn't that warrant some caution?

"I believe you called about a disturbance," he said casually. He held up a badge, "Detective Heights." The detective zeroed in on Jake's injury with newly piqued interest. "Mr. Parson, is there anyone else hurt?" His hand slipped under his jacket, resting on his holster. "May I come in?"

"Please. Yes," Jake said stepping aside. "I thought other officers would be here."

"I'm sure that's not necessary," Detective Heights offered exposing the sleek silver pistol strapped to his chest. The detective scanned the room. His attention landed on Christopher. "You all right, young man?"

Christopher nodded his head up and down, showing more fear than he had originally when Sirena held a gun pointed at his face.

The detective turned his sights to the dazed figure slouched against the wall. "Looks like you won."

"Here's the gun she used." Jake held it out away from his body like it was smelly trash.

The detective gladly took it, gripping the barrel without considering fingerprints. He checked the bullet chamber before shoving the gun in his waist.

He leaned over Sirena and pushed her eyelids open one at a time. He slipped his hands under her arms lifting her to her feet. He used the wall to hold her upright while he checked her for more weapons. "Ma'am, can you hear me? I'm going to need you to come with me. You're under arrest."

Sirena remained groggy but at least stood up with his help. She gripped his sleeve. He held her steady before pulling her wrists in front of her and clipping them together with restraints. Their slow stride only a few feet seemed to take forever. When they reached the front door, he looked to Jake for assistance. "Could you get the door?"

Jake felt awkward, not sure why. His few moments of heroism came to an anticlimactic halt. "That's it?"

"An officer will be here to take your statement," the man said with his hands full. "You might want to get that looked at." Meaning the bullet graze on Jake's head.

"Yeah, will do." Jake watched as Sirena was put in the backseat of the small car, not very detective-like. More like an economy sized rental car. The detective gave one last wave before rounding the turnstile and speeding off. The knot in Jake's stomach remained. The weight on his chest lightened up a bit. Still, he had an uneasy feeling.

Everyone else breathed out a collective sigh. Venus, Bliss, and Christopher slowly untangled themselves. The silent noise of the big clock over the fireplace, the raspy inhales and exhales of Jake's unstable breathing, and the shifts of fear to relief blanketed the confusion of what-tha-hell just happened.

"I'm taking you to the hospital right now," Venus announced. She took a few steps then stopped. "Oh God," she looked up. Jake looked up too. The distinct black hole in the ceiling was directly above the twin's nursery.

All of them bound up the stairs in record speed. They found Jezzy squatted in the corner with her arms wrapped around Lauren and Henry.

"Mommy!" Lauren broke free then Henry. They both rushed into their parent's arms.

Jezzy stood up. "Who else she shoot?"

"She's gone. The police arrested her," Bliss said.

"She needs to be put under the jail." Jezzy went over to the floor and tapped with her foot. "That bullet could've hit these children. Madness." She went to the nursery bathroom and came out with a clean towel. "Mr. Jay, you should get to the hospital. I don't want nothing to happen to you. I'm going to be expecting combat pay. Dodging bullets is extra."

"Me too," Christopher said. "I want an increase in my allowance."

Jake shook his pounding head. "Let's just be grateful we're all okay." He shifted his attention to Venus. She kept her eyes down or closed, while holding Henry. She still hadn't found her footing.

It donned on Jake only then. "Wait a minute? Where's Mya?" He tore out the bedroom door down the hallway calling out Mya's name.

"She's already gone. She went to school," Bliss said catching up to him.

Jake dropped his head in his hands while he wished the ringing sound would stop. Her gentle hands rose and squeezed his shoulders. "It's okay. We're all okay," Bliss said, trying to sound sympathetic. For this brief time, her heart seemed to soften towards him. "Your family is safe. That's all that matters," she said, holding her voice steady. She'd been shaken up and was doing her best to keep it together too.

Jake turned around and pulled his sister-in-law close for a hug even if she hadn't wanted one. He was convinced a hug could save a life. You never knew who you were helping with that one act of kindness. This time, it was his own. He hoped she didn't feel the tears rolling down his cheeks and onto her shoulder.

He was finally able to accept the fact that everyone was safe. He could breathe again.

Bliss patted him gently on the back. "You did good."

There was heavy knocking and doorbell ringing all in unison breaking up their nurturing moment. Jake slid a hand down his face to make sure the evidence of his mini-breakdown was all clear. "It's probably the police. Someone's supposed to come and get a statement."

"Or the ambulance. Make sure you let them clean that area," Bliss said genuinely concerned. Maybe finally they could be friends.

"I'm straight," Jake assured her before he traveled down the stairs two at a time, holding his head ringing with pain from each step. He was more concerned about hearing loss than a scar.

"Yeah, I'm coming," he said hitting the landing as gently as possible.

He opened the door, greeted by a line of officers, four or five deep all in defense mode. This was more like what he'd expected the first time. Now he couldn't fathom why giving a statement would require that many officers. Jake narrowed his eyes in confusion. "What's going on?"

"Sir, we're responding to an emergency call. A woman with a gun," the first officer spoke softly with caution. His eyes shifted to Jake's injury.

"She's been arrested already. A detective came almost immediately."

Two of the officers who were in front gave each other a questioning look. "We're first on dispatch, sir. Did the detective show a badge and state his name?"

"Yes," Jake replied matter-of-factly, but a name wasn't readily available in his memory. "I saw the badge."

"So, the woman you called about is gone?"

"Yes, gone. An officer put handcuffs on her and took her out of here. We all saw it, my wife, sister-in-law, nanny, all of us. Call your station. Check your dispatch. She's probably already booked by now."

The officer wasted no time. He got on his police radio. "This is Officer 412 responding to a call at Wind Song Road. Has there been an earlier response team at this address?"

"No. You are the first," the woman's radio voice echoed back. "Do you need back up?"

"No back up, thank you." The officer gave Jake an official side eye. "Is it all right if we take a look inside, sir?"

Jake stepped back without hesitation opening the door wider. "Please do." He was starting to think he imagined the last hour of his life. A detective came, flashed his badge, and responded to the situation. Was it a dream?

Two of the officers stepped inside. The others dispersed around the property. Their heavy presence moved throughout the living room, kitchen, and hallway. They took note of the broken vase and scattered flowers. They paid even closer attention to the smudge of blood on the wall.

"Did you know the woman who entered your home and attacked you?" The officer was standing directly in front of Jake.

"Yes. Sirena Lassiter. She was in prison for an attack on my wife. She's the biological mother of my son who lives with me, and my wife. She wasn't supposed to make any contact with him but suddenly she's out on parole trying to kill my whole family."

"She came to your house, threatened you and your family. You were pretty angry about that?" The question posed by the officer was loaded, full of suspicion.

"Wouldn't you be?"

"Yes, definitely. If someone came in with a gun and waved it in front of my children, I'd be extremely upset." The officer's innuendo hung in the air.

"Look, she's not here. I wrestled with her to get the gun, but that's all. She walked out of here in handcuffs escorted by one of Atlanta's finest." Jake swallowed the ball of anxiety trying to grow in his throat. "You want to talk to my wife and her sister who saw the whole thing, or are you going to stand there acting like I'm the guilty party here?"

The officer took a deep breath. "Domestic disputes can get nasty. We have to cover the full possibility of what might have taken place here."

"This wasn't a domestic dispute. The woman is insane. She had to be stopped," Jake responded far too hastily. Best to shut it down while he was ahead. "I appreciate you showing up so quickly, officers. Thank you." He held his breath a bit tighter. "Can I show you out?"

He waited until the uniforms and heavy guns belts were completely out of sight before climbing the stairs hoping the women hadn't heard the conversation.

Worrying had become his constant state. Not knowing what was the right thing to do. How much information was too much or not enough? He wasn't sure what to say to Venus.

He couldn't answer the burning question of WTF just happened? Sure there had to be a simple explanation but he couldn't think of it. There were signs he ignored. The man, the detective looked familiar, a face he'd seen before but couldn't place. Then there was the part where Sirena hadn't put up a fight when he told her she was being arrested.

In fact, she'd smiled. A faint genuine smile that he'd attributed to her hazy state. Head trauma. Sirena had even leaned her head on the man's shoulder for a brief moment as if she'd found solace.

There was also the response time. Jake wasn't watching his clock or anything, but there was no doubt in his mind the detective had arrived within single digit minutes of Bliss calling 911, which would make it likely that the detective (or whoever he was) had arrived with his own agenda.

He pressed his ear against the twin's nursery door before going in, preparing for what he was going to say. Conveying the officer's suspicion that Sirena was disposed of by his hand wasn't what he'd call a promising start.

Get a grip. He entered the nursery. He looked over their faces. The calm demeanor of his wife and her ladies in waiting gave him a boost of confidence that his secret was safe. "The police have everything under control. Sirena's out of our hair and we've seen the last of her."

He wasn't always such a purveyor of truth bending. Over the years of being a married man he'd learned to say the opposite of what he was thinking. It worked better that way. Appearing oblivious to what was going on also worked well at times, though very frustrating for his wife.

"Where's Chris?"

"In his room," Bliss answered quickly. She'd already been a witness to his earlier breakdown so she understood it was more than a simple question. "Christopher's fine. We're all fine."

He was grateful for their new found bond. He could trust her to not tell Venus that his tough exterior was all a ruse. Seeing his mini-breakdown was a safe secret between the two of them. Besides, Bliss wanted the freedom to walk out the door and leave this circus tent and there was no way she could do it if Venus was left unhinged. Jake knew her strategic thinking all too well. She wasn't the only one who could read minds.

"So is everybody okay?"

"Okay as one can be after being held hostage at gun point," Jezzy replied first in usual fashion. This episode wouldn't be forgotten or forgiven any time soon. She'd already asked for a raise. She knew her employer would give her whatever she wanted at this point.

"You know, I could use a vacation," Jezzy announced. "Stress leave."

"You know what? That's not a bad idea. As a matter of fact, that would be fantastic. Lets all grab a few things, throw them in a bag and catch a plane for a much needed vacation."

Jezzy did a double take. "I said I could use a vacation. If we all go, then I'm still working."

"It'll be fun. It's Thursday. We can leave tonight and come back on Monday." Jake took ahold of Henry's small hand where he'd latched onto his leg. Jake scooped him up on his hip. "What do you say, big guy? You want to get on a plane and go on a trip?"

"Disneyland," Henry screamed. It was word association. He knew what a plane trip was after they'd gone to Orlando, Florida last summer. Every time he saw an airline commercial, he screamed, "Yay! Disneyland."

"Then Disneyland it is," Jake said to his less than enthusiastic audience.

"We really should get Chris back in school." Venus blinked her dissension instead of speaking it directly. "He's already missed an entire week."

Bliss shook her head, no. "I have orders that need to go out." She was clearly exhausted. She needed a vacation too, she was just too afraid to admit it.

"Then a few more days aren't going to matter," Jake announced making an executive decision. He wasn't taking no for an answer. They were all going to be on the first flight that left the ground by midnight.

"If you can't beat him up, join him." Jezzy was already on her feet moving in the right direction. She began packing the children's bags without hesitation. "What?" She stopped for a moment to give her detractors the stink eye. "What woman turns down a free vacation? I'm not the one."

Chapter thirty-nine

I COULD TELL WHEN JAKE was covering his tracks. He was a good actor, a great actor, but when it came to me, I could see through the mask he was wearing.

I told him a million times not to even bother because I could see the truth. Flashing signals of guilt reflected with a soft twinkle in his shimmering dark eyes. Then there was the way he took in short hard earned breaths like the plug would be pulled at any moment.

"Can I talk to you?" I took his hand and didn't wait for an answer. I led him outside, down the hall, and into our bedroom. I closed the door and kept my voice low. "Tell me what's going on."

He dropped his head as if he was relieved. He was tired of hiding his missteps and I was tired of pretending not to see them.

"So we're supposed to just get on a plane to the happiest place on earth when we're all just miserable? I don't think seeing Mickey and Minnie are going to fix this."

"Okay, so what are we supposed to do, disappoint Henry and Lauren? They want to go, so let's just go." He cupped his hands around my face.

"Are you going to stand there and pretend there's nothing you need to tell me?"

"I swear, I'll tell you every single thing on my mind if we can just get the hell out of here."

"You see, that's what I'm talking about. You want me to just blindly, follow the leader, right over the cliff. I'm not going to do it. Do you hear me? I'm not going anywhere and neither are my children until I know what's happening."

"How about you start first?" He lowered his eyes in a suspicious gaze.

"What?"

"Yeah, what Sirena was talking about when she said she followed you to your lover's house. Are we going to pretend that didn't happen? Since we're putting all the truth out in the open, lets start there."

I didn't have long enough to think of a good answer. Just as I knew him, he knew me equally well. I didn't bat an eye, not even half a blink or he would've noticed the fight or flight in my response.

I kept my eyes on his and dared not even swallow a breath. "She's insane. That's what insane people do, they live by their imagination instead of reality. I'm not going to defend myself over something a stalker said."

"So last night when you left here, where'd you go?"

"Are you serious? We're not going to make this thing, this mess, about me. That was your personal stalker who just held a gun on this family. Not mine." I said all I wanted to say on the subject then made a move for the door.

"No. Wait." He put out his arm keeping me from passing. "I just have one more question."

"What?"

"Do you still love me?" Jake took my hand as we stood there. He knew I had something to hide but he was willing to let it go if I made the right choice. The decision was mine. Either I told him what he wanted to hear or I would have to confess the whole consorted relationship with Marco.

"I love you. I could never not love you."

"Then pack a bag. I'm asking for your trust because you know I would never do anything to hurt you or our children."

I wanted to tell him I knew no such thing. I stopped trusting him eons ago. All I could depend on was his sensible nature. He hated wasting resources. He hated stupidity, even his own. He hated not being in control, therefore Sirena and the scenario we'd just met with classified as a low mark on his spotless record.

He moved in closer to hold me. I couldn't move away, though I wanted to, my feet wouldn't budge. This was my problem; I could never stand up against his tenderness, his promise to do better. He always brought me back to this place of absolution. His sins wiped clean with one kiss.

"I only need one day—with you, alone." He whispered near my ear. "We can lock ourselves away in our room while Jezzy and Bliss take the kids to the park. No worries. No fears. Just us. Can I have that?"

His lips were soft but determined to get what he wanted. I remembered his kiss and why I loved him so much. He slipped his hands around my waist. "I love you," he said, wanting to hear the words back.

"I love you, too." It was the truth. What other choice did I have? Jake and I had been through so much worse than this. A gun wielding stalker was a blip on our marital screen.

I was ready to push delete on the memory file and let myself be swept away in the heat we'd created. The rush of danger pushed behind us, replaced with gratitude for being alive. Too bad the doorbell rang—again. We both had perplexed expressions of what now.

"I'm guessing the ambulance. A little late, but they aren't ones to miss an opportunity. Go ahead and start packing." He took a few light steps before turning back toward me. "I love you," he repeated or in other words, don't let me down.

I waited a few moments standing in one place, still unable to move. I feared if I sat down I wouldn't be able to get back up. The thought of packing sandals and sundresses seemed daunting.

Instead I wanted to go back to the nursery and pick up my babies and hold them tight. Passing the stairs, I leaned over the railing just to make sure Jake was okay. I heard him talking in a low steady voice. The other voice I recognized was Detective Brewer's. I stood on the top step where I could hear but not be seen.

Jake deliberately held his tone to a minimum level. "So what are you telling me? She's still running around, free to do this again?"

"No one's more shocked than I am. I told you it was a bad idea to let her get away with the first offense, kidnapping your son. If you weren't so determined to let her go, we could've stopped this whole thing before it happened. She'd be in custody now."

"I know. I get it. But I know what I saw. The man had a real badge. He was a cop."

"Well, whoever he was, he made a detour with Miss Lassiter. She's God knows where by now."

Hearing this made me stop and take a seat on the top stair. I couldn't get up enough nerve to scream, which is what I wanted to do. I'd wanted Christopher to talk to the police and Jake said no. I had no idea he'd outright blocked Detective Brewer from doing his job. Now, none of them were safe.

"If I hear anything I'll give you a call. As for now, keep your head on a swivel. She could be anywhere. And now that we know she has an accomplice, there's even more danger. Keep your family close."

"I can do one better," Jake said. "We're going to Disneyland for a few days." The smugness in his voice only added to the insult.

After the door closed and I was sure he was alone, I marched down the stairs. He looked up surprised to see me.

"I thought you were packing." He knew there was no way out. "Sirena is still loose," he confessed. "I didn't know. I just found out from Detective Brewer."

"How is that even possible?" I could feel the tickle of anger getting stronger. The lip quiver was giving me away. I was tired so there was no need in fighting it. "You knew. The question is, what else? Tell me."

"The man who came in here and arrested her was her friend. Somehow, he and she were together. I found out after the first officers, I mean, the other first officers showed up and acted like I buried Sirena in the backyard or something. They wanted to know where she was and when I told them she'd already been arrested, they nearly arrested me."

He was talking faster now, afraid at any minute he was going to lose his foothold. "I should've told you but I didn't want to scare you anymore than you already were. Being afraid at every turn, that's no way to live."

"And why shouldn't I be afraid? Your ex-girlfriend is still out there thinking I'm in the way of your great love affair. This was her second attempt at trying to kill me.

She almost shot Henry and Lauren this time. What's it going to take for you to understand? This isn't a situation you can mold and shape at will. This is our life."

"This is exactly what I'm talking about. You're blowing this thing out of proportion."

"Really? Then why are you hell bent on getting us out of the house? I'll tell you why, because you don't know. You don't know what Sirena is going to do next or what she's capable of."

"And that's my fault?"

"Yes," I screamed. I wasn't sure how many other ways I could say it. "I'm sick of you pretending like all of this has nothing to do with you. Like we're hens fighting and pecking at each other for no reason, when we all know we're fighting over the big rooster stepping around too cocky to notice."

"I can't control Sirena and what she does."

I pressed my hands to my ears. "I don't want to hear anymore."

"Anymore of what, the truth? If you'd moved to Los Angeles with me none of this would've happened. She wouldn't have known where to find us. She wouldn't have been able to walk right up to our door and walk in here holding a gun. So how is this my fault?"

There was nothing else to say. We were at an impasse where no one was going to sign the peace treaty. I got up to walk away.

"Where are you going?"

"To pack. You're right. If we weren't here she couldn't have found us."

He could read between the lines. "Packing to go where?"

"I'll let you know when we get there."

"Don't do this," he said nearly at a whisper. "The kids have been through enough. Don't make it worse."

"I'm taking control, something I should've done a long time ago. When Sirena is locked up and we're not in danger anymore we'll talk about what happens next. Until then, I think I'm doing the right thing for all of us."

"You have a business to run. How do you plan to do that living out of a suitcase?"

I hunched my shoulders as I continued going up the stairs unfazed by his declaration. "I'll figure it out."

He was right. I hadn't given Two Sisters a single thought. The shipment that was supposed to go out ended up spilling, thank God, from Jezzy's lousy job of screwing the tops on. Sirena recognized the conditioner's scent distracting her enough for Bliss to step in and help Jake make a grab for the gun. In other words, Two Sisters had saved our lives. Selling it seemed like the wrong thing to do.

Chapter forty

SIRENA HAD THE WORST HEADACHE. When she opened her eyes it hurt even worse. Her blurry vision only made her angrier, wishing she'd accomplished her goal instead of making a plain fool of herself.

"You're awake. Good," Lucas said standing over the bed. He held a glass of water. "Drink." He slipped his hand around her neck to help prop her up.

"Oohh. No. Stop." Pain rang through her skull and down her neck. "It hurts."

"You took a nasty blow. That's what happens when you show up to a gun fight with a gun you didn't plan on using."

"I planned on using it."

"No. You didn't or someone would be dead. I hope you got it out of your system now." Lucas sat on the edge of the bed. "I got you out of there, but you were this close to being locked away for life."

"You want a medal?" She shoved a hand to his chest. "If it weren't for you letting Christopher go, I would've never gone there. All I wanted was my son."

"All you wanted was JayP's attention. Well now you got it. I did what you asked. I paid someone to follow him in Los Angeles, drop something in his drink and get him in a compromising position. I didn't even ask the point of your little plan, I simply did it because you asked me to. Harmless. But this...the stunt you pulled stepping in that house with a loaded gun..." he shook his head. "So we've got to lay low for a few weeks until we can hit the road. We'll drive to Mexico."

Sirena shut her eyes. "We? After all this?" She partly wanted him to let her go. Let her be free to drown in her sorrow.

"I think we make a great team. I've got plans for us. We're just getting started, baby." He kissed her softly between the eyes. His piercing dark eyes latched onto hers.

Suddenly her vision was focus sharp. She saw the greed, the power he desired and understood what this partnership was about. She wasn't sure how, but she was going to find a way out. She needed to get off the man juice for a while. Detox.

"How am I expected to trust you again? You don't care about me," she pressed. "You said you were going to pay me for the last job and you never did. Now you want to drag me all over the third world to do who knows what. I rather take my chances here, right here, then get stranded in one of those south of the border jails."

"Baby, nothing like that is going to happen."

"How do I know? I don't feel secure. If something happens to you, I'll have nothing," Sirena whined for good measure.

Lucas was smart and conniving. He was a good pretender but Sirena could tell she was breaking through to him. He massaged his forehead for a few seconds. "Okay, here's the deal. I'll open an off shore account that's just your own. You'll have full access to it," he acquiesced, putting up both his hands in surrender. "Every time we do a job, I'll add another quarter million. But I just can't give it to you all at once, baby. You'll leave me."

Sirena rubbed the side of his face and wished she could pull herself up to kiss him for a better effect. "I'm not going anywhere. I know you're going to take care of me. You always do."

"That's right. Glad you're finally understanding." Lucas smiled that smile, devilish and appealing all at the same time. He walked over to the small desk in the hotel room and flipped open his laptop. "First thing we have to do is get your new name, new identification. Then we open the account. That simple." He tapped a few keys. The computer was purchased on the same day they went to the gigantic electronic store and let Christopher run loose like a kid in a candy store.

She remembered the salesman spouting about connectivity and being able to track all the open accounts with GPS. The joy of technology. Her knowledge of computers was basic, but surely she'd be able to find Christopher again when she was ready with a simple key punch. He loved the e-tablet and wouldn't let it out of his sight. She marveled at how easy it would be next time.

"That's it," Lucas said, closing the computer. "Everything's in motion. All you have to do is think of your new name." He came back to the bed and ran a warm palm over her shoulder. "How about Lucia. Sexy, huh?" he whispered, kissing her on the neck.

"You're an angel," Sirena cooed. "I don't know what I ever did to deserve you."

Chapter forty-one

MY MOTHER STOOD AT THE DOOR smiling. She wrapped her arms around my shoulders and didn't let go.

"Grandma." Lauren tugged on her sweater before pushing her arms up. "My turn."

"Yes, my precious baby. I have plenty of hugs for everybody." Pauletta had cried over the phone when I told her all that happened. She didn't have anything to say except, "Come home where you'll be safe."

My father was also a sight for sore eyes. I hadn't seen him on my last visit when I'd blown through town like a reckless tornado.

"Hey, precious," he said pulling me in for a soft squeeze.

"Hey, dad." I inhaled his familiar Irish Spring soap. He hadn't changed brands once. Always the subtle freshness that let me know all was right in the world. His face lit up even brighter when he saw Bliss come in behind us.

"Mom said it was okay," I told him when his expression U-turned into fear.

"Well, of course it's okay. She's always welcome," Pauletta added as if she hadn't cursed the day the illegitimate girl-child was born. I hoped her change of heart had come on her own terms and not from any spell Bliss might have conjured, which wasn't as farfetched as it seemed. I'd witnessed Bliss change my mother's negative into a positive with a mere touch. I'd also seen it go the exact opposite, from mild mannered happiness, to extreme rage.

This time, Pauletta was on her own. No one had influenced her new found understanding. Over the years, I'd learned not to question my mother's method of madness. She had to make sense of things her way. It was an all or nothing existence if you wanted to live in Pauletta's world.

I was the same way not too long ago. I'd made a conscious decision to change my ways. Compromise had started out as my goal. Somehow I'd veered off the road of compromise and ended down the gully of full submission. If Jake said jump, I asked 'should I wear heels or flats?' How high, was the second question.

Mya pushed her way through the crowded entry. "Hi Grandma. Hi Big Pop." Her pre-teen sullenness had been put on the back burner. Seeing my parents brought a smile on her face I hadn't seen in a long time, for that alone, it was worth the trip.

Jezzy trailed in carrying a couple of suitcases. She wasn't happy about the canceled Orlando trip until I reminded her that Los Angeles was the home of the original Disneyland with way cooler rides. I couldn't leave her behind. Unfortunately, that wasn't the case for Christopher. He wanted to stay with his dad and I understood.

I wasn't sure what the next step would be for Jake and I. My only goal was finding someplace safe where Sirena couldn't find us.

My father dispatched us to the bedrooms that were once mine and Timothy's, along with the den that held a fold out sofa. There'd never been this many guests at one time in the Johnston household. My old bedroom now painted a soft shade of mauve felt cozy and safe. I kicked off my shoes and couldn't resist lying down. It was no easy feat traveling with small children. Lots of Ziplock Baggies filled with snacks, sandwiches, and dry cereal that had found their way down my bra.

The twinkling noise coming from my phone announced a message. I suspected it was Jake. He'd asked me to call and let him know when we'd arrived. That too felt like too much information. My self-induced witness protection program would only work if I kept communication to a minimum. I simply didn't trust him anymore.

'I miss you.'

The message wasn't from Jake. I can't say I was disappointed. Marco's words lit up my screen and made my heart flutter. This was a dangerous time to feel a new connection with someone else. I was too vulnerable.

I wrote back, *Good to hear from you. I will contact you regarding Two Sisters on Monday.*

It wasn't sexy. Barely cordial. The message looked like something you'd type with a gun pointed to your head. I knew the feeling.

"Hey," Bliss stuck her head in. "Your mom cooked."

"Oh. Cool." I shoved my phone in my sweater pocket and sat up like a revived Zombie.

"You okay?" Bliss asked the question already knowing the answer. "I brought you some tea."

I looked at the cup in her hands. "I think I'll pass on the tea. The last time I drank your special brew I hallucinated about Marco DeVon making love to me."

"It's out of your mother's cabinet. I swear, I had nothing to do with it."

I took the warm cup and inhaled the sweet scent. Good old fashioned Lipton with a hint of lemon. "Thank you."

"You're welcome. I'll bring you something to eat too."

"I should probably come in the kitchen and visit with my mom for a while."

"She's fine. All her attention is on her grandchildren. You need to rest," Bliss batted her deep brown eyes. "Stay here. Relax," she ordered.

I sipped the tea and thought about the journey we'd traveled together. We would soon part ways after only finding each other a couple of years earlier. I'd grown dependent on my sister. As much as I didn't want to part with *Two Sisters,* I knew it was what Bliss wanted.

My phone chimed again. Marco wrote: *"Monday is so far away."*

"I'm in Los Angeles."

"Interesting. I have a trip planned for Los Angeles tomorrow morning. I'll see you then."

I rolled over and pulled the blanket around my shoulders feeling a sudden chill. I had enough worries. I really didn't need to add Marco DeVon on that list. My logical mind told me loud and clear this was a bad idea. After a few minutes of staring into my closed lids I opened my eyes and wrote back.

"See you tomorrow."

After I pressed send I felt better. It made absolutely no sense. I was inviting more trouble into my life and yet I'd never felt more relieved. The resounding applause and pat on the back said I was making a decision not weighed down by what everyone else wanted. What Jake wanted always seemed what was first and foremost in my mind. I was thrilled with the rebel spirit. The thought of seeing Marco made me smile. Like he said, we'd figure something out.

Chapter forty-two

THE NEXT MORNING I WOKE UP with Lauren's bent knees curled into the side of my ribs and Henry's hand cupped my over mouth. I was sandwiched between their pajama-clad bodies and couldn't move without peeling their limbs off of me.

I did my best to untangle myself without waking them. The sun was always brighter in California. This wasn't an opinion but a genuine fact. I'd traveled and lived in enough places to see the certainty. The sunglass industry probably wouldn't be profitable if it weren't for Southern California.

I squinted my way through my suitcase to find my robe. My mother liked it cold to sleep at night. I was sure she and Jezzy would get along wonderfully, both needing icicles hanging off their noses to have a good night sleep.

I adjusted the quilt over Lauren and Henry before I slipped out of the room.

Mya had slept in the same room with Jezzy where there was a bunk bed left over from Timothy's childhood. I peeked in on them, both still asleep. Bliss had the guest room downstairs to herself. It was still early but on East Coast time it'd be late in the morning.

I tapped on her door to see if she was awake. "Bliss, you up?" I knocked harder before turning the knob. My mother didn't believe in bedroom locks. When Timothy and I were in our teens, we used a chair shoved under the knob to keep her from bursting inside whenever she felt like it.

The door easily opened. The pullout bed was already put back in place. The plaid cushions neatly set on the sofa and the sheets folded. I panicked for a second before I saw her green suitcase in the corner.

Maybe she'd gone out. Even in the coldest months, the weather was irresistible for a long morning walk. I went to the front door and realized there was a light flashing on a security panel. My parents had installed a security system. The neighborhood had changed. No denying the unkempt lawns and shady figures hanging on the corners.

I assumed all the doors were rigged. If I attempted to check outside for Bliss the five alarm bell would ring waking up everyone on the block.

Then how did she get outside?

"Hey, precious. You up early?" My father stood behind me nursing a mug of coffee.

"It's not that early for me. Have you seen Bliss this morning? Well, I guess you would've seen her, to let her out. When did you get this alarm system?"

"A few months back. Your mother didn't feel safe. Been in this house for forty years. Been fine up till now. It's a damn shame when you can't feel safe in your own home."

"Boy, do I know the feeling." I turned my attention back to the mysterious disappearance of Bliss. "I wonder if mom let her out. She couldn't have left without setting off the alarm."

His eyebrows drew closer together. "Doubtful. Your mom doesn't break ground till way past ten."

"It's no big deal," I said to end the conversation. My father wouldn't understand about these things. Bliss and her strange ability to disappear whenever I was looking for her. "I forgot to tell mom how nice the house looks. You guys did a really nice job on the kitchen remodel," I offered, changing the subject.

"Thank you. I mean that. Thank you for sending the money. We really appreciated it. Your mother couldn't stop telling all the church ladies about the gift her daughter and son-in-law gave. We even had a little left over. That's where the security system came from."

It took me a minute to understand what my father was saying. The gift I'd sent? I hadn't sent any money. Although, I should have. "You're welcome," I'd said after realizing what my father was telling me. Jake sent them the money. No matter what he may or may not have done, Jake loved me. He loved me enough to care about my parents when I was too busy to notice that their house was falling apart and in need of protection. "I'd like some of that coffee, Dad."

"You still take cream?"

"A little. No sugar."

"So you want to talk about all of this chaos your mom's been telling me about. Being held at gun point by Christopher's mother, that had to be mighty scary."

"Terrifying."

"You shouldn't blame your husband. He wasn't the one holding the gun."

"No. Dad, I didn't say I blamed him. I just think he could've done a few things differently."

He gave me a thou-protests-too-much face. He set a cup in front of me. "Ahuh."

"I mean, I don't blame him for everything that happened. Just..." I could feel my logic falling apart. My father had a way of doing that. Instead of being in sales he should've been a prosecutor, one of those guys who sat back and let you dig yourself in a hole.

"Dad, it's a long story. This crossroad that we're at was already in the making. Anything can push you over the line when you're already standing there."

He took a sip from his cup. "I understand."

"I haven't wanted much. I've kept my head down and provided a stable home for our children, but at some point, I needed to come up for air."

"So how's the air?" A sly grin rose on his face.

I took in a deep long breath, exhaling slowly. "Good. Calm. It's nice."

"Enough said. No one can argue with peace of mind." He raised his cup. I raised mine. We gently clinked our orange ceramic mugs together. "Cheers."

Coffee with my dad was a ritual I'd missed. We laughed and talked a while longer before the rest of the household began to stir. I casually wished Bliss could be a part of our session but then selfishly turned grateful to have our father-daughter time alone.

More of me taking back *Venus*.

First on the list, I would learn to enjoy moments without putting a guilty cloud over everything. Second, I'd ask myself what's best for me...at least once a week.

I could already feel my edges softening. The bitterness and betrayal I'd felt toward Jake disappeared into a mild annoyance. By the time everyone was awake, my father and I had made a delicious breakfast spread. The kitchen smelled of country bacon, eggs, and buttered toast. I'd even used the juicer and made a pitcher full of fresh orange juice.

"This is what I call a vacation," Jezzy announced standing in her robe. "Waking up to a good hot meal, priceless."

"Hey, I cook," I said, responding to her not so discreet dig.

"Of course you do." She nudged my father. "If you like the earthy flavor of burnt rice."

"Say what? That doesn't sound like my Precious at all. My baby can burn."

"Thank you, Dad."

"Oh my goodness." Jezzy shook her head. "De-nial is not only a river in Egypt." She took a crunchy bite of bacon. "Where's Bliss? I need backup on this one."

I stayed quiet. There were things I wanted to forget about my sister. I didn't want to think about her curious ability to leave a locked house with a working security system.

"Good morning," Pauletta entered the kitchen fully dressed in a pink velour tracksuit. She leaned in and kissed me on the bridge of my nose. "How'd you sleep?"

"Wonderfully, considering I woke up with Lauren and Henry's limbs in my mouth."

Pauletta chuckled before picking up the remote to the TV. Like my father and his Irish Spring, some things were lifetime memberships. My mother always had to have the television on, even if it was only background noise. Even at night, she couldn't fall asleep without it. "I just love my new kitchen. You see how this new screen folds up and down."

"Only we never fold it up because it's always on," my father added. "Nothing on TV but bad news."

"How else are you supposed to know what's going on in the world?" Pauletta punched up the volume. We all had no choice but to turn our heads to follow the strumming music indicating breaking news. The woman news anchor faced the camera gravely.

"Good morning, we have sad news today. The once popular singer and actress, Sirena Lassiter was found dead late last night in a downtown hotel room in Atlanta, Georgia."

We all gasped in shock.

An old picture of Sirena, smiling and radiant, came on the screen.

The newswoman continued. "Apparently foul play was involved. The Atlanta Police aren't revealing any definite details until they've completed their investigation. The once celebrated pop star sold millions of records before she was convicted and sentenced to prison for stalking and kidnapping her former lover's wife. She was currently out on parole. We'll bring you updates as we receive them." The anchorwoman turned to her co-host sadly. "I really liked her music."

We all stood silent in the kitchen. My father reached over and pressed the power button with no admonishment from my mother.

"Wow," Jezzy said, breaking the stillness and the tension for all of us. "Just wow."

"What do you think happened?" My mother dare asked.

"Maybe she was doing drugs," My father reasonably ascertained.

Jezzy poured herself another cup of coffee. "She messed with the wrong person this time, that's all. When crazy meets crazy this is the result."

"What do you think happened?" My mother asked me again. All three of them studied my face for a response.

"I don't know," I said, still speechless.

"It had to be someone she knew. Nine murders out of ten are committed by someone the victim knows," my mother quoted the statistic from one of her reality crime shows.

"I think she owed someone money," my father chimed.

"No, I say a crime of passion. Henry, I'm telling you, it's the number one reason for committing a murder." My mother had a point. It had to be someone Sirena knew.

"Unless you're a serial killer. You don't need a reason if you're a serial killer."

Jezzy put up her hand like a kid in the classroom with the right answer. "I know. Maybe it was that guy who pretended to be a policeman. Maybe he was sick of her lies and manipulation and finally snapped."

"That's possible," Henry said. "He's the most likely suspect if you ask me. When your mom told me about that man coming into your home pretending to be a detective, it sent chills down my spine. You just can't trust anyone these days."

The inside of my cheek began to sting from where I'd bitten down too hard. "Like you said the first time, she must've been mixed up with the wrong people." I stood on shaky legs and took a second to get my balance. "I need to check on the kids."

"I'll go," Jezzy said with an unusually sympathetic tone. "You stay and talk with your mom and dad."

"No. Really. I need to go," I said with a hard squeeze of my hand on Jezzy's arm.

She understood, letting me pass. "We'll keep the food warm."

"No. Don't worry about it. I can't eat." I rushed to my room where the twins were still sleeping. I grabbed my cell phone and dialed Bliss's number. It didn't bother ringing. The message greeting was a cheery Bliss instructing the caller to go take on the day and she'd call back when she had a chance.

"Bliss, where are you? Call me? It's an emergency." I held the phone to my chest since I was truly speaking to the air.

I was worried that it was Bliss who was responsible. I knew it was ridiculous. We were thousands of miles away from Atlanta. Sirena was killed while we were in Los Angeles, right? I shook the ludicrous fear out of my head.

Yet, I couldn't stop the chills moving up my arms. Visualization she called it, seeing what you wanted to happen and sending it up to the heavens. The 'how' was left up to a higher power.

"Mommy," Lauren softly stirred before she climbed out of bed and into my arms.

"Hey, sweetie." I wrapped my arms around her and kept a tight fist grip on my phone.

"I'm hungry," she whispered.

"Grandpa Henry cooked a big breakfast with pancakes." I kissed her soft cheek before putting her down. I pulled her tiny pink robe out of the bag. She slipped her arms in and knew how to tie it by herself. She and Henry were three years old and I couldn't believe how fast they'd grown. I wanted them to stay babies forever. I at least wanted them to stay unaware and innocent until all the dark clouds had moved past Jake and I. Sirena being gone wasn't the relief I'd hoped to feel. Instead I was more afraid than ever and I wasn't sure why.

I jumped when I heard the light knock at the open bedroom door. Bliss stood oblivious to the panic spreading through my veins. "I'm back."

Chapter forty-three

"WHERE WERE YOU?"

Bliss stared through me for a second before answering. "I was with Nigel."

"Nigel?"

A sly smile rose on her lips. "You're meeting with Marco today, aren't you?"

"Yes. We're meeting. But he's not going to be here until this afternoon. I assumed he was coming alone from Atlanta." My mouth was dry with confusion making it difficult to speak. "Something happened to Sirena," I said before the giant ball in the back of my throat silenced me.

Bliss stuck her hands into her jacket pockets. "That's a shame. I'm famished." She turned and walked away.

By now little Henry had awakened. "I have to go pee-pee, mommy."

I trotted him off to the bathroom. I was still floating in disbelief. The last hour was surreal. I did my best to wash the fog from my mind.

After breakfast, I called Jake. He answered on the first ring. "Did you hear? Is it really true?"

"Yeah, I got the call from Detective Brewer. She was found last night."

We stayed quiet listening for the other to make the first move. Death had a way of putting things into perspective. Problems and issues that seemed too difficult weren't so important anymore. "It's all over the news here. She had a lot of fans."

"I want to see you," Jake pleaded. "I need to see you."

I was already brimming with regret. "Of course." I wiped the onslaught of tears from my eyes. "I'll come home. Give me a few days. My parents haven't seen the kids in a while and they're enjoying their visit."

That quickly, we were back on track. We both wanted to bury our past resentments and get on with our lives as a family. I twirled my wedding ring around my finger and wondered how I'd ever contemplated being without him. "I miss you."

Jake sighed with relief. "I miss you, too."

"How's Christopher?" It was one of the first questions on my mind before Jake and I began mending fences. This had to be hard for him too. No matter what he thought of Sirena, she was still a part of his life.

"He's been quiet. No tears that I've seen. I think he's torn between relief and sadness." Jake cleared his throat before continuing. "He'll be okay. He's resilient, always has been."

"What about you?" I asked, knowing it probably wasn't what he wanted to talk about, not so soon after we'd kissed and made up.

"I'm just glad it's over," he said. "Sirena wasn't going to change. She was never going to stop coming after us."

I bit my bottom lip to keep it from shaking. "Yeah. Well, I still hope they find whoever did this to her. It's all so scary."

He didn't respond. Instead he stayed on the phone and talked about my parents, how they were doing. I told him about their new kitchen, how beautiful it was, and how much they appreciated his gift.

"Why didn't you tell me?" I asked with a renewed gentleness. "It was such an amazing thing that you did, giving them the money. I had to pretend I knew about it, but I was impressed and embarrassed at the same time. I didn't want my dad to know you'd given them the money without telling me as if I wouldn't have approved."

"I wasn't sure. Everything's been so icy between you and your mom since Bliss came into our lives."

Now it was my turn to be silent. I didn't know what to say in regards to my sister. She may have been a force all her own but she still needed my protection. I would never let anyone think or speak badly of her. No matter what I knew in my gut to be true she was still my baby sister.

"We're all getting along fabulously. Even Jezzy is having a good time and you know how hard that is."

Jake chuckled. "Yep. I know. Listen, I gotta go. I promised Christopher I'd take him to the field and do some drills. He's gunning for quarterback next season."

"Oh, yeah. That's great. I'm glad you two are getting some quality father son, time."

"I'll call you later." Jake sounded a world apart from the depleted person he was an hour earlier. We were good for each other, there was no denying it.

I hung up realizing I was going to be late meeting Marco. I now felt guilty about agreeing to see him. Business, I told myself. I'd keep it professional knowing it would be difficult.

***

Marco and I were friends now, whether he liked it or not. I would've never gotten through the last few weeks without his shoulder to cry on. There was no need in regretting a minute, not even a second of the time I'd spent with him.

I saw him sitting in the hotel lobby where he was reading his telephone in one hand and a folded newspaper in the other. He wore a white shirt open at the collar and jeans. He looked like a Berkley college professor instead of a CEO of a multi-million dollar company. I waved at him.

"Now I see how you stay in the know."

"Information overload is a curse." He stood to greet me.

"Good to see you." I could see that he wanted a hug but I kept a safe distance. I barely leaned in and gave him an air kiss on the cheek.

"Are you all right?" He sensed the distance between us was more than physical. His expressions were so telling. I liked that about him. He didn't try to hide what he was thinking.

"I'm great. Really great. You know you didn't have to fly all the way out here. You and Nigel really take your business relationships seriously. It's the weekend," I chided. "Don't you two ever take time off?"

"Nigel? He's not here. I came alone," Marco said, leaning in closer. "I thought we could spend some time alone. No pressure. I booked you a full massage in the spa here. I even heard they have awesome fresh baked cookies." His wicked sexy smile usually worked. He was surprised when I looked heartsick. "What's wrong? Just tell me."

I licked my dry lips before I could speak. "I assumed Nigel was here. Maybe I was mistaken. He didn't come to Los Angeles with you?"

He shook his head, no. "Let's get some coffee. We can talk somewhere quiet." He put out his hand and I took ahold, unsure if I could keep my balance on my own.

Bliss had lied. Not a surprise. I was tired, so tired.

"I know you flew all the way out here for me," I blurted before we took another step. I hated being what he'd already accused me of becoming. *Friends take advantage of you.* Friends expect honesty but are angry when you tell the truth. Friends take each other for granted and then one day they decide to move on and get new friends.

It didn't help to look away, not when I'd memorized every detail of him. "I can't see you anymore. I really, really, appreciate you, and everything." The words were getting stuck in my throat. "But that's what I came to tell you and give you this." I dug into my purse and pulled the papers out. "I signed for the full sell of Two Sisters. I don't think it's a good idea if I work with you so the company is all yours." Just saying the words overwhelmed me. Letting go of the business was like letting go of Bliss, and him.

"It's for the best," I continued. "Okay?"

"Okay," he said clearly disappointed, taking the contract and softly gripping my hand in the process. "You have to do what's best for you."

"Thank you." I backed away. My heart was thumping erratically, torn between staying and going.

"Your welcome." He watched me with those intense concerned eyes. His heavy gaze followed me until I was no longer in the building.

I took a deep breath once I was outside. The Los Angeles sky was clear blue. I could see the mountains a good distance away. That view would've never happened a few years ago. The smog that plagued the city had been greatly reduced over the years by regulating businesses and car emissions. No one liked the work it took to make things change.

I understood the hard process of making things happen. First came the mistakes, then the lessons to be learned, then came the difficult decisions made from those lessons. I'd made my share. I'd learned. Like the smog lifted, I could see and breathe again.

***

I wasn't sure what I was going to say to Bliss. I drove without music to hear myself repeat the same thing over and over; *you lied. Why?*

The house was quiet when I arrived. Mom and dad took Mya and the twins to Disneyland. Jezzy was more than happy to tag along. I knocked on the guest room downstairs. I knew before I let myself in that Bliss would not be there. I knew her suitcase would be gone. No note. Nothing. No trace she'd ever existed.

I sat down. I had a feeling I wouldn't see her again. The prospect of losing her weighed heavily on my heart. I'd wanted answers. She knew that I was coming with questions she didn't want to face.

Knowing what she was capable of, was knowing too much. Like any relationship, having too much information wasn't healthy. Besides, whatever she'd done, it was because of me. I pushed my shoulders back. It was time to move forward. I wouldn't cry. I was done with crying.

Chapter forty-four

IT WAS CLOSE TO MIDNIGHT when our plane landed back home. The airport was nearly empty, a rarity since Atlanta Hartsfield was one of the largest airports in the country. The twins were cranky. Jezzy could hardly walk from her swollen ankles and achy knees.

I wasn't that much better off with the spasms moving through my lower back. The one thing I was grateful for was that Jake was standing at the exit waiting with a bouquet of colorful balloons and a sign that said, 'I love you.' Christopher stood next to him with heavy lids but smiling nonetheless. "Hey, Mom." He threw his lanky arms around me.

"Hey, sweetie."

The twins could barely contain themselves when they broke loose to run into their daddy's arms. Mya wasn't far behind screaming, "Hi, Dad!" Her big cheesy grin exposed dimples I'd forgotten she had.

Then it was my turn. I inhaled Jake, slipping my arms under his coat, around his waist. His chest had been my place of solace and protection for so long. It felt that way again. We kissed passionately but briefly.

"All right, you two, get a room," Jezzy said moving past us to the baggage claim. "Come. Help me with the bags, Chris."

The kids squealed with delight. "Daddy, we saw the ocean."

"We sat in tea-cups."

"We ate squider."

Jake paused. "Squider?"

"Squid," I corrected. "They ate calamari and Mya told them it was Squid. She even pulled the picture up on her iPhone to show them. They screamed and gasped, then a minute later they were eating it again. They loved it." We stayed wrapped in each other while we walked. "They really had a great time. So did I, but I'm glad to be home, with you."

He kissed me on top of my head. "I don't know what I'd do without you."

"Good thing you'll never have to find out," I said welcoming the sincerity back in my words. The ambivalence was gone and buried. I knew what I wanted the minute I saw him waiting for us at baggage claim, standing there like a man in love. I was the lucky one. I wouldn't forget again.

* * *

When we arrived home, the twins had fallen asleep and had to be carried up to their rooms. Christopher headed out for an overnight stay at a friend's house, something I wouldn't have been comfortable giving permission for. With Jake taking the parental reins I could relax for a change.

"Go to our room. I have a surprise waiting for you," Jake whispered with a kiss.

I obliged. There was nothing I wanted to do more than lie down. I took the last heavy steps before turning the corner of the hallway. I passed the room Bliss stayed in telling myself she would be okay, wherever she'd disappeared to.

I scooted into our bedroom, kicked off my boots and laid flat on my back staring up at the high ceiling and wood beam. I was glad to be home in my own bed.

It took me a minute to recognize the sound humming in my ear. The low vibration was the motor running in the spa tub, the one we never used. I forced myself up, back on my feet. I walked to the master bath and opened the door. The lights were dimmed. Three candles lined the outside of the tub. Rose petals floated on top of the bubbling heated whirlpool.

Jake knew the way to my heart. The clothes came off. I sank into the center of the perfectly heated water. I leaned back on the soft towel Jake had placed on the end as a pillow. My tension sailed away with the gentle lapping of water at my naked body. I let it all go.

And so I did. I asked nicely. That wasn't good enough. "Fuck me," I ordered turning over and pulling him close. "Please, baby."

He happily went in for the kill. The weight of his body plunging me into another spiral. I flexed my hips to get the fullness I'd demanded. Within seconds he was ravishing what was left. Enjoying his spoils. He lifted me up for better entry and reached where no man had gone before.

I fell into a lucid trance, unable to do more than sail into Utopia. Mumbled words tumbled from lips. His name was the only thing that mattered. I whispered the only comprehensible thing that passed for the English language, "Jake, oh God."

Afterward we rested in between panted breaths, our chests rising and falling. I realized I was finally home. No matter how far I thought I could run there was no place else I wanted to be but in Jake's arms.

His hand rested on my waist with his head listening to my rampant beating heart. "I was so scared I was going to lose you," he said quietly.

A tear trickled down the side of my face and onto the pillow. "I know. I'm sorry."

He placed a kiss on my navel. "I'm sorry too, for ever making you think you were anything but first in my life. I love you. I need you." He rose on his elbows. The room was lit enough to see his eyes glistening. "Everything is going to be okay now."

"But, are you okay? I mean really okay? Do you want to talk about it?"

"Sirena's not our problem anymore. So, yeah. I'm good with that," he said with relief.

"At first I thought this was another one of her tricks. Like it was another woman but she wanted us to think it was her."

"Yeah, I know what you mean," Jake sighed. "I thought the same thing, but Detective Brewer brought pictures. I was the only one he knew that could identify her for sure."

Do they know what happened to her?" The mood was officially over. I may as well take advantage of it and find out as much as I could.

"She was found with head injuries at the Palomar Hotel. There was a struggle. That's all I know."

"I had the craziest premonition that Bliss had something to do with it."

"How? She was with you in Los Angeles. You told me she was there in the morning so how could she have anything to do with Sirena?"

I was dangerously close to pointing out things we both swore we'd never talk about. Besides, it was me who looked mentally unstable when I spoke of the strange activities I'd witnessed being around Bliss. Jake never saw anything. He only had my word to go on. But he'd felt it too, her ability to unnerve him was proof enough. It took a lot to make Jake uncomfortable in his own skin, something Bliss did naturally.

"All I can say is however it happened, doesn't really concern us. I'm just glad it's all over." Jake rose from the bed kissing me lightly on the lips. "I told Mya we'd take turns reading chapters."

"That's nice. What book is she reading?"

"The Secret Life Of Bees," he announced. He was going for father of the year since he'd already won me over.   He disappeared into the bathroom closing the door. The shower came on.

I stretched before throwing my feet over the side of the bed landing on his jeans, shirt, and jacket. I picked them up and heard something fall out and hit the floor. I felt for it in the dark. I landed on the weight and size of a credit card. I examined the smooth white card with only a magnetic strip. I flipped it over to read, Palomar Hotel.

Wait a minute, what? My hand shook holding a key for the hotel where Sirena was found. The questions were spinning right along with the room.

I heard the water stop in the shower. I pushed the clothes back on the floor and shoved the card haphazardly underneath as if I'd never seen it. I rushed under the blankets trying to stop my entire body from trembling. *However it happened doesn't really concern us.*

Jake came out with the steam swirling behind him in a light haze. He pulled his robe tighter and came straight over to me. He grazed my forehead with a kiss. "After I read with Mya, we can meet downstairs, have some tea."

"I think I'll stay here. I'm tired after the long trip home." I tried to keep my voice from shaking.

He moved around and picked up his clothes off the floor. He took everything to the closet where they'd probably still be on the floor but out of the way. Once he slipped on his drawstring linen pants and a T-shirt he left to go read with Mya.

I popped up and checked the floor again. The card key was left behind. He hadn't seen it. I picked it up and held it for a few minutes pacing and contemplating what I should do.

What did it mean? And did I really want to know?

Jake wasn't capable of what my wild imagination was conjuring up. The answer was, no. It wasn't possible. He had nothing to do with Sirena's death.

So what, he had a room key to the same hotel Sirena was found. I was being irrational. Yes, this time, I admitted to the very thing Jake liked to accuse me off, blowing things out of proportion. Seeing the mountain instead of the molehill.

In the bathroom drawer I grabbed a pair of scissors. I cut the plastic in half, then again until it was a pile of shards. I pushed the tiny pieces into my hand.

I slipped on my robe and tiptoed down the stairs and out to the garbage on the side of the house. It was still a few days away from trash pick-up. In that time anything could happen, a knock at the door announcing Jake as a suspect. The first place searched was always the suspect's trash.

Even in tiny pieces I felt like there was too much information being put out for someone to find and accuse my husband of doing the worst thing a human-being could do. *Thou shall not kill.* I went back inside with the chopped

was already gone. So I left. I didn't tell Brewer anything or I'd be a suspect."

"Oh, you think?" I was crumbling inside. I was undeniably hurt that he'd still trusted her enough to meet after all we'd been through. After fear and disbelief came something I wasn't prepared for, crushing sadness. I was ready to give up. I couldn't fight anymore.

He wrapped his arms around me. My arms remained limp at my side. "Baby, please, understand." He dropped his head on my shoulder. There was nothing else to say. The room fell silent while we held each other.

* * *

I woke up the next morning and pretended it was all a dream. Neither a good dream nor a bad one, just a vivid picture fueled by my imagination.

For the sake of our love and family I could pretend we lived in that vacuum where nothing could come between us.

I made coffee, sat down at the table, and settled into the peace and quiet of the house. Not having anything to do for Two Sisters left me empty with too much time on my hands so early in the morning.

I did something I hadn't done in a while. I decided to go out for a long brisk walk. I dressed quickly and made my way back downstairs before anyone else woke up. *Me time* had been something I'd avoided. Too much time to think led to problems I didn't want to address. Now, it felt like a gift I owed myself. Fresh dewy air greeted me as I hit the door.

I started out slow but picked up the pace after about a quarter mile. I circled the main block and was back already. I figured I might as well leave the private community and venture to more open space. What good was living behind a gate when anyone and everyone could come and go without warning? How many times had Sirena sailed past the security shack as if she belonged?

I stopped myself from speaking or thinking ill of Sirena. It wasn't good to have evil thoughts of someone who'd gone on to the great beyond. Whether she was spending her time in eternal damnation or looking down upon me from heaven, I didn't want her eavesdropping on my conscience. Besides, I was free of Sirena for once and for all. If I kept bringing her up in my mind, I was the fool carrying her around like a bad penny.

I pushed against the cool wind that suddenly picked up rustling the leaves in the trees surrounding me. I turned on the main road and stayed on the dirt edge. The whistling of the wind kept me from hearing the car trailing behind me. I eventually heard the hum of an engine and scooted closer to the edge.

When the car didn't pass, I looked back trying to figure out exactly how much room they needed. I was just one person.

The car was trailing behind, matching my pace. When I sped up, so did the car. I came to a dead stop. That's when I saw the man intently staring at me. He took off his sunglasses and laid them on the dash. He slowly pulled along side of me. "Mrs. Parson," he called out. "Can I speak with you for a moment?" He held up an ID badge.

I realized he was the same detective, the one who'd taken Sirena but never arrested her. The very same man who'd tricked us into believing he'd arrived early on the seen before any other cops had responded to the 911 call.

I looked around realizing there was no one else around. No one would hear me scream. Running would be useless since he had a car and I was on foot.

"What do you want?"

He smiled. "Wanted you to give your husband a message for me."

I stepped back, not sure what he was about to do. My heart was racing but my body was growing numb with fear. I stood there, scared to move.

"Tell him, an eye for an eye, and all that good stuff." A one sided grin appeared.

"What are you talking about? I don't understand." I tried to catch my breath. Panic was taking over. Nervous bile seeped into my stomach threatening to come up my throat.

"Well, it's simple. He took someone I loved. In return I will take someone he loves." His dangerous grin was followed by a menacing glare. "Does your husband love you?"

I stopped hearing him. His mouth continued moving. I took a step back, then two, before I took off running. From the dense ground cover where I'd ducked into the trees I could still see his car driving by slowly. I kneeled down, shaking in fear. I reached into my sweatshirt pocket and pulled out my phone. I pushed the button to dial Jake. He answered on the first ring and I could do nothing but sob.

"Babe, what's going on?"

"He's here, the man. The one who took Sirena, her friend, he's after me. I was walking..."

"Wait, whisper, babe. Where are you?" Jake went into immediate panic mode. "Tell me where you are."

Before I could say another word I felt a tug pull me backwards. He'd caught up with me, grabbing my hood and dragging me to my feet. The phone dropped. I could hear Jake yelling my name.

"I saved your life before, did you know that? Now this is how your husband repays me? By taking the only person I cared about." He easily squeezed the fabric of my sweatshirt choking me without any effort.

I struggled and clawed at his hands. "Jake didn't hurt Sirena. He had nothing to do with it," I hissed, growing slightly light headed. Tears streamed down my face and nose. He was taking me to his car.

"Is that what he told you? Well guess what, everything is because of him. Everything," he snapped in my ear. "She's gone because of him."

"Please, please, don't do this."

He fumbled with his key trying to get the trunk unlocked.

"Payback is a bitch," he said before getting trunk popped opened. It was my last chance. I wedged my face

ratchet squawk. Her wings flapped for attention and I thought of Bliss.

There were no accidents, she would say, only the power of intention. That bird sweeping into the driver's window at just the right moment with only one thought, to make the detective disappear, and he had. He was gone in an instant. I didn't have to be afraid anymore.

The bird flew away with a proud stretch of her wings. I was safe, my children were safe, that's all that mattered.

* * *

Once I was home, I could really breathe again. After a long hot shower I wanted to put on the most comfortable clothes I owned. I combed through my drawers and couldn't find my favorite sweatpants.

I went on Jake's side searching in his drawer in case they were put in the wrong place. I nearly tripped over a black Nylon sports bag on the floor. It was heavy and barely moved from my foot getting caught in the strap.

I tried to push it out of the way only to find it too difficult to move, not even an inch. "What's in here, a body?"

Of course I was only kidding. But now I was curious. There was a good chance my sweatpants were in there. The zipper wouldn't slide, stuck on something. I used what strength I had left from the earlier struggle and managed to rip through whatever was on the other side.

Inside were neatly labeled stacks of one hundred dollar bills. The cash Jake was supposed to pay to Sirena to make her go away. Inside was also a folded piece of paper, a receipt from the cash withdrawal. $100,000 just like he said. I went to close the bag. It was stuck again. Shredding dollar bills wasn't the smartest move.

I reached inside and tugged realizing it wasn't paper this time, but fabric. I yanked until the fabric gave way landing me on my butt and holding Jake's blue dress shirt, now torn, or had it been torn before. I looked closely and noticed dried brown stains speckled all over the front and sleeves. *Blood?*

I rushed to the bathroom. I thought I was going to be sick. I threw water on my face. I washed my hands but they would never be clean. My eyes were bloodshot. My nose was red too. I stood at the sink looking in the mirror.

I talked myself out of hurling him on the mercy of an insane justice system. I could never bear witness to what I found.

I heard the bedroom door open. Jake made his way to the bathroom.

He found me, where I'd curled myself in a ball, my knees under my chin, frightened and in shock. "Babe, you don't have to be afraid anymore." He kneeled in front of me and took my hands, bringing them to his lips. "I'm not going to let anything happen to you ever again. I love you," he whispered. "Do you understand? You're safe now."

A quiet tear slipped down my cheek. I nodded yes with determination. *Safe.*

We were safe in our silence. I wouldn't speak of it, ever. I closed my eyes and leaned against his shoulder and prayed for forgiveness, for both of us.

***

Acknowledgments

The journey as a writer is often a secluded one. Silence is part of the deal. When it's time for me to finally lift my head up after completing a book, I'm grateful to the people who are still there. My family, friends, and readers I am forever in your loving debt. You complete me, XXOO's

Trisha R. Thomas